FAMILY ALWAYS FIRST

The Henchmen History

OMEGA BLACKPRIDE

NEWMAN SPRINGS PUBLISHING
320 Broad Street
Red Bank, NJ 07701

First originally published by Newman Springs Publishing 2021

ISBN 978-1-63692-904-0 (Paperback)
ISBN 978-1-63692-905-7 (Digital)

Printed in the United States of America

This book is dedicated to

1) every Black man in America trapped in the system;
2) every Black woman in America that's lost a loved one to the system; and
3) all the Black families stuck in the struggle…

Thanks for being my inspiration.

"Know for certain that your descendants will reside as aliens in a land not their own. Where they shall be enslaved and oppressed for 400 years. But I (the Lord) will bring judgement on the nation they must serve. And after this you will go out with great wealth…" (Genesis 13–16) Chapter 15

Disclaimer

The information contained within the pages of this book is exclusively subjected to the interpretation of the author and may or may not be entirely accurate. All modifications of stories altered from the original event is strictly for entertainment purposes.

However, this is a nonfictional documentary that has been based on and inspired by true events. The characters are real, the stories are real, and I offer no apologies for keeping it real.

The author assumes no responsibility for actions of the reader nor of their use of the information contained within this book for any negative purposes. Consequently, all names have been altered to conceal the identification of actual persons. Any similarities of characters to actual ppl are merely coincidental and unintended.

The reader is therefore encouraged to read responsibly...and respect the truth.

Acknowledgments

First and foremost, I must give honor to Ifa and the Yoruba African Culture for guidance, wisdom, and prosperity.

To my ancestors Alethea and Eddie Davis for spiritual guidance. To my seeds Shaunteona, Shy'ion, and Skai Jennings—who carry both my name and bloodline... (I love y'all to death!)

To all my family especially my big Sis Teion, who always believed and never doubted my vision... (First Fam Salutes, Sis!)

To all the real rights that continue to properly represent the true meaning of Blood and Family...

My Father's Son

One of the earliest memories in my life taught me the most valuable lesson that any real man of honor should know: "Never trust a **rat**, a **snake**, or a **coward**."

Waking up from a long night of tossing and turning in a bed that I shared with my older sister (Teion), I sleepwalked lazily to the refrigerator. I was only six years old, but I still remember this day clearly.

I grabbed a pack of cheese, sat Indian style on the floor with the fridge still open, and ate slice after slice of cheese. Damn, that cheese was good, so good that I fell right back to sleep in front of the fridge with the door wide open and empty cheese wrappers scattered all around me.

"Ima beat your ass, boy. Get up. [Smack] *What I tell you 'bout blundering in the refrigerator?* [Smack] *Get your ass back in bed* [smack], *and Ima tell your daddy too* [smack]."

I can't remember how many more smacks to the head I caught trying to haul ass back to bed, but I made it. Waking Teion up in the process by slamming the door, I jumped in the bed and hid under the covers.

"Shawn, why Mama yelling at you, and what you done did?"

Too scared to talk, I ignored her while still hiding under the covers, praying that my mom was finished with her ass-whipping warpath. After a while, my mom stopped yelling long enough for me to feel safe enough to speak. *"I ate all the cheese."*

"Again? Ooooh, you gone get a beatennnn."

"No, I ain't. Ima hide under these covers aaall day!"

Hearing footsteps in the hallway and assuming it was my mom, I balled up tight in a fetal position under the covers.

"Teion, go help your mom with breakfast while I talk to this little rat," I heard my father say.

Hearing the calmest of his voice let me know I wasn't in any more trouble. It was something about my dad that always made me feel safe. His voice alone was enough to scare the shit out of me, so I rarely did any wrong on his watch. We shared the same bloodline and the same name, and he was my idol.

Sitting on the edge of the bed and pulling the cover back from over my head, he laughed and said, *"You did it again, huh? Guess you must really like cheese a lot."*

"Yes, Dad, it's my favorite!" I answered as honest as my six-year-old mind would allow.

Suddenly, there was no smile on his face and no laughter in his voice, and this was the part of him that scared me the most. *"Ain't no rats in this family, Shawn."*

Lost and not fully understanding what was going on, I asked, *"Dad, what's a rat, and what's a family?"*

"A rat is a rodent that loves cheese. It will do anything for cheese including getting trapped and dying—but that is not the type of rat I'm speaking about. A rat is also a person with a big mouth who tells everything, and they can't be trusted." He went on to explain that snakes and cowards were similar to rats and are never to be trusted. *"Snakes hide. Cowards run."* He told me to never run from a fight or hide under covers. *"Those are things that only weak men do."*

He said family was everything and all that mattered in life and to always put your family first no matter what. *"Your mother and sister are to be protected at all times, and if anything should ever happen to me, you'll be the big man of the family."* He then got up, grabbed my ankles, pulled me out of the bed, held me upside down in the air, and said, *"If you ever catch a rat, snake, or a coward, drop them headfirst off the tallest building you can find. They don't deserve to live."*

He then flipped me right side up, swung me around on his back, told me to hold on, and ran out the room. We ran through the entire house, yelling at the top of our lungs only to end up in the kitchen with my mom and sister.

"Big Shawn, why is y'all making all that damn noise, and why you got that damn boy on your back? That's why he so damn crazy now."

"My boy ain't crazy. He just comes from a bloodline of warriors," my father said while letting me off his back.

"Warrior my ass. Y'all just crazy. Teion, cut that stove off and put them plates out. Lil Shawn, go wash your hands, and Mr. Warrior Bloodline, you need to take this damn trash out."

See, my mother was a real live firecracker, the second to the youngest in the family of eight with only two girls. She didn't play. Her first line of defense and discipline was to whip ass. Her real name was **Faye,** but everybody knew her as Feisty Faye. My mom was, still is, and will always be one of the strongest women I know.

"Lil Shawn, say the grace," my mom said as we all sat at the table for breakfast.

"God is great. God is good. Let us thank You for this food. Bow our head, we all are fed. Give us, Lord, our daily bread... Amen," I said excitedly while stuffing a crispy piece of bacon in my mouth!

Boom, boom, boom! The entire house shook as the door flew off the hinges.

My mother screamed, my sister cried, my dad stood up, and I just sat there, shocked—seeing ninja turtles dressed in all black running in our house with guns. *"Everybody, ooon the ground nooow!"*

My dad stayed standing as my mother pulled my sister to the ground, protecting her with a motherly hug while screaming for my father to get on the floor. *"Shawn, please get down."*

Hearing my mother scream, seeing my sister cry, and watching my father stand, surrounded by three ninja turtles with guns pointed directly at his face while the others tore our home apart; I stood up, wrapped my entire body around my father's leg, and yelled, *"Leave my daddy alone!"* I screamed as loud as I could while still hugging his leg.

Finally, the turtles lowered their weapons. By this time, my mother and sister had maneuvered around the table, hugging my dad's opposite leg *"Mr. Jennings, we have an outstanding warrant for your arrest. You are wanted for assault with a deadly weapon with intent to kill. We'll give you ten minutes here with your family before placing you under arrest."*

"Damn" was all I heard my father say.

It was as if he picked our entire family up off the floor in his embrace. I was no longer wrapped around his leg. I was in his arms; we all were. He gave my mother instructions on what to do and who to call, told my sister to look after me, sat me down on the counter, and said, *"Stop crying and look at me. You have to be the big man of the family now, okay? You have to protect your mother and sister. I'll be back, but you got to be strong. No hiding and no running, okay?"* He then lifted me off the counter and told me to go stand with my mother and sister.

That was the last time I ever saw my mother and father hug each other. Our last meal together and the last time we stood as one family. My life from that point on would be hell-bound.

"Mr. Jennings, you have the right to remain silent. Anything you say can and will be held against you."

I watched my father get handcuffed and walk out the kitchen by the turtles. He stopped at the door and looked back over his shoulder at all of us. His eyes locked with mine, and his last words to me were *"Family always first, and ain't no rats in this family, son…"* I didn't know it at the time, but those words would mold the direction in which my life would take from that point on.

Walnut Hills

It would be five long years before my dad made it back home, and when he did, he was a changed man.

Gone was the street-smart hustler with words of wisdom. He was now a full-fledged follower of Christ. I still loved my dad; but I was just too young to grasp any real concept of religion, and that put a lot of distance between our bond.

My mom was strong, but not strong enough to hold on for five years. She eventually moved on and found another man, and by the time my dad got out, I had a one-year-old little sister named Terry. Not to mention that while my pops was away, I had started running with the older kids around my neighborhood, and we were into a lot of mischievous things.

My older cousin (Dennis) stayed two houses down from me. His mother (Shirley) was my godmother. She had four kids, but Dennis and I were the closest. Dennis had a friend named Don, who stayed at the top of the street right by the bus stop. Don came from a family of three, with his older brother (Noon) and baby sister (Erica). Don was slightly older than Dennis, so we all pretty much followed his lead.

Every morning, we'd all meet up at the bus stop along with the other neighborhood kids. Our bus stop was like a swap meet for kids, and it was Dennis and Don's operation. We swapped clothes, copied one another's homework, traded toys, and did it all. My bus always came first because I was still in elementary, so I never knew what else took place after my bus came.

Until one day, we were at my godmother's house getting ready for school. Dennis asked me, *"Do you want to play hookey?"*

Not knowing what he was talking about, but I knew it sounded fun, I answered, *"Yes, but what's that?"*

"It's when you skip school, silly. Just don't get on the bus when it comes. We're going to act like we are going to school, but when she leaves for work, we coming back to the house."

So we left out as if we were really going to school and linked up with Don at the bus stop. I guess Dennis was telling Don that I was rolling with them because Don looked at me and started laughing.

"You ever had some pussy?" Don asked.

I embarrassingly shook my head.

"Do you even know how to fuck?"

I again shook my head, embarrassed.

"Well, you gone learn today… Go hide behind that house. Your bus coming up the street now."

I took off running behind the house, concealing my body while peeping my head around the corner. I saw my elementary school peers getting on the bus, and it was right then and there that I realized none of the kids my age were really my friends. Yeah, I played with them sometimes, but I spent more time with Dennis and Don than them.

About fifteen minutes later, Dennis and Don along with several more neighborhood kids including three girls joined me behind the house. We watched the school bus pull off and waited patiently for my godmother to leave for work. Finally, we saw my godmother's car drive past the bus stop.

Dennis gave Don a nod, and Don gave us all the instructions, *"Split up in groups of three, one girl in each group, and walk back to Dennis's house one group at a time. That way, we don't draw no attention just in case somebody watching."*

Don, Necee, and I were in the last group, and instead of going directly to my godmother's house, we stopped by Don's house first. He was in and out in no time; when he came out, he had a VCR tape in his hand.

By the time we made it to my godmother's house, the guys were in one room, and the girls in another. My godmother's garage had been converted into a den, and that was where we all met up. Don put the VCR tape in and pressed *Play*…and for the first time in my life, I saw people having sex. My heart sped up, my dick got hard, my entire body got hot, and not once did I blink. I was glued to the TV and lost in a trance. When I finally did look around, I noticed Dennis, Don, Cedric, and two girls were missing. I left out the den curious as to where they had gone and what they were doing.

As I walked down the hallway, I saw Cedric come out the room sweating, smiling, and naked. I heard moans coming from the room, and Cedric was standing there smiling and naked. Finally, he stepped aside and opened the door. *"Go in and get some. Its only pussy. Don't be scared,"* he said.

Looking inside the room, I saw Dennis and Don in the same bed under separate covers with the two girls beneath them. Both girls were moaning, and both guys were pumping and humping to the finish; but for some reason, I didn't want none. Not from them girls anyway. I wanted Necee. So I went back to the den, passing Kippy in the hallway on his way to the room where everybody else was at. He warned me as he passed, *"She acting stuck up,"* but when I got to the den, she was still watching the porno tape all by herself.

Necee

Now Necee was only fourteen with a well-developed body. I secretly had a crush on her. I used to smack her butt hard as I could and take off running. She would always yell after me and sometimes give chase. Sometimes instead of smacking her butt, I would grab it and squeeze as hard as I could. Man, her butt was so soft it was like squeezing a cloud.

So one day when I smacked her butt, I took off running, and she gave chase. I was one of the fastest runners in my neighborhood, so I laughed because I knew she couldn't catch me. I looked back to see where she was at and somehow lost balance and fell. *"Shit!"*

She was on me in no time. Pinning my arms to the ground, she was bigger, stronger, and outweighed me. Wasn't nothing I could do. *"Got your lil bad ass now,"* she said, sitting on my chest and slapping me upside my head and twisting my earlobes. She then reached back, stuck her hands in my pants, grabbed a handful of dick and balls, and started pulling and squeezing hard as she could. *"How you like that, huh?"*

I screamed and begged for her to stop, and finally she did, not before making me promise to never touch her butt again. She was still sitting on my chest with my arms pinned down when suddenly she asked, *"You like me, don't you? You want to be my lil boyfriend?"*

I could hardly believe my ears. The same girl that had just beat me up and that I had a crush on was asking me to be her lil boyfriend. So of course, I said, *"Yes."*

She put both her hands on the side of my head, leaned over, and kissed me hard.

Now here we were watching a sex tape. I knew she wasn't a virgin, but I also knew that the only reason she was acting stuck up was because I (her lil boyfriend) was around.

I was only in the fifth grade, eleven years old, and here I was in a house full of older kids, playing hookey and watching a sex tape with my girlfriend. Truth be told, I was a virgin. I had never had sex and didn't know what to do. My neighborhood was full of kids of all ages, so it wasn't unusual for kids my age to be sexually active. In fact, almost all the boys over ten were having sex... (Sorry, Moms. I'm just being honest) And this was my initiation.

So I sat down beside her on the couch. Before I could even get comfortable, she got up and closed the den door, making sure it was locked. The lady on the TV had her legs spread-eagled atop the man's shoulders, almost wrapped around his neck. He was slow, stroking her good, and she took it all, making sounds of pleasure.

Necee came back to the couch, started undressing, and instructed me to do the same. It wasn't long before we were both naked. *"I only made you my lil boyfriend because I knew you had a big dick, I found out that day I beat you up."*

Confused but only because I had never compared my penis to anybody else, so I didn't know rather it was big or not but proud it had gotten me a girlfriend.

The lady on the TV was in the same position, and by now, the dude was pounding her full force. Necee pointed to the TV and said, *"I want you to do me just like that."*

I tried my hardest not once but twice. The first time lasted about three minutes. The second was better and longer but still couldn't hold back. She felt like heaven, and till this day, the hucklebuck is my favorite position. Necee told me it was okay, but I would have to take my time with girls my age because of my size.

We both got dressed, and I unlocked the door. It wasn't long before Dennis, Don, and the rest of the gang made their way to the den. By this time, Necee and I were both acting as if nothing happened. When the older guys tried to get with her, she said her stomach was hurting. I felt like a king. I had just lost my virginity to a girl three years older than me, and she was dissing the older guys because of me. Damn, I felt good.

When it was time for school to let out, we all went our separate ways. Necee and I waited at the bus stop to meet up with my sister. Normally, I would've ran off with Dennis and Don to go terrorize the neighborhood, and normally, my sister would have to come find me. But not today.

Necee and my sister were good friends, so when the bus came and my sister got off the bus, first thing she said was *"What y'all done did?"*

"Nothing," we both said at the same time.

"Y'all done did something. Y'all two can't stand each other, and now y'all both waiting for me at the bus stop after y'all done skipped school."

Damn, my sis was sharp. I didn't think she'd peep game, but she did. But still, I was just as sharp, so I played it off. I smacked Necee on her ass as hard as I could and took off.

"You lil bastard! Ima beat your ass when I catch you!" she yelled after me.

Wrightsboro, a.k.a. "The Motherland"

Around the same time I lost my virginity, we lost our house. Actually, our house was paid for, but my dad had spoiled my mom to the point that she wasn't used to working. The father of my youngest sister (Terry) turned out to be more interested in using drugs than being a father. He left my mom high and dry with another mouth to feed. By this time, my dad was out of prison, but he and my mom had gotten a divorce. My dad let my mom keep the house and walked away empty-handed. I salute my dad for that because I know he only did that for his kids.

I came home one day to see my Uncle Harold's truck parked out front and packed with our property. My mom and Grandma were in the house also.

"Don't start asking me all them questions. Just go help your uncle put that stuff on the truck," my mom said soon as she saw me.

I couldn't help it. I had to ask, *"Ma, where we moving, and why we moving?"*

There was no way in hell I was letting my mother get away with not giving me an answer. This hood was all I knew. My friends were here, and this was the only home I ever had. My mom started yelling, cursing, and threatening to whip my ass. My uncle must have heard all the commotion because he came in and told me if I didn't take my ass outside, he'd whip my ass also.

Now my Uncle Harold's nickname was Gator; and I'd seen for myself what his definition of an *ass-whipping* was, and I wasn't trying to feel that. Plus, word was Unc had a body under his belt. The streets say back in the day, he killed a White man for beating up his brother (my Uncle Bernard) and got away with it. They're both deceased now, so it's safe to say my Uncle Harold was a killer; and I feared him more than my dad… RIP, Gator. I ain't forgot you, Unc!

So anyway, I took my lil ass outside. I was so mad I didn't even realize I was crying. I felt as though I had just got double-teamed by Mom and Uncle. I ended up at my godmother's house. Seeing my tears, she asked me, *"What's wrong?"*

I told her I didn't wanna move and that my mom was making us go stay at my grandmother's house.

She told me not to worry. *"Ima come get you, and you can stay with me anytime."*

That was like music to my ears. My godmother had always been like my second mom; so I knew she was serious, and I was definitely going to take her up on that offer. Walking back home later that night, I was no longer mad at my mom. Although I didn't want to leave my hood, knowing my godmother had my back made me feel better. I got home and saw that most of our belongings had already been moved. My sister didn't seem to care much about moving. I guess she wasn't as attached to the hood as I was.

My grandmother only stayed at about a fifteen-minute drive up the street. We would still be going to the same school, so that wasn't a problem. The only thing that I hated was leaving all my friends behind and the fact that my grandmother stayed down a long dirt road. She owned plenty of property and a few houses thanks to my granddad who made some wise real-estate investments. Her house sat in the middle of five acres of land surrounded by woods. My grand-dad, when he passed, had willed each of his eight children a half acre of land. Plus my great-grandparents had also left my grandmother their land also. My Uncle Harold stayed right across from my grand-mother. That land is still in my family. I plan on getting me a nice big house built on it in the near future.

The neighborhood was called Wrightsboro, a.k.a. "the Motherland," and almost everybody was some kin. Even if we weren't kin by blood, we were kin by marriage, and we all carried it like family. Nobody locked their doors, and if you messed with one, you dealt with all.

Being that both Walnut Hills and Wrightsboro were located on the outskirts of the city limits, we were called and considered to be the country, so whenever we went to town, we had to have one another's backs. One thing the kids in town would soon learn was, wasn't nothing sweet 'bout them boys from the country. We had big guns and weren't afraid to bust them.

My Uncle Harold's oldest son's name was Donald, and we became tight as brothers. My other Uncle Mike's son's name was Lil Mike, and we also became tight as brothers; but he only came to my grandma's house on the weekend.

Every weekend, my grandma would cook Sunday dinner, and it would be people from all over the Motherland pulling up to get a plate. My uncles would bring their ladies and friends. My mom would be helping my grandma cook. The music would be blasting. They'd start playing spades, getting drunk, and talking shit. Donald, Lil Mike, and I would be outside riding our go-carts and dirt bikes. We'd steal a few beers, go hide in the woods, and get drunk. I grew to love the Motherland more than Walnut Hills mainly because we never moved out and everybody was like family.

My grandma held our family together like super glue. I swear it ain't been the same without you, Grandma… RIP. Damn, I miss those Sunday dinners.

Lakeside

Around this time, I had just started middle school. My mom had remarried, bought another house, and was pregnant again with my younger brother (Avyd). We stayed down that same long dirt road right across from my grandmother on the land my grandfather had left my mom. My mom's husband (Big Al) was a former college football star who everybody said had the potential to go pro but for some reason, didn't. Word was he dropped out of college in his fourth year to be with my mom. He was now a top chef at a world-class restaurant (Blockadd Runner) located right on the beach. My mom had just dropped my lil brother Avyd, and within nine months was pregnant again with my lil brother JB.

We had it rough, but like what 2Pac said, we had enough. Her husband, Big Al, was a good provider but had started drinking and hitting her. Now here I was, twelve–thirteen years old fighting a grown man and trying to defend my mom.

Truth be told, that shit drove me crazy. I literally lost my damn mind. My teachers started calling home, saying they couldn't get through to me. My grades started failing, and just like that, I stopped giving a fuck about everything. My mom started thinking I was crazy because I was straight acting up, but it was all that shit going on at home messing with my head.

My older cousins were hustling crack by now. Donald was called Murder One and had moved to go stay with his mom. Every time I saw him, he had a pocketful of money and was fresh. Same for my cousin Lil Mike; he was doing his thing too. Even my older sister Teion was selling weed and seeing some paper. She gave me some to sell, but that shit was moving too slow. It seemed as if I was the only one still waiting on my mom to buy my clothes. I started having to wear my sister's clothes just to stay fresh.

And then *bam*! I just snapped the hell out. I was tired of all that shit! Tired of fighting my mom's husband! Tired of not having no fly gear to wear! Tired of not never having no money! Tired of struggling and tired of giving a fuck!

I caught my first case at thirteen for pistol whipping a dude and having a weapon on school grounds. All behind a bitch-ass nigga I thought was my friend. Over a damn soda…

I had already been kicked out of all the schools, so I was going to Lakeside, an alternative school. My class consisted of kids of different ages that had been kicked out of their schools also. Kalvin was one of the dudes I linked up with, and we became cool. Kizzy was this cute redbone that knew how to manipulate any weak-minded dude. She was fine, and having come from the hood, she was street-smart too.

So one day, we were all at the lunch table. Kalvin got up and went to do something—I guess to use the bathroom. So anyway, he had left his drink, which was a can soda on the table. I grabbed the soda, took a swig, and honestly, ain't think nothing else of it. We did this often; it wasn't nothing new. But when Kalvin came back before I could even tell him I got some soda, Kizzy's lying ass told him, *"He spit in your drink."*

I'm thinking like *I know you don't believe this bitch,* and that's exactly what I said. *"I got some soda. I didn't spit in your drink. I know you don't believe this bitch."*

I was only thirteen at the time, this stupid-ass, clown-ass dude Kalvin was sixteen. He actually started flipping on me over this shit and then called me out to fight. Now the dude was bigger than me, and I knew I couldn't beat him. But like what my dad told me, only cowards run, and I wasn't no coward. Plus my mother's husband was like 6'4 and 240 pounds, and if I survived fighting him, then fuck Kalvin.

We went outside and squared up; he ended up getting the best of me. He put me in a headlock, punched me in the face a few times, and then pushed me on the ground. He acted like he was going to stomp me, but I grabbed a stick of the ground and backed him down.

I was embarrassed as hell. I had just got beaten up in front of everybody, but it wasn't over. I come from a bloodline of warriors!

That night when I got home, I went over Gator's house. I knew where he kept all his guns, so it was easy for me to sneak in and steal one without getting caught.

The next day, I couldn't wait to get to school. I had stolen a .38 revolver from my Uncle Harold, and Kalvin was a marked man. I saw him standing with his back to me, talking to that snake-bitch Kizzy. I walked right up behind him and blindsided him with the pistol. *"Bitch-ass nigga!"*

The first blow split his face wide open. He hollered, grabbed his face, and spun to my direction. I smacked him again. *"Think shit sweet?"*

"Aahh, noo, noo. Please don't shoot me. I'm sorry, man."

The second blow split his shit again and dropped him. He balled up like a baby. I put the gun in my back pocket and stomped him all the way out. All the frustration I had toward life, I took out on him. When the school officer came, I was still stomping him out. It was blood everywhere. I didn't stop till they maced me, and the only reason I stopped then was because I couldn't see or breathe.

Because of my age, I was arrested and taken into Juvie Hall. I was given a court date and released to the custody of my mother. As soon as I got inside the car, she went off on me. *"Shawn, what the hell is your problem? I do all I can to make sure you got what you need, and you still doing this dumb shit! I give up, Shawn. I can't do it anymore! Your lil brother and sister look up to you, and I can't let you lead them down this road. I can't do it. I done lost you. I can't lose no more."*

My mother cried, and inside I cried too. I knew I was lost. It was something going on inside me that was pure evil. All I cared about was family. If you weren't family, then anything goes. I tried to control it, but I couldn't. I wanted so badly to tell her (my mom) that it was partly her fault that I was acting this way.

I had two sisters, and my mother raised me not to hit girls. But here it was she letting her husband whip her ass and mine too. Every time they fought, I jumped my lil ass in it and got my ass beat, but I didn't care so long as he got off my mom. Most times, my older sister wasn't home, but when she was, she was jumping in too.

I remember one day, I cut class and came home early. My mother would usually be at work around this time but was at home. But by this time, she had pretty much let me do what I wanted, so it was a no-questions-asked as to why I wasn't in school. I guess she didn't hear me come in or knew I was in the house. So as I was walking to the kitchen, I heard my mom in her room; and it sounded like she was crying, so I opened her bedroom door. *"Ma, you okay?"*

She tried to turn her head away from me and hide it, but I had already seen it. Her mouth was busted, both lips swollen. And I wanted some instant action with Big Al, but he had already fled the scene. My mom fussed me out for not knocking on her door and told me she had made a mistake and fell. Some sorry excuse. I knew she was lying, but I went along with it.

My mind was already made up. I was going to kill Big Al. He had to die. I was tired of this shit.

As soon as I left, I cut across my grandmother's yard and headed over to Gator's. My plan was to steal another gun, but when I went to the stash, it was empty. Gator had moved all the guns. *"Damn!"* I was mad as hell. I guess after I got caught with the .38, he was hip to my shit. Now my plan to kill Big Al wouldn't work, but still the warrior in me came up with another one.

I walked back to the crib, went to my room, and turned on some 2Pac. I lifted my window, rolled a blunt, blew some smoke, and cried. It was like 2Pac was the only person in the world that knew what I was going through. He was the only one that felt a young-nigga pain, and I was hurting hard on the inside. I was young, thugging and feeling like the world ain't giving a fuck about me.

Earlier that day before I left for school, her husband had told me to cut the grass, which was why I cut classes and came home early. But after seeing my mom's mouth busted open, I told myself, *"I ain't cutting shit. Fuck him, and fuck that grass."*

I was really ready to kill this man. I stayed in my room all day listening to 2Pac. Usually, I would go get on Teion's nerves, tease

Terry, or play fight with Avyd. But not today. I had murder on my mind in the worst way.

It didn't take long for my plan to go into effect.

As soon as he got off work and drunk a couple of beers, he was pounding at my door. *"Didn't I tell you to cut the grass this morning?"* he yelled through the door.

I opened my bedroom door. *"Yeah, you did, but I didn't. And you are not my dad, so I ain't gotta listen to nothing you tell me to do!"*

It took a brief second for what I said to register, but when it did, it was on. He pushed me hard in my chest. I flew backward but stayed on my feet and gripped my baseball bat tight. He charged. I swung (*pop!*). I swung again (*pop!*), connecting both times. I kept swinging.

Finally, he grabbed me and slung me across the room. I landed on top of the nightstand, breaking the lamp and falling on the floor in the process. He was 6'4, 240. *"Oh, you think you tough, don't you?"*

Before I could answer, I heard my sister screaming, *"Get off my brother!"* First, she hit him in the back of the head with a chair, the she jumped on his back and started choking him.

By now, my mother was at the door, screaming for us to stop. He slung my sister off his back. Luckily, she landed on the bed. My mom stepped in the room and got between us. *"Y'all stop!"* was all she kept yelling. She now had a scarf wrapped around her mouth to conceal her busted lips.

The warrior in me was wide-awake, and I wanted to see this man bleed. I let out a loud battle cry, *"Aaaaaaaahhhhh!"* while staring Alan dead in his eyes.

"Shawn, stop! Stop, Shawn! Stop that shit right goddamn-it now!" my mom yelled. I was possessed and ready to die to defend my mother's honor. But she didn't get it. Instead, she kicked me out the house and made me go stay with my dad. I wasn't trying to leave my mom and sisters at the mercy of Big Al; but nobody understood, and I didn't know how to tell them. It was me against the world.

Leland

I spent summers and occasionally visited my father, but like I said, my dad was a changed man. All he did was work and go to church. Not to mention he stayed deep in the country, and there was nothing to do out there.

My dad had remarried also and bought another house. His wife had two kids, Vallin and Raymond, from her previous marriage. Plus she had given birth to my lil sister Kesha. It really wasn't that bad. It's just I knew my dad wasn't going to let me run wild; and that's what I was used to, so I wasn't trying to change that.

My mom had already told me my dad was coming to pick me up. I heard her, but I wasn't listening. In my mind, I wasn't going nowhere, and that was that. So by the time my dad came to get me, I had forgotten all about what my mom had told me. *Knock, knock, knock.* I knew it was my dad at the door, so I ain't making no attempt to answer it. My sister did not know that (1) my mom had already told me to pack; (2) that Dad was here to get me; and (3) that I wasn't going nowhere.

So anyway, my sister went and answered the door. I stayed lying on the couch. I heard her and my dad talking but couldn't understand what was being said. Finally, after about ten to fifteen minutes of talking, my sister came back in the front room and told me, *"Daddy outside. He said come here."*

Now any other time, I would've been happy as hell to see my dad, but not this time. I started to run out the back door and hide in the woods until he left, but this was the same man that taught me that only snakes hide and only cowards run. So I got up off the couch and went to the door, which was still open, and shut it right in my dad's face. I never showed my face, so my dad didn't know who shut the door; and it was only out of respect for my mother's husband that he never came in the house to begin with. I went and lay back down on the couch as if nothing ain't happening.

After about five minutes, my sister asked, *"Where Dad at?"*

"Ion know. I guess he outside," I answered with attitude.

Like I've been telling y'all, my damn sister was sharp. She knew me like a book; I could never get one over on her. She went and opened the door again. This time, my dad came in, and from the look on his face, I had just pissed him off. He came and stood over me and told me to get up.

"I ain't getting up, and I ain't going nowhere."

He snatched me right off the couch and dropped me right on the floor. It happened so quick I didn't even have time to think about what I was doing. I just reacted. I hopped up, swung, and connected all at the same time. As soon as I felt my blow connect, I felt bad inside. So instead of swinging again, I just stood there with my guard up, looking my father in the eye. I loved this man, but I wasn't leaving my mom without a fight. So here we were—father and son, two warriors, the same bloodline—about to battle.

My dad fought me like a grown man. We tore the entire house up from the front room, to the kitchen, in the dining room, out the front door, and on the patio; and by the time I got inside the car, my shirt was gone, and I only had one shoe on. I never packed any clothes; I went to my dad's house just like that.

My dad just kept staring at me as he was driving and was shaking his head. Finally, when we pulled up in front of the house, he just looked at me and said, *"Fear no man, not even your own father. Those who walk with fear will die a thousand deaths as a coward."* He then started smiling and told me, *"Don't worry about no clothes because we was going school shopping first thing in the morning."*

Now my dad's house was completely different from my mom's. It was more structured; we woke up on time, went to bed on time, did our homework together, ate together, prayed together, and went to church every Sunday (shout-out to Grace Baptist). It was no such thing as doing what you wanted to do in my dad's house. He was king of his castle; even my stepbrother and sister respected him. For the first time in a long while, I was in a peaceful household, and it felt strange. My dad kept me in a child's place and didn't have to worry about fighting no more. It felt weird because up until then, all I knew was fighting. Don't get it twisted; my mom's house was full of love also, but it's the mind state of the man that dictates the harmony within his household. And Big Al's mind state wasn't stable. Every time he got drunk, he got violent, and it was a fuss or fight.

It's crazy because even though my father's house was peaceful, I still found a way to get in trouble. Well, actually, we didn't get in trouble because we never got caught. Let's just say we found a way to have fun, me and my stepbrother Raymond.

Raymond

Now my stepbrother was a smooth criminal. Till this day, he doesn't have a criminal record. Let's just say he's a traveler and does a lot of driving from state to state. It's funny because even as kids, he was the driver.

After about a month of watching how I move and what I was into, he called me to our bedroom. First, he gave me some money then showed me some crack and asked me if I knew how to sell it. I mean, I had seen it plenty of times, but I had never sold any. He then went on to explain the price on each size when breaking down a gram from nickel rocks all the way to 50 pieces. He explained the difference between a smoker's 50 piece and a hustler's 50 piece. *"A hustler's 50 piece was called a double up and should always be a 1.0 or better on the scale."*

As we were talking, I heard a car horn. Raymond got up and looked out our bedroom window. *"I'll be right back,"* he said, leaving out our bedroom. I got up and looked out the window. I saw that it was Rod, Raymond's older cousin. When Raymond came back in the room, he sat down, reached into his pocket, and pulled out a ziplock bag full of double ups. He then told me, *"Ima show you how to sell crack so you can keep some money in your pocket and stay fresh."* He had a closet full of Nautica, Hilfiger, Polo, and all different-colored Air

Force Ones. He was able to hide the fact that he hustled because he also had a job, so my pops and his mom didn't have a clue.

Later that night, he woke me up and whispered, *"Be quiet and get dressed."* He told me we were sneaking out the bedroom window, taking the car, and going to sell some crack. I already told y'all my dad stayed deep in the country, so the only way we could make money was by going to town. Now I was always down for some fun, but this adventure right here was out of my league. I had never even thought to try some shit like this. Plus, I knew if my dad found out, we would be in serious trouble, but I couldn't back out. This sounded like some major fun, and I was tired of being stuck deep in the country with nothing to do.

So I got up, got dressed, and crawled out the window. Our bedroom window was right in front of the driveway, so I ducked down by the car and waited on Raymond. When Raymond came out the window, he got in the car, put it in neutral stood by the driver side doorway and pushed. We pushed the car out the driveway, up the road past the house before actually getting in and cranking it up.

Brah was nice behind the wheel, could drive his ass off, and was only fifteen. Before we went to town, we stopped by this spot called Springhill. This was where Raymond's older cousin Rod hung out at with Bengy and Ish, his cousins also. Raymond introduced me to everybody. We all just sat out front of the trailer park and served cars as they pulled up for crack. I only had three grams, so it wasn't long before it was all gone. Raymond was sharing his sales with me. Plus Bengy and Ish let me get most of the nickel and dime sales.

My pack was gone. I had close to 300 dollars in my pocket, and we hadn't even made it to town yet. That was the first time I had ever had that much money. I was still only thirteen years old. Before we left for town, I had given Rod 200 dollars, and he gave me five more double ups.

"You family now, so Ima look out for you. Just keep the money in the fam. Ima make sure Raymond good, and he gone make sure you good."

From that day forward, I considered them all as my real family and Raymond as my real brother.

By the time we made it to town, we had already sold most of our crack. In three hours, I had made like 500 dollars and still had two double ups. When we got to town, all we did was get some weed and drove through the projects.

I had called my lil girlfriend at the time (Michelle) and asked if she could sneak me in. She said, *"Yeah."* So my bro dropped me off over there and told me I had an hour to get right. He had something lined up with his girl (Kathy), so I assumed that's where he was headed.

Michelle

Chelle was this shorty I went to school with—I mean that literally. She was 4'11", a cute face, and pigeon-toed. After Necee, I had hit a few stragglers here and there, but somehow, Chelle had worked her way to my heart. Ion know what it was, but I think it was 'cause she didn't trip about my home situation. Before I went to stay with my dad, I used to wear the same clothes damn near every week and my sister's clothes too. But Chelle ain't seem to care about that; she still gave me some play.

So anyway, my brah dropped me off over Chelle's house with an hour to get right. Now Chelle and I were close. We spent hours on the phone almost every day. And from what she told me, I was only the second guy she had been with. We had done it once before, but it didn't go right. It was blood everywhere when we finished. Somehow, during one of our conversations, I asked her, *"Have you ever been ate out before?"* She said, *"No,"* and I always kept that in mind.

When she came to the door, she only had on a T-shirt and panties. We tiptoed up the stairs and made it safely to her room. Once we got on her bed, she laid back and pulled her T-shirt off. I grabbed her panties and pulled them down and off her ankles. Everything about Michelle was bite-size; nipples, titties, ass—everything was the perfect size. I was still fully clothed. I hadn't removed one piece of clothing.

The first thing I did was tongue-kiss her with deep passionate kisses while positioning myself in between her legs. I kissed her from the mouth all the way down, stopping briefly to take a mouthful of each bite-size titty, sucking and biting gently on each nipple. I kept kissing until I was breathing directly on her pussy. I took a deep breath (smell test); she smelled like water. Then I licked to see what she tasted like; she tasted like clean flesh. Then finally I stuck my mouth on her clit and just started sucking it.

Man, I made a mess. I ate her out for damn near the entire hour and never let up. She came right in my mouth multiple times, and by the time I actually got up in her, she was soaking wet. I wrote my name on her heart that night. My first time eating a girl out and her first time getting ate out, and this time, there was no blood or bleeding... I did my damn thing!

When Raymond pulled up to get me, I hopped in smiling. We rolled up and traded stories all the way home. He was the one that taught me, *"Lil brah, you got to eat them first so they don't bleed. They still tender."*

Yeah, brah, that was some good game you gave me; and Chelle, thanks for that special memory.

Everything was running smooth at pop's place. Big brah gave me helluva game and made sure I stayed fly with money in my pockets. I had transferred to South Brunswick, the new face on the schoolyard. Plus I was fly, so I had a lot of attention from the young ladies. I had so many girls calling my dad's house Pops decided it was time for *that talk*.

My pops was old school with it. He came in the bedroom one day and told me, *"Let's take a walk."* I'm thinking I done did something wrong, but I could tell by his body language he wasn't angry.

So anyway, we went walking. After about the first five minutes, he was unusually quiet, then suddenly he spoke, *"Your mom told me she bought you some condoms. I know you having sex, but I'm not buying you no condoms. Don't let me catch you having sex in my house."*

I went along with it mainly because (1) there were no girls in the neighborhood; (2) I did most of my dirt at school; and (3) I had secret transportation where me and brah were jumping fences, climbing in and out windows, and most definitely pulling up!

After he got that off his chest, he told me, *"Your mom said you'll be going to court soon."* I had actually forgotten all about the situation. He told me I should come out okay since I was young and that was my first offense ever. I mean, I thought I would be good too.

Blue Clay Road

Until I showed up at court and saw Kalvin soft-ass sitting with his mom and the school officer. Kalvin was a rat; he was ready to tell everything, and that's exactly what he did. He made sure to leave out the fact that he had bullied me. Which was really the only reason why I pistol-whipped him.

The school officer testified too and told the judge that the only way he got me to stop was by macing me. And that after he cuffed me and he patted me down, he found an empty .38 revolver in my back pocket. So if you were wondering why I didn't shoot Kalvin, now you know. I didn't have no damn bullets.

The judge then requested that my mom get on the stand. They wanted to know how a thirteen-year-old boy had gotten hold of a firearm. My mom couldn't answer because she didn't know, and I never told the police nothing except I found it in the woods. My mom broke down in tears and told the judge she couldn't control me and that I needed help. Seeing my mom in tears almost broke me down too. I knew her tears were my fault.

As my mom was crying and trying to explain to the judge how it seemed as though I had just changed overnight, I heard somebody behind me laughing. I looked back and saw it was my juvie PO (Ms. Holmes), and I assumed she was laughing at my crying mother. I couldn't help it. I tried to ignore her, but when I turned back around, she started laughing again. Here was my mother up here, crying tears of pain, and this bitch is laughing like this shit's a joke.

So I turned back around, stood up, and asked her, *"What the fuck so funny?"* The entire courtroom got quiet. All I could hear was my mother sniffing, trying to hold back tears. My lawyer told me to sit back down, but I wasn't trying to hear it. I pointed to my juvie

PO and tried to explain, *"She was laughing at my momma. This shit ain't funny."*

The judge hit the gavel and yelled for "Order! Order in the court!"

I refused to sit back down or turn back around. All I kept doing was pointing at my PO and asking her, *"What the fuck so funny?"* She never answered, and next thing I knew, the bailiff was escorting me out the courtroom handcuffed behind my back. I ended up in a holding cell by myself; they made me wait in there all day. I was literally the last case they heard, and on September 28, 1994 (my birthday), I was sentenced to juvenile detention confinement indefinitely up until my eighteenth birthday or until I showed signs of rehabilitation. Shit had just gotten real, and I was in for a ride… The warrior in me was on high alert.

My first day at juvie was pure hell. For the first time in my life, I was stripped searched, sprayed with lice spray, and given a shower, sandals, and jumpsuit. I had met two other guys in the holding cell, J-Rat and Doggfaze. All three of us were getting processed in. We had already formed a bond on the van ride to have one another's back. Doggfaze knew my cousin Murder, and J-Rat had heard how I had pistol-whipped Kalvin. Plus all the commotion I caused in the courtroom had the guards thinking I was crazy.

As soon as we hit the tier, the dudes started yelling, *"Fresh meat, fresh meat!"* and making catcalls. I ignored that shit but took a mental note of which cells it came from. Doggfaze spoke up, *"Fuck y'all fagot-ass niggas. Do that shit when we face to face."*

I guess dudes saw we weren't scared, so they shut up. They split all three of us up in different cells. My cell mate was a kid named P-Nap. He went to Lakeside also. We knew each other but ran in different circles. He gave me the rundown on how shit was being ran.

"We come out for breakfast at 6:30 a.m. Lock back after breakfast and come back out at 8:00 a.m. for school. Stay out from 8:00 till 3:30 with a lunch and recess in-between. Lock back at 3:30 till 5:00, eat dinner at 5:00, and shower at 6:00. From 6:00 to 9:00 is free time. On the weekend, we get to stay out till 11:00."

Nap was a cool celly. We did push-ups, 300 every day, and kicked it a lot. He was in on a drug charge, and everybody who knew him spoke highly of his hustling skills; but Nap was kind of anti-social. He never spoke or dealt with nobody when we came out our cell. He never played basketball or nothing. All he did was walk laps around the fence, and when we were in the cell, all he did was read the Bible whenever we weren't doing push-ups. No lie, Nap read the Bible three times back to back, from front to back within two months.

So one day after showers and I came back to the cell, I saw Nap was balled up in the corner with his back to the wall, sitting on the bed and holding his Bible. At first, I ain't thinking much of it, but when I looked at his face, I saw he looked frightened. So I asked him, *"You okay?"*

He just stared at me with a crazy look in his eyes then said, *"I just saw Jesus."*

At first, I laughed; but I saw it in his eyes that he was serious, so I was like *"You for real? What happened? How He look?"*

He said, *"I was in here reading my Bible, and the room got filled with a blinding light. It was so bright that I couldn't see. All I heard was a voice, and it said, 'I am Jesus.' Then the light went away."* I ain't know what to say, so I just shut up and listened; but seeing how serious he was made me think either this dude was really crazy or he really saw Jesus.

Because of my outburst in the courtroom, the judge ordered a mental health evaluation. They actually thought I was crazy for real. So that meant I had to stay behind while J-Rat and Doggfaze left for training school. Our bond was already formed; we had already started calling ourselves the Henchmen. If one fought, we all fought. It wasn't no fair ones unless we were fighting one another, which we tended to do from time to time, all in the name of brotherly love (shout-out to all the homies on Blue Clay road that showed me love).

After my mental health evaluation, it was determined by the docs that I officially had ADHD (attention deficit hyperactivity disorder). I was prescribed Ritalin, and before I go any further, let me take a second to explain to all the parents who have ADHD children what Ritalin is doing to your child.

Ritalin and Attarol are anxiety suppressants. However, after the suppressant wears off, your anxiety returns twice—sometimes three times more powerful. Those drugs don't cure hyperness; they only suppress it. The more doses you take, the more you'll need, which is why you can always tell when a child who takes those drugs hasn't had their meds. They can't sit still because they have excessive energy due to the imbalance that the suppressant creates. My advice is, if you have a hyperactive child, put them in all the after-school programs you can. Don't let your child become dependent on those drugs. Half of the dope fiends I know were once considered ADHD, and Ritalin and Attarol were the drugs that paved their road to self-destruction.

When I started taking Ritalin, it made my mind move slow. I felt like a damn zombie. I was literally sleepwalking. I hated that feeling. I like feeling alive and sharp, so I started hiding the pill under my tongue and spitting it out.

That worked fine for a while. But the case manager at Juvie Hall told the courts that the medicine wasn't working, so they put me on Attarol; and that shit almost killed me. I couldn't eat nor sleep, and my hair started falling out.

My mom had told me she was trying to get a crazy check for me and that the meds would help when she went to DSS to state her claim. I was down to play crazy for a check, but that shit was too strong. The next time my mom came to see me, I told her, *"I'm not taking no more of the medicine."* She didn't even argue with me after I told her how I couldn't eat and showed her where my hair was falling out. She was like *"Don't take no more of that shit, Shawn."* She called one of the staff members over to the table and told them, *"Don't give my son no more of that damn dope-fiend medicine."* They told my mom because it was court-ordered, they had to offer it to me, but it was up to me if I accepted it. I never took that shit again! (And again, I repeat to all parents who have ADHD children: do not let your child become dependent on those drugs.)

Samarkand Manor

Now that my mental health evaluation was over with, it was time for me to leave Juvie Hall and get transferred to training school. Nap and I said our goodbyes and promised to link up with each other on the outside. During my ride from Juvie Hall to training school, I was accompanied. Lil Dave talked for the whole entire ride nonstop; he was the entertainment. He and Titus knew each other, so I just sat back and listened. I eventually dozed off to sleep, and when I awoke, Lil Dave was still talking as we were pulling up to the training school.

It was nighttime, so I couldn't see much besides the dorm we pulled up in front of. We spent our first night in the disciplinary dorm, went to orientation the next day, and were designated to our housing unit. When we got to our dorms, we were instructed by the staff to stand in front of the office while they made arrangements for our housing. As I was standing there peeping out the scene and talking to Titus and Lil Dave, I heard somebody say, *"War before peace,"* the official Henchmen greeting. I looked back and saw Doggfaze and J-Rat standing there, smiling. *"I'm my brother's keeper,"* I said, smiling and properly greeting my Henchmen homies.

They all ended up knowing one another; Titus, Lil Dave, J-Rat, and Doggfaze were from the Southside. The housing staff had to come out and tell us to stop cursing out so much. J-Rat had already gone and made some dudes move, so Doggfaze, Titus, and I were assigned to the back porch. It was an open-style dorm room with eight beds, four on each side located all the way in the back of the building. Lil Dave was also assigned to the same building; his room was on the back hall right next to the back porch. I told Doggfaze, *"We have to look out for him. That lil nigga crazy."* All he wanted to do was talk, and if you ain't listening, he wanted to fight. Crazy shit is, he could fight his ass off. He eventually became Henchmen, but by that time, he had beat so many people up wasn't nobody messing with him. Titus never officially became Henchmen, but he was with us on whatever. It wasn't long before we had the whole Samarkand Manor screaming, *"War before peace, and I'm my brother's keeper,"* and throwing up *H*s. We had started a movement without even trying, and even though it was never talked about or nobody actually said it, I was looked at by all as the *"Head Henchmen."*

So one day, we were all in the gym, and the Henchmen homies was playing ball against this squad from Queen City (Charlotte, North Carolina) that call themselves the Charlotte Dons. I wasn't playing; I was actually coaching but was busy spitting game to this girl named Tina Martin. She was from Charlotte too (Tina, if you're reading this, holler at me). Next thing I know, I see Lil Dave arguing, and out of all people, he picked the biggest dude to fuss with.

So I go over, and by the time I got there, the homies had already swarmed around Dave. And dude, I could tell they were ready to bang out. The dude from the Dons started explaining what happened, which was that Dave had pushed him out the air and because of that, he wanted to fight Lil Dave. Now I already told y'all before: *"Ain't no fair ones with this henchmen shit. You fight one, you fight all, and I told dude the same thing."* Actually, my exact words were *"You too big to get a fair one with my lil brah. If you fight him, you gone have to fight me."*

Not only was the dude big but he was stupid also. What he did next got his ass beat and his nose broke. After I told him he would have to fight me too, his response was *"Well, whatsup then?"* But after he said that, he turned his head; I guess to see if the Dons had his back. I stepped in and punched him as soon as he was turning his head back in my direction—left hook (jaw) and right hook (chin). I stepped back and squared up. He dropped his head and rushed me; I grabbed his head and directed it to my knee. I felt his nose break on my knee then saw the blood. *"Bitch-ass nigga. Henchmen shit."* He ran off, holding his bleeding nose, but by this time, everybody was fighting. It was like thirty of us; even dudes who weren't repping a set were riding for their cities on both sides.

After the dude ran off, I just started running up on dudes and swinging. Maaaann, they locked all our asses up. Dave, Titus, and I got sent to the IDP building. We never saw normal population again. Doggfaze and J-Rat got transferred to another training school; their sentences were about over with anyway. They both only had six months and had already done four. Titus, Dave, and I were stuck in the IDP (Indoor Dormitory Program), and in this program, we were confined to one building twenty-four-seven. No going out to school, going to the gym, or having outside recreation with the girls. We were actually in a mini prison. A place where they stuck the worst of the worst. The individuals they felt needed to be isolated.

The only thing we were allowed to do was go to school, which became the highlight of our day. We had this ex-military teacher named Mr. Utley, and he was just as crazy as we were, but for some reason, he took a special liking to me. When I first arrived at the program, he had already heard about the Henchmen and what had happened in the gym. So anyway, one day, he called me to the classroom by myself and started interrogating me. "Where you from? What you locked up for? What gang you run with?" and all these crazy-ass questions. I guess he was trying to let me know he wasn't having the bullshit. Finally, I just got tired of all the questioning, so I told him straight up, *I'm here for pistol-whipping a dude that beat me up and bullied me. My mother got six kids, I'm the oldest boy, and I know how to fend for myself. I don't like to fight, but I will because my dad told me a long time ago that only cowards run.* For a minute, he just stared at me then went to his desk, grabbed a stack of paper, gave me the answer sheet, and told me to grade the papers.

From that day forward, Mr. Utley was like my mentor. He opened my mind to so much knowledge and Black history. He gave me books on Malcolm X, Martin Luther King, Nat Turner, Clyde Brown, Nathan McCall, and Sister Souljah. For the first time in my life, I was learning, and it was fun. Also around this time, Mr. Utley had put together a newsletter called *The Path*. I was assigned as editor in chief. I had Titus and Lil Dave as my assistants, and together we managed to publish one newsletter a month with various articles. My articles were so in depth that no one believed that a teenager kid was actually writing the article. They accused Mr. Utley of being my ghostwriter, and just to prove everybody wrong, he converted the library into my office and let us work from there. He would check in occasionally to assure we weren't bullshitting around.

It was also around this time when we came up with the acronym for HENCHMEN, which was **H**ighly **E**ducated **N**egro **C**ees **H**is/**H**er **M**ind **E**levate **N**obly. Now not only was **HENCHMEN** a movement but we were also becoming an organization with a legitimate purpose. Mr. Utley, without even knowing it, was helping to sharpen our minds on a more militant level. Every time I finish reading a book, I would pass it to Lil Dave or Titus. I wrote a letter to Doggfaze and J-Rat informing them of the progress we were making.

One day, Mr. Utley called me to the class; by this time, my sentence was almost over. I was showing signs of rehabilitation, and it was almost over. I had served a total of twenty months. Mr. Utley asked me what my plans were, and truthfully speaking, I didn't have any. I was just happy to finally be going home. I had already earned my GED, but I did that just to pass time. So now I was sitting here, talking to my mentor, and I realized I was about to be going back out to the real world to the same old shit without a plan. Mr. Utley was telling me that I had one of the brightest minds he had ever taught. He offered to pay for my college and, as a going-away present, bought me a Guess watch. *"That way, whenever you check the time, you'll be reminded of this place. And hopefully, that'll keep you out of trouble."*

When my day finally arrived, the hardest part of my departure was leaving Titus and Lil Dave behind. Those were my dudes, especially Dave. I had grown to love him like my brother for real. On my final day, Mr. Utley let me give a speech to the class. I had made a lot of friends and a few enemies too. My final words for everybody were to stay focused on getting home and that nothing else was of any real importance besides elevating your mind. *"Mr. Utley might be a little crazy because of his military experience, but if you'll listen and follow his lead, he'll definitely sharpen your mind."* After my speech, I sat down and waited on my mom to come pick me up. It wasn't a long wait; my mom was just as happy as I was about my release. She had spoken with Mr. Utley and read all my newsletters, so she knew I had matured.

The first thing my mom said when I got in the car was *"I got a divorce."* Now I know you would've thought that I would be happy to hear that, but I wasn't. Being locked up gave me a lot of time to reflect, and during those reflections, I learned a lot about life and myself. I realized that the only reason I acted out so much was because my dad wasn't around. I knew I could get away with a lot more with my mom. Whenever a dominant adult male was around, I would listen, but with my mom, I knew she had too many kids to worry about to just focus on me. When she told me she had gotten a divorce, the first thing I thought about was my two little brothers and sister. I figured they would need their dad just as much as I needed mine. So my response was *"Y'all might need to get back together. You gone break the family apart."* My mom laughed it off, but I could tell my response had shocked her. I wasn't as young in the mind anymore. I was fifteen, soon to be sixteen, and Mr. Utley had enlightened me a lot about life. I was a mature-minded young man, and I was ready for the world.

Biscuits and Bricks

I knew that with my mom getting a divorce and having another child (my youngest sister Vanny), I had to step up. Somehow, someway, I had to hold my FAM down.

One of the first things I did was get a job. My dad had a friend that was a manager at Bojangles' on Market Street. Technically, I had to be sixteen to work, but since my birthday was close and he knew my dad, all I had to do was fill out the application.

My first and last job ever was making Bojangles' biscuits. I lasted about three weeks before I realized I was too fly for that shit. Every day, I would go to work fresh, and by the time I got off, I would have biscuit dough all over me from head to toe. So one day, I was in the back making biscuits, and I looked up to see J-Rat at the register. First, I didn't say anything 'cause I didn't want him to see me. Brah was looking like new money—rings, earrings, Cuban link, and just fresh to death. And here I was looking like the Pillsbury Doughboy covered in biscuit dough. I watched for a second as he placed his order and flirted with the ole girl working the register.

All I could do was smile; I could tell ole girl was buying whatever game he was selling. Finally, I stepped up to the front, but he was so busy gaming ole girl that he never looked my way. *"War before peace."* Soon as he heard that, his head snapped in my direction. This fool jumped over the counter and was like *"Oh, shit, my nigga home!"* and gave me a hard hug. *"Yo, brah! How long you been out, and what the hell you doing working at Bojangles'?"*

By this time, all eyes were on us, so I told brah to step outside and talk. My coworkers were cool, but they didn't know me. All they knew was I was a biscuit maker, and that's all they needed to know. When we got outside, I told brah straight up, *"Money tight at the house right now. My mom struggling trying to do everything by herself. Day in and day out, she struggling, and that shit killing me. I only been out a month, but with this job, I'm one less mouth she gotta worry about feeding."*

We talked for a while about a lot of things. His mom (Buckey) had just got out the Feds, and he wanted me to meet her. *"I told her all about you, brah."* And he was running with some cats he wanted me to link up with too. *"I kept the Henchmen movement going brah. Wait till you meet my people."* He then went in his pocket, counted 1,000 dollars, and gave it to me along with his pager number. *"I'm your keeper, brah. Make sure you page me and put 4.5.6 behind your number."*

And just like that, I was back on. I watched as he got inside a money-green Mazda MX-6 two-door coupe. He pulled alongside me and turned the music loud. *"♪It's mine, it's mine, it's mine. Whose world is this…"* he started singing along and pointed at me as Nas was saying, *"♪The world is yours, the world is yours…"* then he pulled off into Market Street traffic. Needless to say, that was my last day making biscuits at Bojangles'. I went in, clocked out, and never came back.

When my mom came to pick me up that night, I told her, *"Making biscuits ain't my thing. It just don't feel right."*

"Well, son, it's going to be a lot of times in life when you have to do things that just don't feel right in order to survive. In case you didn't notice, we not rich, and I'm doing everything by myself now. So you gone have to find whatever your thing is and make it work for you because I gotta take care of your younger brothers and sisters and I'm not getting back with Big Al. So go ahead and get that out your mind." She then went on to explain to me how while I was away, his drinking got worse. He started blaming her for not going pro and continued to hit on her. She started shedding tears as she explained, *"Son, I tried to keep the family together, but it's only so much I can take. You think I want to be doing this by myself? I don't, and like you just said, it don't feel right. But guess what? Ima make it work."*

Seeing my mother crying always made me uncomfortable, and I knew that the only time she cried was when somebody she loved had hurt her.

It was time for me to step out on my own and become a man. Playtime was over. The streets were calling me, and I couldn't ignore it. The next day, I paged J-Rat. When he hit me back, he told me he and Doggfaze were coming to pick me up. When they pulled up, I was outside, waiting. The first thing I saw was Doggfaze's big-ass head bobbing to the music. J-Rat was driving the same whip from yesterday. We ended up at the mall, and they bought me some clothes. Even when I tried to pay for something, they wouldn't let me. *"Yo, brah, keep your money in your pocket. You just got out. We got you covered."*

After we left the mall, we rode around for a while. Doggfaze was bringing me up to speed on his hustle. It was two cats from NY he was hitting the highway with, Don V and Smiley. Two older cats that had taken him under their wing and put him on his feet. *"Last time I went up top, they introduced me to DJ Jazzy Joyce. I was actually chilling with them in her apartment. They be showing me a lot of love and putting a lot of money in my pocket."* As if to prove his point, he reached in his pocket, pulled out a thick wad of money, and gave it to me. *"That's 2,000 dollars, your welcome-home present. Don't let me catch you with that Bojangles' uniform again,"* he said, laughing at me.

"Fuck you, nigga," I said, laughing too and accepting the money. I knew J-Rat must have told him about the conversation last night. I didn't mind. After all these were my Henchmen homies, and having one another's backs was something we were sworn to.

We eventually dropped Doggfaze off on the Southside and went to J-Rat's grandma's house. First thing he did was go the closet and move some clothes around. When he turned around, he had an AK-47 with two banana clips. *"This my baby right here. Brah, she don't play."* He then sat the AK down, reached under the bed, and pulled out a book bag. He unzipped the book bag and pulled out three pistols. A 17-shot chrome and black 9 Taurus, an all-black beretta 9mm with the wood grain handle and a chrome .38 Smith and Wesson revolver. *"You can have the beretta, but keep it in town. I got a spot for you to stash it."*

After the gun show, he let me know he and people had just hit a bank for 220,000 dollars. They also just hit another lick and left dude stanking for 80,000 dollars. It was a lot of dudes from up top (New York and New Jersey) in the city. One guy in particular was named Hybeeb from East Orange, New Jersey. J-Rat was telling me how he had the whole city shook, so people were blaming everything on him. **Hybeeb was the first one who brought the KSBG, a.k.a. Double II Blood Gang, to Wilmington, North Carolina, in 1997.**

I had heard about the body because it had happened right after I came home, and the hood was speculating hard about what actually happened and who actually did it. Everybody was blaming Hybeeb; now here I was listening to my homie tell me that it was his people. At first, I was doubtful as to whether or not brah was telling me the truth, but when he took me the stash spot (which happened to be in Rankin Terrace at the crib of this chick named Shauntey), I knew he wasn't fronting.

When we got to Shauntey's crib, he told me to stash the gun in the downstairs hallway closet. He then went upstairs and came back with two book bags. *"Look at this shit."* He unzipped both book bags and dumped the money right out on the floor. *"That's damn near 300,000 dollars in blood money, nigga. Frank, pay attention. These mafuckers is Henchmen,"* he said. I had never seen so much money in my life. He said it was damn near 300,000 dollars, but it looked more like a million to me. *"Help me count this shit. My people on the way to pick this up. They should be here soon, and plus they wanna meet you anyway."*

It wasn't long before they pulled up, and when they did, it wasn't what I expected. No fancy car, no jewelry—there was nothing fancy about them at all. One guy was named Kawada. He was light skin and had a medium height of about 5'8–5'9, 190 pounds, with glasses and a permanent smile on his face. The other guy was short and cubby and had brown skin with glasses too. Looking at them both, I really wasn't impressed. I guess by me knowing what I knew, I expected more.

Kawada was the first one to notice me; he asked J-Rat, *"Who's that?"*

"That's my man I was telling you about that I was locked up with. He official. He just getting out."

"Oh, word, whatsup?" Kawada said as he offered me his hand. He still had that smile on his face. I could tell it was only a mask because when I looked in his eyes, they had "I *kill for fun*" all in 'em. After we locked eyes and shook hands, he and his man left. The other guy's name was Shaun too; he never did a lot of talking or said more than necessary.

As time went on and they got more comfortable around me, they began to relax. Actually, J-Rat and I never hung out with Shaun. It was Kawada that helped us take Henchmen to a whole 'nother level. He was hitting so many licks and had so much work he just gave it to us for damn near nothing.

So one night as we were riding around, Kawada pulled the car over and parked. We just sat there for a while. J-Rat was upfront along with Kawada. Out of nowhere, Kawada turned around and asked me, *"You ever seen somebody die?"*

And for the first time, I noticed he wasn't smiling. His face matched his eyes, and I saw the killer within the depths of his soul; but for some reason, I wasn't afraid. It was as if the warrior in me was ready for whatever came next, so I answered honestly, *"No."*

"Well, you gone see somebody die tonight," he said while reaching out his hand to give me a gun. *"You see that house right there with a Ford Explorer parked in front of it? Ima get out and go lay under the truck. When the dude come out the house, I want both of y'all on each corner to start walking towards him. We gone box him in. If he get to the truck before y'all get to him, Ima be waiting for him. This nigga worth at least 100,000 dollars and work, so don't fuck this up. If you have to shoot him, aim for his leg. We need him to tell us where it's at."*

We watched for nearly three hours, waiting for the dude to come out, and when he did, we was on him. J-Rat came from one direction; I came from the other. Kawada was lying on his back under the truck with a sawed-off positioned on his chest. As we approached, J-Rat pulled the Taurus out too soon. I could see the reflection of the chrome gleaming off the streetlight. The dude froze, looked both ways, then turned, and tried to run back to the house. We closed in on him.

He fell clumsily, trying to run up the porch steps. *Smack! "Nigga, you know what it is. Where it's at, and who else inside the house?"* J-Rat said after slapping dude with the gun.

"Man, please, my kids in the house. Just don't shoot me, man, please. Ima give you everything."

By this time, Kawada had ran up and pointed the sawed-off dead in his face *"Nigga, Ima ask you one time where it's at, and if you lie, Ima kill everybody in the house before I kill you."*

"Okay, okay, it's inside the TV. You gotta remove the back panel. It's all there. I swear, that's everything."

"Get up," Kawada instructed and walked the dude back inside the house. Once we got inside, Kawada told me and J-Rat, *"Search the house and tie everybody up."*

The only person in the house was a girl, and she was sound asleep. I woke her up by gently tapping my pistol on her forehead. She let a short scream. I put my finger to my mouth and told her, *"Shhhhh, we not here for you. Go hide in the bathtub and be quiet. Your man downstairs begging for his life. Don't lose yours behind a bitch-ass nigga."*

She walked nervously to the bathroom, which was connected to the bedroom. I told her to lie face down on her stomach, ripped the phone cord out the wall, and tied her hands behind her back. *"That's loose enough for you to get out of, but count to 1,000 before you move."*

By this time, I made it back downstairs. I saw Kawada and J-Rat stuffing money from the back of a floor-model TV inside a trash bag. Dude was laying at an odd angle in a puddle of blood and appeared unconscious. And that's exactly how we left him.

Southside

We split the lick 60/40 between me, J-Rat, Kawada, and Shaun. J-Rat and I ended up with 30k a piece and a nice amount of work. I was cool with it; I mean, all I did was run up on a nigga and tie his bitch up for 30k. That was light work. Come to find out Shaun was the mastermind behind all the licks. He would go buy work from all the big-time dealers, gain their trust, and then turn us loose on them once he knew where they kept the stash.

Around this time, I had started hustling and hanging on 10th and Castle, a block located on the Southside right down the street from the notorious housing projects called Jervay. The Henchmen movement had expanded all over the entire Southside, and the streets had nicknamed me Frank White. Due to that fact, the 10th Street extended from Jervay to Castle and stretched all the way to the BO. We also called ourselves the Dime Squad. It was on Castle Street that I met a lot dudes that would later become Henchmen. My homie Killa Black and J.V. were both from the Bottom but would come chill on Castle occasionally. We eventually became real good friends and started hitting licks and hustling together. Killa Black was real dark skin and had a way with words and women. A real slick talker that a lot of dudes hated on because he got a lot of attention from females. J.V. was a natural loner; the only company he kept was a dog. Most times I saw J.V., he always had a pit bull with him. If he didn't have his dog, he had one of his younger cousins with him and always wore a lot of black. Needless to say, they both became Henchmen, and we all put in a lot of work together. My older cousin Murder was hustling in Jervay and running with this cat called Ty-Dow. Ty-Dow had a younger brother that was my age named Lil Illy, and we hung out a lot too. My mentor at the time was this cat named Uncle Wise.

Uncle Wise was Godbody, a real sharp 5%-er that always dropped jewels on us all. He'd always pop up on Castle, spark a blunt, and dropped the day's mathematics. He was the one that introduced me to the 5% Nation of Gods and Earths. Then you had my cousin Polky and Ghetto. These two hustled in Jervay also. Polk was wild; Ghetto was wild, so everybody just pretty much stayed clear of these two wild niggas. Only thing was, they both were just as smart as they were wild, so that kept a lot people off balance and out of their business by playing crazy. It was Ghetto that showed me that sometimes it's best to play stupid and let people underestimate you. That way, they won't view you as a threat. Don and Noon were hustling on Castle also. They pretty much had it on lock and got a lot hate for that. Being that they weren't from the Southside, dudes felt like they could try them. Noon was more of a hustler; Don was more of an enforcer, and he wasn't going for the bullshit. I respected the fact that they had put it down and built a spot for dudes likes myself to come and get money in town. I was considered a country boy just like they were, so I knew firsthand how some (not all) dudes from town be hustler hating.

10th and Castle became like my second home. Most days, you could find me posted in the front of the store and getting my grind on. It wasn't long before the hate came my way. I was hitting so many licks, but nobody really knew besides the few people I actually took with me.

Me and J-Rat had kind've drifted apart. He, Kawada, and ole girl Shauntey had started snorting heroin. Every time I went over Shauntey's house to check in with him, he'd be nodding out. They had so much money from hitting licks the only time they ever really left out the house was to re-up when they ran out of dope. It got so bad I went over there one day determined to get my dude some help. Kawada and I ended up fussing, and next thing I know, I was fussing with everybody in the house. Kawada was mad because I was telling J-Rat, *"You hustling backwards, brah. You got all this money and wasting it on getting high. That's some crackhead shit."* When I said that, Kawada got mad at me and told J-Rat, *"You better get you lil friend before I hurt him."* He had that same killer look in his eyes. I looked him right back in his eyes and told him, *"You ain't gone do shit to me!"* From that day forward, we established a mutual respect. J-Rat had fallen off hard. He was still fly and had money, but that dope had my homie moving messy.

At this time, I was staying on Hall Street. Murder, Ty-Dow, and I shared a two-bedroom apartment. It was on the low, and nobody knew we stayed there. I spent most of my time on Castle Street or at my older sister's crib. She stayed on the Southside in a project called Houston More and was still doing her thing with the tree.

I had met Buckey (J-Rat's mom), and she was the first female OG I had ever met. Actually, she was the plug. She was giving us dope for next to nothing until she found out J-Rat was snorting it, and she cut us off. It wasn't until she realized that I wasn't snorting dope that she started back-dealing with me.

One day, she called me over to the house and was asking me if I had seen J-Rat. *"If you see my damn son, tell him I said bring his ass over here."*

I already knew where he was at, and seeing Mama Buckey worried was enough to make me go deal with all the bullshit that came with going to Shauntey's house. *"I got you, Ma. We gone come through here later on."*

When I left from there, I went straight to Shauntey's house. When I got to Shauntey's house, he was sitting at the kitchen table, nodding; and oddly enough, there was nobody else home. *"Brah, Momma wanna see you. She worried because you haven't been by the house in a while."* He tried to brush me off with *"Ima go by there later on,"* but I knew better. *"Nah, brah. We 'bout to go see Ma now."* And before he could even disagree, I put his ass in the headlock and applied pressure. *"Nigga, you gon' leave out this damn house today, even if I have to drag you ass outta here. You in here laid up with this trifling bitch snorting that poison. Fuck wrong with you fool?"* I damn near choked his ass out.

When it was all and done, we was pulling up at Momma Buckey's spot in Brooklyn Square. That same night, Mama Buckey gave me a whole ounce of dope and told me, *"You don't owe me nothing. Just make sure my son okay out there on them streets. You the closest thing to a brother he gone ever have.*" Back then, dope was 30–40 dollars a bag, 300–350 dollars a bundle; and the shit she was giving me could take a three. Even till this day, J-Rat and I still tight as brothers (RIP, Mama Buckey. I still got your boy's back).

It wasn't long before word got out as to who was hitting on all the licks. J-Rat and Kawada were still moving messy. For the most part, I had fallen back. 10th and Castle was a gold mine, and it was so much money up there I really didn't need to hit no more licks. Plus I had the dope, and the plug really loved me. Crack money is good, but dope money is great. I could take 1 oz. and make 2 ½, bag up 120 bundles off each oz., and let 'em fly for 250 dollars a bundle, and I was only paying 6,000 dollars an ounce. I was making damn near a 30,000-dollar profit. The only thing I didn't like about selling dope was I had to go on the Northside to a project called Taylor Holmes to sell it because that was the only dope spot in the city at the time.

No one suspected me of being involved in all the shit that was popping off around town. I was a country boy from Wrightsboro, and they were too busy blaming Hybeeb to really know the truth. Plus I had taken Ghetto's advice; I always played stupid when I heard people gossiping about things I knew they knew nothing about.

So when word did get out, my name was never mentioned. However, the dude we hit for the 100,000 dollars was from New York, and word was his people were asking around about who was responsible. The plan was to lay low and deal with them according to the code *"Real niggas move in silence,"* but like I said, that dope had Kawada moving wild and reckless.

I'll never forget, I was right there on 10th and Castle when Kawada and Shaun pulled up. Shaun got out and walked to the corner store. He acknowledged me with a nod, which wasn't unusual because he never spoke much. I walked to the car and kicked it with Kawada until Shaun came back out the store. My last words to both of them were "Be safe."

I can't say for 100 percent fact because I didn't actually see it myself, but the streets say when Kawada and Shaun left Castle, they went to Jervay. And when they got there, one of the dudes that was supposedly *asking around* was out there. Kawada started shooting and ending up hitting and killing the dude, but the saddest day of all Jervay history took place also. Nine-year old lil Poppa caught a stray bullet to the head while sitting in the car, waiting on his mother to take him to the store. Man, that was one of the saddest days for all of Jervay. That was one of those moments in life when I honestly couldn't think straight. The streets were calling for the blood of the same dudes that had put me on my feet.

Luckily, J-Rat wasn't with them when that shit happened, but that still didn't stop Big-Homie Stace from running up in Shauntey's house and kidnapping his ass. The only thing that saved J-Rat was the fact that he wasn't with them when that shit happened. Stace was one of the OGs in Jervay, and he played fair with everybody; but in a situation like this, he was serving street justice, which nobody could really fault him for.

At this point though, it was just too much going on. I wasn't scared, but I also wasn't stupid; and I damn sure wasn't trying to get cased up. So I got low, packed up, and moved to Raleigh for a while with my older cousin Diamond. I had to; wasn't no telling how things would play out back in the Port City, and I wasn't about to stick around to see. I was on I-40 that same night... (Raleigh, yo!)

Raleigh

Diamond was my first cousin on my father's side. He had told me to come to Raleigh and lay low. So I figured now was the perfect time to do just that. When I pulled up, I was in an apartment complex called Stony Brook apartment located in North Raleigh. Diamond had a nice spot—three-bedroom, two-bath—and he stayed there by himself.

That first night, it just felt good to just be able to relax and put that bullshit behind me. I fell asleep as soon as I got all my clothes in the crib. I didn't even unpack. I was exhausted.

The next morning, I woke up to the smell of weed and breakfast and 2Pac rapping 'bout *so many tears.* For a second, I forgot where I was at. The first thing I did was reach for my gun. I had brought my 17-shot black-and-brown beretta and two twin chrome and black .357s. The beretta was my favorite; she never jammed, and that's why I had her under my pillow.

Once I realized where I was at, I took a deep breath and relaxed. My mind was playing tricks on me. Diamond came in the room with a blunt in his hand—just what I needed to wake up and get my mind right. *"It's some food in there if you hungry, fam."* He had a habit of addressing everybody as family or fam. *"I'm about to go handle some BI. When I get back, we gone talk."*

"Man, pass that. I can't eat shit until I get my medicine in me," I said, laughing and reaching for the blunt.

"The weed in the closet at the bottom of that chest with all the clothes in it. It's only one pair of white pants. Grab them and make sure you put the pants back at the bottom. I gotta go handle this BI," he said, leaving out and never passing me the blunt.

For a second, I just laid there and let my mind wander. I started thinking about what my life would have been like if I was born with a silver spoon in my mouth. If I ain't have to hit licks and hustle to survive, I never knew the feeling of not having some type of worry. If it wasn't one thing, it was another. Damned if I do, and damned if I don't.

I wasn't stressing about money. I was doing okay financially. I had my own spot, had brought a decent whip, and helped my mom out with bills and school shopping. I was holding down damn near all my family and friends that were locked up. All this at seventeen years old. I was feeling like NORE on the song called "Sometimes."

> ♫*Sometimes I wanna chill and lay*♫
> ♪*Sometimes I wanna cry and pray*♪
> ♫*Sometimes I get drunk all god damn day*♫
> ♪*Sometimes I wanna ride and smoke*♪
> ♫*Sometimes I got money and I still feel broke*♫

Those were my exact same thoughts at this moment. I was tired; my entire mind, body, and soul were exhausted from hitting licks and hustling. I just wanted to chill and enjoy life, something I had never taken time to do. I decided right then and there that it was time for a vacation.

I got up out the bed, stretched, scratched my balls, smelled my hand, and decided I'll shower before I ate.

Quick break…for my female readers only. When you see your man scratch his balls and then smell his hand, it's called the nut-smell shower check. Most dudes do this because we can't always feel the sweat on our balls, but it leaves an odor; and if your nut sack smells sweaty, it's definitely time for a shower. It's basically the same or equal to when females stratch their scalps and then sniff their nails. Oh, what? You thought we men didn't peep that? Yeah, we peeped that, but we ain't say nothing because them micro braids were too expensive to be taken out so soon. I guess you could say that's the female version of a nut-smell shower check called the

scalp-sniff hair-wash check...but that was for the ladies—only for the ladies. Break's over.

So anyway, after I showered, I grabbed some weed out the white pants that was at the bottom of the chest. I noticed fam was holding; he had like ten pounds of weed buried at the bottom of the chest. I guess he wanted me to see that so I'd know what all was in the house. "Point given, point taken." Fam was sharp, and I could already see I was 'bout to enjoy my vacation in Raleigh, a.k.a. The Capitol.

By the time I rolled up and ate breakfast, Diamond was coming back through the door. *"Whatsup, fam? I see you finally got out that bed,"* he said as he sat down, pulled some stacks out, and started counting.

"Yeah, man. I had to. Don't nothing come to a sleeper but dreams and bad breath. And ain't neither one of them going to put that shit right there in your hand inside my pocket," I said, pointing to the money he was counting. I got up, washed my plate out, went to the front room, and sat down on the couch. *"Let me guess, that's weed money you counting?"* I asked.

"Yeah, this just a lil something to start the day with. All I mess with is weed. All that other stuff bring too much attention. You know I'm still on the run from that shit in Jersey, and the last thing I need is them people on my ass."

"I feel you. I'm trying to duck they ass too."

"Yeah, I heard your name floating around in the air, that's why I kept telling you to bring your ass up here. It's sweet around here. All I do is sell weed and fuck these college hoes. Most days, I'm in the house by seven, and if I do leave out after that, I make sure somebody else driving. But whatsup with that situation back at the house?"

From there, I pretty much told him how it was going down and what happened with Kawada and Shaun. How big-homie Stace was head-hunting for their ass and had already kidnapped J-Rat.

After I finished talking, fam got up and went to the room. He stayed back there for a while before yelling, *"Come here!"* When I got to the room, he was on the phone saying, *"That's my fam, fam. My blood family, his pops damn near raised me. He right here,"* then he handed me the phone.

"Hello."

"Whatsup, Mr. Frank White, a.k.a. the Head Henchmen?"

"Whatsup? Who this?"

"Big-homie Stace."

"Oh, word, whatsup? I ain't have nothing to do with that, and truthfully, that shit wasn't even supposed to go down like that. That was just some crazy shit."

"Yeah, I know you ain't play no part in that, but you gotta be more mindful of the company you keep. That situation could've been handled a lot more smarter, and all this extra shit would've been avoided. Lil homie lost his life for nothing, and ain't no amount of money can bring him back. I ain't got no personal problems with you or you man J-Rat. But them other niggas gotta answer for that dumb shit. Your man J-Rat was just at the wrong place at the wrong time, but he good. I been hearing how you been holding down 10th. Make sure you holla at me when you get back."

"A'ight, bet I will," I said, handing fam back the phone. I just stood there and listened to them talk for a while. From the way they were kicking it, I could tell they were homies for real. I waited till they finished their conversation and asked fam, *"How y'all know each other?"*

"That's who I caught the case with in Jersey. We both got popped. I took the charge, and he beat the case. I been on the run almost four years now." He went on to explain that his father's side of the family was actually from East Orange, New Jersey, and that he, Stace, and Big Red were actually the ones who had introduced Hybeeb to the city of Wilmington. *"After we got popped, it was too risky to keep going back and forth from state to state, so we just moved the whole operation to NC."* After that, he let me know that Kawada and Shaun had been arrested, but it was still best if I laid low… He ain't have to tell me twice.

I ended up staying in Raleigh like four months. I did the same shit Diamond was doing: sell weed and fuck college hoes. We hustled at a spot called Melvent Court; at the time, that was the biggest weed spot in Raleigh. Diamond introduced me to George and Ty, two well-known cats from Wilmington that had moved to Raleigh and made a name for themselves. They had all the weed and all the hoes. Life was good and fun in Raleigh…until my money got low from all that partying and having fun. I spent more time at Crabtree Mall than I did hustling, and now it was time to bounce back. It was Henchmen season. The thing I liked most about Raleigh was dudes that had money showed it. They stayed fly, had nice fancy cars (the Acura Legend was in high demand for every big-time dope boy around this time), heavy jewelry, and were overall easy targets. You see, in the Port City, dudes don't move like that. Most dudes, especially dope boys who got money, try to hide it. They know not only are the police watching but the streets too. They know that bragging and boasting only brought unnecessary attention, which was why we kept it simple whenever we stepped out.

These dudes in Raleigh were what we called **walking licks** in the Port City. At any given time, they were worth at least 10,000 dollars. I remember we hit club Plum Crazy's parking lot. Plum Crazy brought the biggest crowd on Thursday, and we laid them all down, the whole damn parking lot. It was me, Murder, Ty-Dow, Ghetto, Polk, and Wise. Murder and I were the only two that got away. We ended with 80,000 dollars in cash, another 60,000 dollars' worth of jewelry, and had to pay 40,000 dollars to post bond for Ty-Dow, Ghetto, Polk, and Wise.

Diamond was very disciplined with how he moved and what he did with his money, so he wasn't into hitting licks. He had started complaining about his connect shorting him on weed. Every time he'd go cop, the first thing he'd do when he got home was weigh it out, and every time, each pound was two ounces short. That happened like three times, and each time I was like *"Yo, fam, let me Hench that nigga."* But he'd always tell me, *"No."*

So one day, I'm chilling in the crib, smoking weed, and listening to 2Pac rap and tell me about **this White man's world.** Diamond comes in; I knew he had just re-up because he had his duffel bag. As usual, he started weighing the work, and as I was sitting there, watching, I saw he was getting madder with each pound he weighed. Then finally after checking the scale, twisting and turning each pound in various ways, he was like *"Man, fuck that. Let me hold the gun, fam. I just told this nigga 'bout this shit, and he still keep doing it."*

I went and got the gun, but I told him, *"You might as well just let me Hench him before you go all out and don't get nothing out of it. At least if I get him, you gone get back what he kept shorting you on."*

What I said must have made a lot of sense because for the first time, fam finally agreed with me and was with it. *"Fuck him, fam. Go Hench that nigga!"*

I ain't wasting no time. I had to hurry up before Diamond changed his mind. I called up Murder and Ty-Dow and gave them the scoop. Two hours later, they were knocking at the door. When they came in, I sat them down and told them everything Diamond told me, which was that the dude was from Virginia, stayed in Raleigh with some college chicks, moved 'bout a hundred pounds a week, and didn't keep no guns in the crib. Every week, his people pull up in an all-black range 4.6 and make the drop.

We waited till the following week so we could catch him as soon as he got the work. In the meantime, I was watching the spot just to see who came and went and what kind of cars they were driving. Murder and Ty-Dow wanted to Hench him in the parking lot, but I knew it would be better to catch them coming in instead of going out; that way, we could get both the work and the money. But sometimes, things don't always go as planned.

When the truck pulled up, a female got out the front passenger side door, and another female got out the back passenger side. They both were totting Burberry bags. *"That's the work."* But the only problem was, we didn't know how many people were still in the truck. This was something we hadn't planned for. But I was thinking like, if they were sitting in the truck, then that meant them two girls weren't going to be in the house long—which meant the money won't be hard to find once we get in the house.

"Let's go," I said, opening my door and pulling my mask over my face. *"We gon run down on 'em soons they get to the house,"* I said to Ty-Dow. *"Murder, get the drop on whoever in the truck. If they move funny, flatline them."*

With that said, we got out the car and started creeping low through the parking lot. We crept up on the bumper of the truck, crouched low, pulled our guns out, and waited briefly. As soon as I heard them knocking on the door, I took off running full speed from behind the truck. It seemed like everything happened all at the same time.

The door opened, and the two girls turned, saw me, screamed, and dropped the bags. The female that answered the door was just standing there, shocked with my gun in her face. *"You move, breathe, or do anything stupid, you're dead,"* I said, waving the gun and indicating for her to back up slowly up into the house.

Ty-Dow grabbed both bags and told both girls the same thing. *"Get up and back up slowly up in the house."*

Murder had somehow managed to lay the driver of the truck facedown in the parking lot without letting off a shot. I saw that as I was closing the house door and telling the girls, *"Just give me the money so we can go."*

It was only one dude in the house, and I noticed that when I said something about the money, all the girls looked at him. Ty-Dow had him facedown and hand-positioned behind his back.

"Ima ask one more time where it at. But first, Ima put this to your head, and hopefully it'll help you think straight," I said, placing my gun to the back of his head *"They call this execution style,"* I whispered softly in his ear.

He let out a deep breath and nodded toward the closet. *"It's in there, inside the two bags. That's everything."*

As soon as I opened the closet, I saw there were two more Burberry bags identical to the bags that the two girls had the work in. After I got the bags, I instructed all three girls to lay facedown on the ground next to ole boy. Ty-Dow and I went through the house and ripped all the phone cords out and tied all their hands behind their backs. *"Count to 1,000. And if anybody come out this house before I make it safely out the parking lot, Ima shoot you."* And with that said, we were gone, slamming the door shut behind us. Once we left the house, I saw that Murder had stripped the dude (the driver) naked. Plus, he had two Burberry bags also… Jackpot!

When we got to the house, Diamond couldn't believe we actually pulled it off. *"Yo, fam, you fucken crazy, fam. You really got that nigga!"*

In total, we Henched ole boy for a 100 pounds and 140,000 dollars. The two bags in the closet had 70,000 dollars; plus the two bags Murder got out the truck had 70,000 dollars too, and the bags both girls were toting had 50 pounds apiece… Sweet lick!

And just like that, my pockets were back right, and I was about to head back to Wilmington, North Carolina, a.k.a. the Port City. I had to holla at big sis. She was still doing her thing with the weed. I had a helluva weed now, so I had to keep it in the family… Family always first.

Family Always First

The first thing I did when I got back to the Port City was stop out at the Motherland. I had to go check on Feisty Faye and the family. Actually, I had to go stash all that weed and put my guns and money up.

When I got to the house, I saw my cousin Lil Mike's car parked out front; he always checked in on my mom whether I was around or not. He was really like my brother and moved as such. When I went in, I saw him and my mom talking. My mom was saying something about *"prayer and positive energy being the greatest form of protection"* and how she was always constantly praying for us when we was out there doing only Lord-knows-what.

"Hey, Moms, how you doing?" I said, walking over and giving her a big hard hug and kiss on the cheek.

"Let me go, boy, and don't be kissing me. Ion know where your mouth been."

I hugged her harder and gave her a quick kiss on the lip. As soon as I let her go, I ducked low to dodge a slap upside my head. *"I love you too, Feisty Faye,"* I said before turning my attention to the food on the stove.

"Let me get some money, Shawn." It was my lil brother A.B.'s favorite line. Actually, it was all my younger siblings' favorite line. They were always happy to see me.

As I was giving them all some money, I got cursed out by my mom for doing it. *"Don't be giving them kids money all the time because they gon think I spose to do the same thing."*

"Okay, Ma, but what you cooking? Fix me a plate before this fool eat it all," I said referring to my cousin Lil Mike.

We all sat down and ate, everybody except my sis Terry who was too busy talking on the phone.

"Whats up, White girl?" I said, sticking my head in her room, which used to be my bedroom.

"Whats up, brah? Can I have some money?" She was thirteen now, so I knew what time it was.

"Why, your boyfriend ain't give you none? Every time I come over here, your ear glued to that phone," I said while giving her two 100-dollar bills. As soon as she grabbed the money, I snatched the phone from her. *"Who this?"* I asked, but nobody replied. *"I catch you 'round my sister, Ima cut your lil dick off, nigga!" (Click!)* Whoever it was hung up. I just started laughing, gave her the phone back, and told her just like what my dad told me. *"You better stop messing with them cowards that can't be trusted. And oh yeah, call big sis and tell her I'm back and to meet me in the Motherland."*

After that, Mike and I went to Gator's house. As always, he was rocking in his favorite rocking chair with his hat pulled low, concealing his eyes and watching the surveillance camera.

"Whatsup, Gator?" We both said as we came through the door, knowing he was going to start talking shit.

"The hell y'all want? Y'all don't come bothering me till you want something. And Shawn, where the hell you been? I haven't seen you back here in years." That was Unc's way of telling me he has been keeping an eye on me; and like I've told y'all, Unc was a killer, so he knew what was in my bloodline.

"Been laying low, Unc. Shit got hectic, so I had to disappear for a second. But look, I got some things I need you to put up for me. Just can't leave these types of toys laying around. Somebody might hurt themselves with them."

We all went out to the car, and I opened the trunk. The guns were wrapped in a blanket: the AK, SK, M-90, two mini MACs, and like three riot pumps. These were just my big guns; this didn't even include my handgun collection. I opened the blanket so Unc could see what was inside, counted out 1,500 dollars, and handed it to Gator. He grabbed the blanket and went back inside the house and never asked no questions…

For a while, Mike and I were just kicking it and relaxing. When we were young, we hated staying down this long-ass dirt road. But now that we were older and into the streets, it was good to have a lay-low spot and family you could trust. The Motherland was our safe haven. Wasn't nobody in their right mind coming back up in these woods without an invite. Unc already had the surveillance cameras; we could see you a half a mile away. Plus our property was private. And now that I had just dropped off all this artillery, I knew that even if the things I did out in the streets ever led back to my family, they were protected.

Cla, cla claa claa, claaaaaw! We both ducked and started looking around. I knew it was the choppa from how the shot sounded. Unc came out the woods from 'round the back of his house holding the AK in the air with one hand. ***Claaaw, claaaw, claaaw!*** *"I like this mafucka. She chop down trees and all,"* he said and went back in the woods.

Mike and I just started laughing. My mom had come out the patio to see what all that shooting was about. I yelled and told her, *"That's your crazy brother. He just got some new toys."* She just shook her head and walked back in the house.

Mike was telling me how he had just gotten out of rehab and was trying to stay clean. *"Man, that powder had me down and out. I lost my car, my job, my crib, and started fucking 'round with that dog food. I was out there. My dad told me if I went to rehab and got my shit together, he'd help me get back on my feet. All I do now is smoke weed and work."*

After hearing all that, I knew he was struggling, so I told him, *"If you tryna get some weed money, I got something for you."*

His face lit up. He started smiling and said, *"You always there when I need you. I swear, you the chosen one of the family."*

As he was talking, I saw big sis pulling up over in my mom's driveway. *"Yo, sis!"* I yelled to get her attention.

She looked my way and started walking over. When she got to me, the first thing she did was give me a hug. *"Ain't nobody seen your ass in months, and you standing here like too tuff to give me hug. And y'all two better not go getting in no trouble."*

All I could do was smile and shake my head. My sis was always able to read me like a book. As she was talking, I walked to the back of the car and opened the truck. I had all the weed in a trash bag, thirty-seven pounds total. I took seven pounds out. *"Man, will you shut up and come get this? I didn't call you out here to hear no damn lecture. You still doing your thing with the Tree? Well, here, take that,"* I said, pointing to the five pounds of weed. *"And this for you."* I gave Mike the other two pounds. *"I got plenty of this shit, but I'm only dealing with y'all two. Don't bring nobody to me. I don't care how much they spending. I'm charging y'all 700 dollars a pound, but I know right now, pounds of kind bud [Baby Dro] going for 1,300–1,600 dollars. So it's a win-win no matter which way y'all play it. You can whole sale or break it down."*

Boom! Boom! Boom! (Unc was playing with the pump.) My sister damn near jumped in my arms. *"That's Gator. He out there in the woods with some toys I gave him to hold for me."*

"Oh, you think you Frank White for real," my sis said.

"Naah, I'm just holding down the fam, like Pops told me to. I'm 'bout to put the rest of this weed up and hit 10th. Whatsup with E-Boogie? He still doing his ones and twos?"

"Yeah, you know how Boog do. He only move when the moment right, and only he knows the right moment."

"I gotta check in with fam and see what he into. Make sure you remind me to do that... Ima fuck with him."

10th and Castle... Guts and Glory

It was pretty much the same ole shit on the 10th—plenty of money being made and drugs being sold. I saw a few new faces, but for the most part, the Dime Squad remained the same.

(It was a lot of talk around the store about Tone-X. Word was, he had made it to the big screen. Tone-X was a good friend and family member of Uncle Chris who owned the store on 10th and Castle. He became legendary for his performance on Russell Simmons' *Def Comedy Jam*. The hood was proud of his progress and the fact that he would always shout-out the Port City before his performance. Last I heard, he was still doing his thing on the *Breakfast Club* morning show in Charlotte, North Carolina, on Power 98 and still shouting out the Port City... Much love, my Port City brethren.)

When I stepped in the store, I saw my Uncle Chris and Aunt Janice both behind the counter. Uncle Chris owned the store, and his sister Janice sometime worked the register. They both were good people and treated me as family. I use to stash my work right in the chip rack. Every time a sale came, I'd go in the store and discreetly buy a bag of twenty-five-cent chips. Every now and then, Uncle Chris would say something slick to me just to let me know he knew what I was up to. *"You damn sure eat a lot of chips"* was his favorite line.

Around this time, Don's brother Noon pretty much had the block on lock. Don himself was locked up, so I had started dealing with Noon. It was Noon that gave me the secret recipe. Before dealing with Noon, I was buying my work already rocked up. So one day, he brought me some powder instead of crack.

"Naah, I want some hard. I can't sell this."

He was like *"What? Man, you don't know how to cook roc?"*

I answered honestly, *"No, I usually cop ready roc."*

He went right to the stove with it. *"Never buy ready roc when you purchasing weight because you don't know what the hell you buying. Fish scale is good for snorters, but oil base is better for smokers. Plus you can stretch it more. The oil residue make the soda burn like coc and don't clog up their stems up. But it's a special way to stretch oil base."*

From that point on, I kept what the base-heads referred to as that *"butter scutter."* Noon gave me the game, and I took it and ran with it.

At the time, Don was locked up, but he used to call the store on three-way. I spoke with him a few times, and he was telling me, *"Just hold it down till I touch. We gon paint the city red."* He already heard how the Henchmen movement had adopted the Red Bandanna to symbolize *"Blood in, Blood out."* Plus he started calling himself **Big Red,** a.k.a. **Red Storm** and was rocking with some sex, money, murder homies.

Overhaul 10th was sweet, so sweet that I got caught slipping. My first adult felony charge ever was a coc charge. I was caught slipping by Hargrove and Hagan, two notorious known police officers who were known throughout the entire Port City as H & H. Even their car had a nickname; it was all white caprice that we called *"that hard white."* Every day when I hit the block, the first thing I wanted to know was whether or not *that hard white* was riding.

On this particular day, I was sitting across the street from the store in front of the church; they rolled right up on me. I discreetly tossed my pack behind me, but I had a 50-dollar piece in my other hand. Before I could think what to do with it, they were standing right in front of me. *"Stand up and let us search you."* I stood up and tried to drop the rock and step on it, but they saw it. Hagan tackled me, Hargrove grabbed the rock, and off to jail I went. Simple possession—I got out the same night. That was the first time me and Terry Jackson met and did business.

Terry Jackson was a bail bondsman that showed a lot of love when it came to posting bail for the homies in the hood. Also around that time, it was another bondsman named Herb Newton who also showed a lot of love also. They both were two successful Black men who knew and understood how oppressive the judicial system was and still is toward Blacks. Terry and I would eventually form a good business relationship, and because of that, I was able to stay out of jail at a discounted price... (Shout-out to Terry Jackson for showing mad love to the struggle.)

Then I got caught slipping by a jackboy named M. Bells. Actually, I got set up by a snake-ass wannabe Godbody cat named Needy, whose word ain't shit. He used to be on 10th too, but I can't recall him ever getting no major money.

So one night, it was me and my man Killa Black (RIP) hugging the block. I saw Needy and really ain't thinking nothing of it because we both were Godbody. So he asked me, *"Frank, you got change for a hundred dollars?"* I was like *"Yeah"* and went in my pocket, but as I was going in my pocket, I turned my body sideways because I was trying to use the streetlight to see the bills. Plus I had way more than a hundred dollars on me. I couldn't see the bills, so I just grabbed probably like three hundred dollars and was turning back around, counting out the one hundred dollars; but when I turned around, Needy was gone, and M-Bells had a gun in my face. *"Give it up."*

"You got it. It's yours, homie," I said, handing the dude my money and keeping my hands up. I thought he was going to pat me down, but he didn't. He just back-stepped and ran off into the darkness.

About two days later, I saw Needy. *"Peace, God."*

"Peace," he responded.

"Whatsup with that shit the other night?" I asked him. I guess he could tell I was strapped because of my body language. It wasn't even cold outside, and I was dressed in all-black army fatigue outfit.

"Yo, word is bond. I ain't know where that nigga came from!"

"Word?"

"Yeah, word is bond, brah. You know I wouldn't do no foul shit like that."

"Oh, a'ight," I said, dismissing the thought of doing him dirty.

In my heart, I felt like he was lying. But according to the universal laws, I couldn't doubt his word unless I could show and prove that he was lying, and I didn't have any proof. Truth be told, I wasn't sweating three hundred dollars; that was chump change. It would be years before he actually had the heart to let it be known that he set me up. Just so happened he told somebody and they told me, and I never saw him again after that.

About a month later, I got caught slipping again by the same nigga, M-Bells. I will never forget; it was Bike Fest weekend. Myrtle Beach is only an hour away from Wilmington. Noon, as well as all the other niggas holding weight, had already left. So I ended up having to get some ready roc from this cat from Jervay named Boo Green. He told me, *"I'm 'bout to hit the highway, so get all you can because I'm not coming back till Monday."* I call myself being slick by staying behind and getting all the money while most of the other hustlers were gone. I ordered up a half a key (18 oz.). When I went to the stash, I grabbed my gun as I was counting out the money. Something told me **"Take your gun with you,"** but I ain't listening. On my way out the house, I went and put my gun back in the stash. There was no need to be toting a gun if I wasn't beefing with nobody.

I was standing right across the street from Jervay in front of Bob Johnson corner store. I saw a car pull up, and three dudes got out. *"If you ain't from Jervay, give it up."* They laid, like, five niggas down, myself included right there on the side of the store.

This was all my fault. For one, I should've straightened this nigga the first time when he got me for that three hundred dollars. Two, I never should've went against my gut feeling. Something told me to bring my gun, and I didn't listen. Now I was standing here looking down the barrel of a big-ass chrome and black .45 getting robbed for 13,000 dollars.

"Oh, nigga, you holding," he said as he pulled money out of each of my pockets and held me at gunpoint. I had a lil over three thousand dollars in each four pockets, and every time he pulled out a knot, I saw his eyes light up.

"Bell, what the fuck you doing? That's my people, yo!"

I looked up and saw my cousin Polky—no gun, chest out, and barking on Bells *"The fuck you doing, Bells?"*

Bells ain't saying shit—just back-stepped away from me and then turned around and ran down Dawson Street.

"You all right?" Polk asked once he reached me.

"Hell no. That nigga just got me for 13,000 dollars, and that's the second time I let that clown catch me slipping."

"Man, you can't be out here slipping. You know better than that."

"Yeah, you right, but Ima see that nigga. He gone pay for that. Word!"

Polk was a distant cousin of mine, and from that day forward, whenever Noon wasn't around, I'd deal with Polky or his right-hand man Ghetto.

Also from that day on, it wasn't no such thing as leaving out the house without my pistol. I had made up my mind that the next nigga that tried to rob me was gonna feel my pain. I had plenty of guns—just never saw no point in toting a gun if I wasn't beefing. Now all that was out the window, and it didn't take long for me to make an example.

It was two older cats named Herb and J-Black. They pulled up wanting to purchase three grams for 125 dollars. I had already served them before I actually counted the money. When I noticed it was short, I told them, *"I'm not taken no shorts."* The nigga Herb said some slick shit like *"I'll take all your shit, lil nigga."* After he said this, he walked back to the car, opened the passenger door, sat down, reached under the seat, then stood back up, and was acting like he was adjusting a gun on his waist. What this dummy didn't know was that for one, I had already been robbed twice by the same person. Two, it wasn't going to be a third robbery. And three, I was strapped the whole time. When he started walking back in my direction, I let him get within five feet and pulled.

He threw his hands up. *"I ain't got no gun, I ain't got no gun!"* he yelled once he saw my pistol.

Boom, boom, boom, boom! *"Just for faking, dumb-ass nigga."*

A few days later, I was back on the block, and Hargrove pulled up. I wasn't dirty, so I didn't care. I was leaning against my car, eating a fresh seafood platter from Zero's. Hargrove came up. *"You need to hurry up and finish so I can arrest you."*

I damn near choked off my food. *"Arrest me for what? I'm not dirty, and I don't got no warrants."*

"Yes, you do. You shot that man up here the other night. One of the bullets hit him in his dick. You got him good."

"Man, Ion know what you talking 'bout. I ain't shot nobody."

"Okay, but I still gotta arrest you and serve this warrant."

Come to find out this nigga took charges out on me. Herb pressed charges, and J-Black was listed as a witness on the warrant. I couldn't believe that I was actually getting an attempted murder charge after these clowns were the ones who started this shit.

My bond was 150K dollars. This was my first serious adult felony. I ended up calling Terry Jackson, and he was like all I needed was 15K and he could get me out.

I went upstairs to the 5th floor (Juvie block); I was only seventeen. I saw a few faces that I hadn't seen in a while. My man Lil Freddy was big-homie Stace's young gunner; he was in there. My homies Big B, Birdie Bird, and Lil Illy were in there too. Then I met my cousin Diesel Bomb for the first time. I ain't even know we were family until then… I stayed in jail for about two weeks, long enough for my mom and big sis to post my bail. As soon as I touched down, I was back at it.

My money was looking funny between posting bail and getting a good lawyer. I spent damn near 30K dollars, and I still owed Terry 5K dollars. My lawyer was a beast—Jewish descent, formerly employed by the attorney general's office, and a Master Mason named Thomas Hicks. Between Tom and Terry, it was no way possible I could sit in jail long. **(Time out! Time out!)**

But this is for my really highly educated Negroes only. I'm 'bout to drop a heavy jewel on you, so do like Frank…and PAY ATTENTION!

Okay, for those of you who don't know, the word Mason is derived from the Latin words Mass and Son (meaning "child or person of light"). It's a direct reference to the highest degree of the Kemetic education system.

The 33 degrees of lessons within Masonry enlightenment stages only represent a fraction of the 360 degrees of instruction that make up the ancient wisdom of the original Kemet people.

The country we now call Egypt was first called Kemet by its original inhabitants. Kemet literally means "the country of the Blacks." Contrary to popular belief, Egypt is not in the Middle East. It's part of Africa.

To understand ancient Egypt, we must first fully understand Africa as well as the original AFRICAN CULTURE, WHICH GAVE BIRTH TO THE ORIGINAL AFRICAN MAN. Only then will we truly understand the relationship between Ancient Egypt, Africans, Afro-Americans, and America.

Most Masons are unaware of their links to the original African culture through their associations with the Kemet study. Mostly because many of them never advance beyond the 33rd degree of Master Mason.

Their organization is a society of secrets, not a secret society. The three branches of Masonic Order are the Scottish Rite, the York Rite, and the Prince Hall Rite. Both the Scottish and the York Rite come from Great Britain. The Prince Hall Rite was founded in the former British colony, what we now call America. History within the Masonic order reveals that the revolutionary war was fought because of conflict between two Masonic orders for control of the new discovered American land. The Scottish and York Rite eventually deaden their beef and started back acknowledging each other as Masonic brothers.

This is why we Henchmen greet one another with "War before peace" or "I'm my brother's keeper." This also how we (Henchmen) align ourselves with Prince Hall Masonic order.

The Prince Hall Masonic order was founded by Prince Hall, an African American who had been denied membership into the Scottish Masonic Rite. The Prince Hall Lodge was created exclusively for African Americans. The majority of African American Masons are affiliated with the Prince Hall Rite...

Now that was some real food for thought for my highly educated Negroes. If you didn't know, now you do. But it gets a lot deeper than that... That's just the surface, so stay tuned and continue to read as I elevate your mind... Now time in, and let's get

it! (See Anthony T. Browder (*Egypt on the Potomac*) for more African or Egyptian historical facts)

Now on top of all the bullshit I had just found out, I had a baby on the way. It was like karma caught up with me, and this was just the beginning.

No lie. Like three weeks later, I'm back on 10th in full-fledged grind mode. It was some New York cats that called themselves The Goodfellas. They had 13th and 8th Castle on lock. And a lot of dudes were dick-riding them because they had the best prices and solid team. My cousin Murder was tight with both Lonny and Lamont. Plus, Murder's mom, my Aunt Sheryl, was cool with Sunny. Sunny, Lonny, and Lamont pretty much operated as the head of the Goodfellas. It was something about them dudes I just didn't trust. My pops had taught me how to spot a snake, and every time my cousin brought them dudes around, I sense a snake.

So anyway, being that 10th was in-between 13th and 8th, they started trying to take over the block. I wasn't having it, and neither were the rest of the Henchmen—me, Killa Black, J.V., Doggfaze, Face-Off, Murder, Ty-Dow, Lil Illy, Lil Freddy, G-code, Ghetto, and Polky. The entire squad shut their ass down.

It all started with them first trying to get me to get down with them. They sent some goons to holler at me about joining the Goodfellas. You see, the Goodfellas was really just a lot of sex, money, and murdering niggas that had migrated from up top to the south. They basically were trying to take over the entire Castle Street strip. The only thing that was stopping them was the fact they knew the Henchmen weren't going for it.

When they came to 10th to holler at me, I saw right through their bullshit.

"We heard you doing your thing up here. It's a lot of money running through 10th. We could just give you the work and let you handle it, but you gotta let some of our people post up here with you," they said.

"Why would I work for y'all and only make a percentage of my profit when I could keep working for myself and get 100 percent profit? No disrespect, but I'd be stupid to accept your offer. That would be a bad bizzness decision on my behalf."

After that, they sent a hitta at me. I damn near killed him.

I was standing right there on 10th in my usual spot right in front of the store—me and a few more guys from the block. When the dude walked up, I thought he was going in the store, but he stopped short and pulled out on us. *"Y'all niggas know what it is. Run that shit. Empty out your pockets!"* I'm thinking like *Damn, not again.* I just got out of jail for shooting a nigga that tried to rob me, and now this shit. I had my gun stashed in the chip rack. I had already emptied my pockets, but then this nigga pointed the gun directly at me and was like *"Take me to your car."*

Being that dude didn't have a mask on, it was easy to see that he was from 13th. In fact, he was with them niggas when they offered me to be a part of the Goodfellas. I knew this shit was personal. They were mad that I had turned down the offer, so now this was a "get down or lay down" tactic.

My car was parked down the street in the dark, and for him to know that, he had to have been watching me. So when he said that, I froze up for a second, then he said, *"Ima count to 3, and if you don't start walking, Ima pop you."*

As soon as he counted to 1, I sped around, ran in the store, and grabbed my gun out the chip rack. There was no way in hell I was letting nobody walk me to my death, not when my gun was only a few feet away.

"Duck down," I told Aunt Janice, and by this time, my homies were running in the store too. Dude came in the store after he picked up the money and started saying, "Didn't I tell…" **Boom, boom, boom, boom!** I put four hollows in his chest plate and blew ass back out the door. I stepped out the store. **Boom, boom!** I put two more in his chest at point-blank range and ran off.

This dumb-ass nigga had put his gun in his back pocket; I guess he thought he had a sweet lick. Another dummy that had to learn the hard way about the Head Henchmen. 10th and Castle was my block, my spot. NO DOPE SALES, NO CRACK SALES, NO NOTHING UNLESS I SAID SO.

And just to be on the safe side, I went out to the Motherland and hollered at Unc. That same night, we pulled up on 13th and chopped everything moving down. ***Claaa, claaa, claaa, claaaw! War before peace, mafuckas!*** I was tired of playing with niggas. It was wartime, and I was war-ready... The warrior in me was wide awake and bloodthirsty...

Learning from Losses

My money was low, but my cousin Polk had told me I could shop with him. He and Ghetto were like the only dudes in the town that weren't dealing with them cats from New York. They had their own plug but had to get it, which was worth it because the number was nice.

So anyway, Polk told me he could get me a half a joint for 10K. I ain't asking no questions. I was hurting financially, and what he had just told me was what I needed to hear. We met up at the Hilltop and got some drinks, and after a while, I told him, *"I got the money with me now,"* passing him a small-size brown paper bag with ten stacks across the table. *"When you gone be ready for me?"*

"Give me 'bout a week. I got you," he replied.

About a week later me, Polk, Ghetto, and Ralow were all at Angie B's house, waiting for the work. I knew something was wrong. The vibe in the air was off, and we had been waiting for a while. Finally, we got word that the mule had gotten popped at the bus station. When the six o'clock news came on, I saw my first cousin Kesha (my Uncle Gator's daughter) in handcuffs. I never knew she was the mule until then; she was only nineteen and had just got popped with a brick of coc. And just like that, I had taken another loss, but the biggest loss was when Polk blew trail and got twenty-seven years for that same brick (Kesha folded and told everything).

The situation with Polk is definitely worth mentioning because the city lost a good man due to his incarceration. However, I don't fully fault Kesha neither. You see, prior to her cooperation with the law enforcement agency, she sat in jail for six months and kept it silent. Polk was supposed to post her bail, but he never did—which, in my eyes, was a major violation to the Code Of Honor. Although I don't agree with what she did, I see the logic in it. Her only way out was Polk posting her bail or snitch. So when he didn't post her bail, she only had one option left.

My personal opinion is that the reason they gave him all that time wasn't necessarily because the drugs but more so because of the death of Kenny Hall... Kenny Hall was also a good dude and a well-respected OG throughout the entire Port City. Kenny and Polk ended up falling out over a broad named Donna. One day while in Jervay, they exchanged words. Polk pulled and bust at Kenny, but his gun jammed. Kenny pulled, bust back, and ended up shooting Polk five times (damn near killed him). A couple days later, I rode with Ghetto to the hospital to see Polk. He was still in the ICU, recovering from surgery as I stood by his bed and watched him take shallow breaths. My gut instincts told me he'd pull through. In the old ancient African Yoruba culture, it is believed that in order to save a life claimed by death, another life must take its place. Kenny was killed the night before; somehow, Kenny's female cousin Ke-ke felt I had killed Kenny. Every time she saw me, including at the funeral, she would make a scene by yelling *"I know you killed my cousin"* repeatedly. Ghetto was Polk's right-hand man and was eventually charged with the murder of Kenny Hall, but the chargers were later dismissed. After the key witness, S. Miller admitted under oath that he had been told by detectives to place Ghetto at the crime scene in exchange for a shorter sentence on pending drug-indictment charges. Polk was mastermind in his own rite; he played chess using real people as pieces and the entire world as his chess board. This, in my opinion, is why the system saw fit to sentence him to all that time... Hold your head, (Polk) fam, and RIP Kenny Hall.

What I learned from all this was that **you can't beef and get money. Beef is bad for bizzness.** I was damn near broke. It seemed like for every three steps forward, I was taken five steps backward. The only thing that kept me from falling all the way off was Henchmen and hitting licks. I had hollered at Ty-Dow, and he had a nice lick lined up for me. All I had to do was go in and get it. The door was unlocked. Dude girl had told for us where everything was at, and just like that, I was back on. Twenty-five K and eighteen ounces of ready roc was sitting right there in the mattress just as ole girl said it would be.

All Ty-Dow wanted was 10K dollars and 5 oz. *"Get back on your feet. I know you need everything you can get right. Just be safe and don't get caught slipping. Frank, PAY ATTENTION!"*

"These mafuckas is definitely Henchmen," I replied, quoting one of our Henchmen mottos.

It didn't take long for me to get back on my feet. I had to take my grind across town to the north side (Taylor Holmes). Castle was too hot to hustle on. Damn near every night, we go head-hunting for Goodfellas. Wasn't nobody stupid enough to be standing out on the block with choppa bullets flying everywhere. Plus most of the residence from Jervay were being evacuated. Jervay was being torn down and remodeled. All the money was going to the north side, so I went with it.

Big-homie Stace was on the north side too. We had finally linked up, and he was showing a lot of love. Murder, Ty-Dow, G-Code, Lil Illy, Lil Freddy, Doggfaze, and I were hanging tight 'round this time. The Henchmen homie Toka was rocking with us too, but he was stationed out east in Creek Wood. Plus, Uncle U (Wayne Sidberry) started schooling us all on how to properly hit licks and apply pressure. Gloves and mask became essential and mandatory on all missions. The one thing I learned from Uncle U is something he always used to tell me: *"You don't need a gun to rob a bitch nigga. A bitch nigga is a weak nigga, and weak niggas gon always fear the strength of somebody stronger. You don't gotta take it from 'em because they gone give it to you."* RIP, Uncle U. I raised a nation with the advice you gave me.

I started fronting work to some of the dudes from the north just to build good relationships. I mean, after all, I was on their territory in their projects, and I already had enough beef with the Goodfellas; so there was no need to make more enemies.

However, some things you just can't avoid, and like what 2Pac said, **"Watch for phonies, keep your enemies close, and watch your homies."**

The Hilltop

So one night, we all decided to head to the club (The Hilltop). This particular night, all the Henchmen homies as well as a few cats from the north were wearing red bandannas and brown Dickies suits. We got a lot of attention because of what we had on; plus it was odd to see dudes from the south and north side hanging together. We grew up fighting each other at the skating ring, but as we got older and more mature, we put all that behind us.

See, at this point, my whole objective was to let it be known there was no outsider or out-of-towner about to govern our land. The Port City was my home, and we (Henchmen) were gonna govern our own land. And if you were from out of town, you either go through us or get dealt with. Truth is, a lot of OGs respected what we was doing and how we were bringing it. Uncle Chris, big-homie Stace, Terry Jackson, Redstorm, Noon, Bob Johnson, Uncle U (Wayne Sidberry)—these were all OGs and well-respected elders within the black community who had given me their blessings to govern our land, so that's exactly what I was doing.

So anyway, as we were all in the club, Ty-Dow came in and started talking crazy because he was the only one without a brown Dickie suit and red bandanna. At first, I really ain't paying him no mind until he looked directly at me and said, *"Ima start robbing y'all niggas."*

Now this is supposed to be my main man, but right now, he was acting like he got some hidden hate in his blood toward me. We were in the club, in front of everybody, and this nigga was talking stupid. But instead of making a scene, I waited till he left then followed him to the bathroom. Once he went in the bathroom, I went behind him. *"Yo, man, you can't be talking reckless like that in front of everybody!"*

"Nigga, I made you. I'm the one who showed you how to bust your gun. I'm the one that showed you how to hit licks."

His response had confirmed my suspicion, but hearing him say that shit had me lost for a second. So I was just standing, looking at him like "The fuck is up with you?" By that time, Uncle U came in the bathroom and got in between us and was like *"Y'all niggas chill out with this silly shit,"* but I was cool, calm, and collected. I knew what this was about because I had seen it before. This was hate. I had seen this so many times before, but it hurt harder when it's coming from somebody you really got love for. The fact that I was young, doing my thing, and no matter how many times I fell off or got knocked down, I managed to bounce back. Now my right-hand man was trying to take credit for all my blood, sweat, and tears.

When shit calmed down, we all cleared out the bathroom and went our separate ways. Ty-Dow went to the bar, and I went and sat down; but the more I thought about the shit he had said, the madder I got. So I went to the bar and sat down beside him. I looked him dead in his eyes and told him, *"Niggas wanna kill me but ain't got the heart to look me in the eyes and spark"* (an old-school Jay-Z verse back when he and Sauce Money were on Clue mixtapes).

From there, we started arguing again, and all he kept saying was *"You better go get your gun!"*

"Nigga, ion need no gun for you. I'll give you a fair one," I said as the homies got in between us again.

This time when they split us up, I left out the club and went to the car. When I got to the car, I grabbed my gun, and just that quick, my mind snapped. As soon as I gripped the gun, I cocked it and put one in the head. For a second, all I saw was red, and it felt like a demon had entered my soul. Here I was plotting on murdering my man. This shit wasn't right, so I shook it off and put the gun under the car tire and went back inside the club. Telling myself that in a worst-case scenario, the homie and I would just fight. Truth is, I had a lot of love for Ty-Dow. His family was like my family and vice versa. His brother Illy was one of my close friends and Henchmen homies.

So with all that in mind, I was like "Ima just leave that shit alone," but as soon as I got back in the club, I saw him headed my way. The homies tried to stop it, but it was too late. As soon as he got to me, he said, *"Whatsup, nigga? You strapped?"*

"Nah, nigga. I told you I don't need a gun for you."

I swung and connected a solid left to his jaw. He stumbled back a couple of steps and lifted his arm with his hand still inside his jacket pocket—**boom, boom!**—and started shooting at me. From there, it was like God had hit the slow-motion button on life. I felt like Neo from the movie *Matrix*. I swear I saw the first bullet coming at me, ducked, and dodged at the same time. The entire club was going crazy now. Everybody was running and screaming.

I got low and blended with the crowd.

Boom! *Right next to my ear, I heard the bullet whistle past my ear.*

Boom! *I felt the flesh rip from my neck (damn, I'm hit).*

Boom! *One to the back and out my collar, chipping my collarbone in the process (damn, I'm hit again).*

Out the club, jumped over the rail, ran to the car, and grabbed my gun. *"Blood in, blood out"* was all I kept saying to myself. Running low through the parking lot and back toward the club, *"Ima kill this nigga!"*

My own homie, all over nothing—a damn Dickies suit and bandanna. Too many people running in the opposite direction. Couldn't get a clear shot, started feeling dizzy, seeing doubles, getting weak and light-headed.

All I remember was Allycat, Killa Black, and Uncle U pulling up and yelling, *"Get in!"*

My last words to them was *"Blood in, Blood out"*...**and then I passed out!**

Shaunteona

While I was unconscious, I was dreaming, and in my dream, I was a king standing on the balcony of a castle with my newborn daughter in my arms. Beneath the balcony, the entire area was surrounded with my family and friends. I raised my daughter high above my head to show the crowd and place a princess crown upon her head. After crowning her and hearing the crowd cheer, I placed her safely back in the crib. The crowd continued to cheer and hold their hands out toward me. I walked to the edge of the balcony with the intention of pulling them up to share my wealth, but when I extended my arm, they started pulling me over the edge of the balcony. Finally, I broke free, snatching my arm back...

I woke to my mother and sister standing over me and a nurse trying to put an IV in the same arm I had just snatched away from my people in the dream. My first words were *"What day is it, and what's my condition?"* I asked the nurse.

"Its six o'clock, Saturday morning. You've been shot twice. One graze wound to the left side of you neck. Another centimeter and it would've penetrated your jugular vein. The other was to the left side of your back. I'm assuming you were ducking down because of the angle of your exit wound. Had you been standing straight up, instead of exiting out of your collar area, the bullet would've penetrated your heart.

"You are under a forty-eight-hour evaluation because you lost a lot of blood and we had to do a blood transfusion. From the looks of things, you seem okay, but I gotta take you downstairs for a CAT scan later on. Just thank God that you still alive because one wrong move could've literally ended your life. Your pants and shoes is right there in that bag. Your jewelry is in the safe. When I take you for your CAT scan, I'll stop by and get it."

I was trying to talk the nurse for as long as possible to avoid having to face my mom and sister. As soon as the nurse left out, I looked at both of them. *"I heard some gunshots in my sleep, and something told me it was your ass. Alleycat came by the house and told me what happened. I been told you I didn't trust Ty-Dow. Now look,"* said my sister.

My mom picked up right where my sister stopped at. *"You just need to slow down, son, and stop doing so much. I hear your name at work all damn day. Everybody that ride the city bus seem to have a story to tell about Frank White. Slow down, son. You heard what that lady just told you. You got shot twice in two areas that could've easily cause you death. You're lucky to still be alive. It's time to chill out, son."*

I heard everything they both were saying, but I was ready to get out this damn hospital and get my revenge. *"I'm okay. Y'all can go home. Just bring me some clothes."*

My sister looked at me and said what I was thinking out loud. *"Shawn, leave it alone. Don't go looking for that boy. It ain't worth it."*

"I'm good, sis. Just bring me some clothes."

After my mom and my sister left, the detectives came. *"I don't know nothing. HOW I GOT SHOT, WHO DID IT, OR NOTHING."*

They left, but just the sight of them made me nervous. I had to get the hell out of this hospital. By the time the nurse got back, I was sitting straight up in the bed, just staring at my shoes because I couldn't tie them. Both my neck and shoulders were sore and aching. I had managed to remove my IVs and put my pants and shoes on.

"And where do you think you're going?" she asked while adjusting the bed to support my back. *"Scoot back and get comfortable. Ima wheel you downstairs for your CAT scan."*

Once we got downstairs, I reminded her to get my jewelry. *"I'll be right back,"* she said. But as soon as she was out of sight, I got up and got the hell out the hospital.

Blood In, Blood Out

I laid low at my BM's (Steph) house for a while and healed up. Really, I was just sore as hell for the most part. Lil Mike and I were really plotting on Ty-Dow. He (Ty-Dow) had sent me word that he ain't mean to take it that far, that he was drunk, and if we could just squash it. Okay, I felt and understood what he was saying. And maybe I would've forgiven him had he shot me in my leg or somewhere nonthreatening, but this guy had actually aimed at my face and ran me down. Ain't no forgiving that. Drunk or not, some shit you just gotta be a man about and held accountable for, and this was just one of those times when there was no nice ending going to come at the end of the story... Blood in, blood out!

I knew he would eventually come to the projects, so every night, we played the shadows, waiting. Lil Mike and I would dress in all black camouflage and wait right outside his sister's house. The war gods must've heard my thirst for revenge on this particular night. He (Ty-Dow) pulled up about twenty feet from where we were and didn't even see us. In fact, he walked right by us in route to his sister's house.

"We gon wait till he come out and hit him from both sides once he get in the car," I whispered quietly to Mike as I walked across the street and hid in the darkness of the alley right next to Dreego's corner store. When he came out, his swag was on a thousand. His body language was saying, "Yeah, I just shot you," or maybe I was just bugging and wanted a reason to feel good for what I was about to do. Either way, it didn't matter. As soon as he got in the car, both me and Mike stepped out the darkness. Mike was closer than me and made it to the car first. By 'bout three seconds, we both started hitting at the same time.

Boom, boom! I heard him holla, *"Nooo, stop! Don't, please!"* and watched as he jumped in the back seat.

Boom, boom! I sent two from the .357 in the back seat right behind him.

Boom, boom! We both were shooting simultaneously. I watched as he dived back over into the front seat of the car. *"Nooo, Frank, please!"* he yelled as he opened the driver side's door and fell out the car and tried to crawl under it for cover.

I ran up on him and looked down on him just as he was rolling over. I raised the gun and had every intention of putting the last three hollows in his face. Actually, I thought he was already dead. I swear, as I stood over him, I saw his soul leave his body. It was like he had exhaled his last breath.

You see, some things in life we'll never understand because God never intended for us to know his secrets. However, that night, God made it very clear to me not to shoot Ty-Dow in the face. As I raised the gun, I heard myself thinking about Lil Illy and Ms. Edner. And if that alone wasn't enough, what happened next really spooked me. When I aimed at his face, I swear I saw Lil Illy. I dropped my aim, shook my head briefly, and looked again. This time, when I looked down on him, I saw his mother's face. You see, a lot of times when people write, they tend to learn on their imagination for creativity. However, sometimes you have situations that are beyond a basic level of commonsense comprehension skills.

And as I stood there, I knew that this was a moment when both the forces of good and evil were playing tug-of-war with me. It seemed like a long time, but really, this had all taken place in a matter of seconds. Either way, it was time to go; I heard some people start screaming and took off running back down the alley… From that day forward, my cousin Lil Mike was known to the streets as Face-Off! My no. 1 hitta!

It didn't take long for word to spread about what had happened. I figured the best thing to do was contact my lawyer and see if I had any warrants. My lawyer told me I was clean but that he had been hearing my name in a lot of stuff. His exact words were *"You're public enemy number one, and they want you off the streets for good."*

The streets were still buzzing about Ty-Dow getting shot five times. Word was he died twice, but they managed to bring him back both times. About three weeks later, my cousin Face-Off turned himself in. Ty-Dow told his mom, and his mom told the police; but they also had two witness. Ty-Dow's sister and cousin had seen Face when he ran back in the cut. The same way Ty-Dow had walked right past us going to his sister's house was the same direction Face ran in after the hit. I went in a totally opposite direction, and nobody ever saw me or knew I was there except Ty-Dow. Neither his sister or cousin actually saw me, but they felt I was involved; and that's what they told the Ds, but that wasn't enough for a warrant.

Ty-Dow stayed in the hospital for about a month, and during that time, his mother (Ms. Edner) had reached out to me to have a sit-down. Truthfully, I was skeptical because I was a nervous about her talking to the cops, but I eventually agreed. I mean, this wasn't just some random person; this was somebody that I really had a lot of love for. Plus I was trying to calm the situation down so Face could beat the case "NO WITNESS, NO CASE..."

So anyway, I finally agreed to have a sit-down with them when Ty-Dow got out the hospital, which was a few days later after we had that conversation. When I got to the house, his mother answered the door, gave me a hug, and told me, *"Y'all need to stop this mess. What's wrong with y'all?"*

I was speechless, seeing the hurt in her face and hearing it in her voice. I wished I could've erased all this shit, but I couldn't. The fact still remained that her son had tried to kill me, and I couldn't forgive that. After about five minutes of motherly talk, she told me, *"Ima go and get him so y'all can talk."* I wasn't expecting to see what I saw, and it kinda threw me off mentally.

Ty-Dow had lost a lot of weight and could barely walk. At first, I didn't even recognize it was him. He was walking with a portable walker, with IVs attached to it that were connected to his body. Finally, he made it to the couch, and his mother helped him sit down. She then left out the room and gave us some privacy.

For a while, neither one of us said nothing. We just sat there in silence, shaking our heads.

Finally, I spoke. *"Why, what the hell was you thinking?"*

"I was drunk. I didn't mean for it to go that far."

"You tried to kill me, man! I was looking dead in your eyes when you fired those first two shots at my head!"

"I was drunk. I ain't mean for none of that shit to happen."

"Look at where you being drunk got us. You shot up! Face locked up! Your mother stressing! And ion know how to explain this shit to Illy! All this shit for nothing over a damn Dickie suit and red bandanna! All behind this shit! I said, taking off my necklace, bracelet, and watch. I then pulled out all the money I had in my pockets and sat it down next to the jewelry on the coffee table. *"All behind this shit?"*

He just kept shaking his head, and by now, we both had tears of frustration running down our faces.

I knew that I'd never be able to trust Ty-Dow again, and that's really what hurt the most. I knew that after I left this house and he healed up, it was a strong possibility that eventually, I'd have to kill him. We had done too much dirt together, and I knew I could never trust him again. Even as we were sitting here right across from each other, I knew in the back of my mind that whatever bond we shared before could never be rebuilt.

"Frank, I died twice, and each time, I fought death with all I had. I fought until was tired and exhausted and had no more life in me. The first time I came back, I woke up in the hospital with my mother and sister standing over me, praying. I had just enough energy to tell my mother with my sister what happened. I thought I wasn't gone make it. I felt death creeping back on me. This time, I wasn't afraid. I was just tired, so I closed my eyes. And it was then that I was alone in a dark tunnel. All I heard was a voice, and the voice asked me did I wanna live. The voice told me that if I wanted to live that I needed to follow it. The voice then gave me instruction on how to get out the tunnel: FOLLOW THE LIGHT. When I awoke again, all I seen was light, and I knew that God had spared me. Frank, man, I don't want no more problems. I told myself, my mother, and God that if I made it out that tunnel that I was gone live right."

I wanted so bad to really believe what he was saying, and a part of me did. I knew he had good intentions but also know how the streets work certain lines you just don't cross. And with that in mind, I got up and left, leaving both the jewelry and money on the coffee table.

"You can have that. Ain't none of that shit worth the love I had for you."

And just like that, one of my best friends and right-hand men became an enemy.

Baby Mama Drama

After all that, I just felt like it was time for me to start paying more attention to my newborn. My baby mother and I had fallen out over some of her scandalous ways. I let that keep me away from my seed, and I was wrong for that. After I got shot and had that dream, I felt like the spirits were trying to tell me something. So I started back kicking it with my BM Stephanie. She was cool people, but the thing about our situation that was weird was we were never in a relationship. I met Steph after the club on Christmas night in 1997, and nine months later (9/23/98), she gave birth to my Christmas present. We both were young and barely knew each other. Plus I had just started talking to Trice before I found out Steph was pregno.

The reason we fell out was because I had found out she was dealing with another dude, which really was no problem if she just would've told me instead of letting me find out in a way the could've gotten me harmed.

So I was over at Steph's house bonding with my daughter who's only five months at the time. As I was sitting, somebody started knocking on the door. I was expecting Steph to go answer the door, but she didn't move. Plus she got this scared look on her face, so I was like *"You gone answer the door?"*

She was like *"No, that ain't nobody."*

So now I was confused, and at the same time, I was thinking like *"I'm not 'bout to have my daughter in no house where her mother scared to answer the door."* So I got up, handed my daughter to Steph, and answered the door. I saw two dudes, and one of them asked if Steph was there. I said, *"Yeah,"* unlocked the screen door, and let him in.

I went and got my daughter back from Steph and told her, *"You got some company."*

Now as I was sitting here holding my daughter, I heard the dude finally ask Steph, *"Who that?"*

"That's my daughter daddy."

Dude was like "Ooh, shit, my bad. Whatsup?" and offered me his hand. I just stared at his hand then looked him in his eyes. *"I don't shake hands with strangers,"* I said, placing my daughter down on the couch beside me and standing up. The dude was trying to tell Steph to convince me to shake his hand. Finally, he saw I wasn't shaking his hand, so he left it at that. But he made sure to let it be known that he and Steph were fucking. Before he left, he told Steph, *"Ima be back tonight."*

After that, I just fell back from even dealing with Steph. Like I said, had she told me, I wouldn't have cared, and the only reason I was upset was because I wasn't scrapped that night. If I knew she was dealing with somebody, I would've never went over without a scrap. But now all that was behind us. We were cool. How we got back cool was a mixture of great sex, manipulation, and me just being on some Henchmen shit.

One day, she called me and was asking why I haven't been by in a while. I basically told her that *"I don't trust you enough to feel comfortable in your house."* We went back and forth until finally I asked her, *"You still talking to dude?"*

"Yeah, but it ain't nothing serious," she said.

"Well, if it ain't that serious, set him up for me," I said, testing her loyalty.

At first, she was hesitant. But when I told her, *"I'll be over there tonight so we can talk about it,"* I heard the excitement all in her voice as she asked me, *"What time you coming?"*

After a long night of some really mind-blowing sex, I laid back and listened as she told the dude everything he wanted to hear. Occasionally, I would instruct her to ask him certain questions. By the time she hung up the phone, I knew enough to make my move…

On the day I went to hit the lick, I took Steph Brother Twizzy with me; he knew where they stayed at. It was easy lick in and out—

18k dollars and 250 bundles of heroin. I gave Twizzy 5k dollars and 50 bundles. Before we even left to hit the lick, I had already given him a gun.

I dropped him back off at Steph's house and gave him my gun too. I went to change clothes, and when I got back, I noticed a lot of Steph's family were at the house. I spoke to everybody and went to the room. I passed Twizzy in the hallway, but his head was down; plus the hallway was dark, so I couldn't see his face.

As I was in the room, stashing some money inside one of my daughter's teddy bears, one of Steph's cousin comes out of nowhere, fussing and yelling. At first, I was lost and not even understanding what she saying. Finally, I just got tired of hearing whatever the hell she was yelling about, so I asked her, *"What the fuck is you talking about?"*

"They kidnapped my cousin because of you and you got him out there doing crazy shit!"

"Who kidnapped who? What the hell is you talking 'bout?"

At that time, Twizzy came into the room, and I saw his face was swollen.

"What happen to you?"

"They kidnapped me."

"Who kidnapped you, and how they get you? And I left you not one but two guns."

"Wild Child got me, and they said they just wanted to talk."

"And you believe that shit after we just Henched him. You stupid as hell! And you lucky they ain't kill your dumb ass because I would've."

During all the commotion, I heard one of Steph's family members say, *"We just need to call the police and let them handle it."*

"Naah, I got this. Let me handle it. Ima take care of it. We don't need no police getting involved. But this nigga just stupid! How the hell he go and get in the car with some niggas we just robbed and leave the guns in the house? That's just retarded!"

Once everybody left out the room, I pulled Twizzy aside and asked him exactly what happened…

"I was in the house, and Double O knocked on the door. When I answered the door, Wild was standing to the side with a gun, and they

told me they just wanted to talk. Wasn't nothing I could do. He had the drop on me. Once I got to the car, it was two more dudes sitting up front. Wild and Double O made set in the back in-between them. They started punching me in the face and pistol-whipping me—telling me they knew it was me because somebody saw me and told them what color clothes I had on. They wanted to know who else was with me." When he said that, he dropped his head. I knew then that he had told them. *"Man, I was scared. I shitted myself and everything. When they smelled the shit, they drove down a dirt road, pistol-whipped me some more, then put me in the trunk. I had to tell them. I thought they was gone kill me. After that, they called Steph and told her they had me. When they opened up the trunk, it was to give me the phone just so she could hear my voice. They closed the trunk back. The next time they opened it, they let me out back at Steph's house. Steph was standing outside on the porch. Wild tried to walk with me to the house, but when we got close, Steph pulled out on him. 'Get the hell away from my house and leave my brother alone!'"*

I started laughing when he told me that. *"She did what?"*

"She had that big ass .357 and was aiming that bitch. And she back that nigga down."

After he told me everything, I knew how to play it, and I wasn't even mad that he told them it was me. They needed to know who they were dealing with. I went to the Motherland, got some play toys and a vest, then went and posted in the projects.

They came through and pulled up but wouldn't get out the car. They rolled down the window. *"Ayo, Frank, we need to holla at you."* I counted four heads.

"A'ight, meet me in the back of the projects." The only reason I didn't let off on sight was because it was broad daylight and there were too many witnesses around.

I had a twin snub-nosed .357 magnums and a sawed-off semi-auto 20 gauge with hallow head slugs. When I got to the back of the projects, I put my mask on, slid across to the passenger seat, got out, crouched low with the two magnums, and laid the gauge across the passenger seat. I waited for a while, but they never pulled up.

To his credit, I was never able to catch Wild slipping. He threw a few slugs; I threw a few back. He ended up catching a case, and that was the end of our beef.

But I did catch Double O late night in the projects with my gun stuffed down his throat. He blamed it all on Wild Child. *"I swear to God, Frank, they made me get in the car."* I literally had this nigga on his knees sucking my gun like a dick, begging for his life. I spared him, but every time I saw him after that, I made him run his pockets—sometimes even without a gun… Bitch-ass nigga, and you told on my man Wayne Burch 'bout that situation with Bootcamp back in the day.

Bodies Dropping

Meanwhile, as me and Steph got back on speaking terms, my girl-friend at the time (Trice) was pregnant. They both stayed on the Northside in the same projects called Taylor Holmes, a.k.a. D-Block. When I wasn't at Steph spot's, I was at Trice's spot. When I wasn't there, I was on Hall Street at the apartment I shared with Murder and Mone.

Around this time, Murder had started hanging with this kid call G-Kode. G-Kode wasn't from the hood, but everybody knew him because his mom taught at the school that most of the kids from the hood went to.

Murder was still up and doing his thing, dealing with snakes from 13th. They had convinced him to believe that they didn't have nothing to do with that situation when the dude from 13th tried to rob me. I wasn't trying to hear that shit, and little did they know I was just waiting to catch their ass the right way too.

For the most part, Henchmen had the city on eggshells. The problem with that was, every time some shit popped off, we got blamed for it. Sometimes we wouldn't even be around and still got blamed, or somehow my name would come up.

In the latest turn of events, my homie J.V. had caught a body and was on the run. From what I heard, the dude pulled up and tried to pull off with homie hanging out the car and somehow ended up slumped. J.V.'s cousin Killa Black was my right-hand man, so just to be on the safe side, I switched cars with J.V. J.V. was OT, but we knew the police would eventually pull the car over because it was in his sister's name.

On that particular day, Trice wanted some J. Michaels Philly; she and her friend Toya were pregnant and had a craving for J. Michaels.

93

I drove all the way to J. M., but it was closed; so I went to Wendy's on Market. I was doing like ninety down Market. I looked in my rearview and saw somebody on my bumper. Next thing I know, I saw blue lights and heard sirens. *"Damn, fucken police!"*

I couldn't just stop in the middle of Market, and truthfully, if I didn't have two pregnant women in the car, I would've tried to lose them in traffic. But I couldn't, so I just turned off Market and pulled over. Just like I thought, police cars started pulling up, and they surrounded the car. They thought I was J.V.

All I had was a bag of weed, and I had already swallowed that. I wasn't dirty, and I knew it wasn't shit they could do to me.

"Cut the car off and get out now!" they yelled over the loudspeaker.

I put that *Above the Rim* soundtrack CD in and let that 2Pac rock full blast. "♪They'll never take me alive, I'm getting high with my .45$♪"

I opened up the car door, stepped out, and stared at them. They all had guns aimed at me.

"Step away from the vehicle with your hands up now!"

I just stood there, staring at them all.

"Fucken pussies. It's two pregnant women in the car, and I'm not going nowhere till y'all put them pistols up!" I yelled over the music. After I said that, I sat back down in the car with the door still open.

I saw one officer out the corner of my eye walking low, approaching the car and ready to fire. He walked right up to the car with his gun pointed directly at my face. *"Cut the car off now!"* he yelled.

I just stared at him and didn't move. He eased closer, kept his aim, reached over the stirring wheel, cut the car off, and snatched the keys out the ignition. By then, other officers had moved in to assist. I slowly raised my hands, stood up, and was placed under arrest. They ended up finding a roach in the ashtray, took 3,000 dollars out my pocket, and charged me with simple possession for the roach.

When Terry came and got me, he told me the same thing. My lawyer and mom had said, *"Your name all over the place. You might wanna chill out for a while. I had the FBI inquiring about how you'll keep posting these bails. They wanted to know your financial history... And that's how it always starts, so you'll need to lay low because they definitely fishing for info."* Plus word was the Feds were in town and had started recruiting. Come to find out Cecil, a.k.a. Merk, told the police J.V. was the triggerman. He later changed his statement, and J.V. beat the case. But in my eyes, he should've never said shit. Period.

And just when I thought it couldn't get any worse... Cousin D had just opened up Club Benjamin. The grand opening was V-day, and the girl group Total was performing that night. We hit the mall 'bout 50 deep; damn near the whole Henchmen squad was in the building.

Cousin D was from Jervay and showed a lot of love. *"Just come out and have a good time. Save that bullshit for the parking lot."* After getting shot in the club, I had thought it would be smart to have some homies stationed out in the parking lot—just in case.

Man, it was sooo many people in the club that night—the Southside, the Northside, the Eastside, the Motherland. The whole entire Port City and all surrounding areas were out that night.

I got up on the stage during Total's performance and started dancing with them, drunk as hell. I fell off the stage, but the crowd caught me.

Next thing I know, my man Tone Harris was whispering in my ear, *"Give me the keys to the car so I can go get a gun. This nigga just spilt his drink all over me and had the nerve to grill me afterwards."*

"Man, it's too much pussy in here tonight for that dumb shit! I can't let you fuck the night up like that. Look at all these hoes. Get one and relax."

There was no way I was 'bout to give him the keys. There were too many people around for that stupid shit. Plus, it was Valentine's Day, and all I was trying to do was get in-between the thighs of this lil thick chick named Queen I had just recently met. After I stepped away from Tone, I saw my big sis in the crowd. I had to go see if she was good. We ended up drunk and dancing the night away.

When the club ended, as I was walking my sis out to her car, I saw something out the corner of my eye. It was Tone. He ran right past me at full speed. I could tell that whatever or whoever he was running from had him scared to death. About five seconds after Tone passed me, a dude stepped out and started shooting. ***Boom! Boom!***

Boom! Boom! Boom! He was shooting at Tone but in my direction. So I got low but put my body in front of my sister. Once I got her safely to her car, she tried to make me leave with her. *"Naah, go ahead. I'm good,"* I said, closing her door and stepping off. When I turned around, the dude was just standing there with his gun out, but by now, some of the homies were strapped too. *"Whatsup with you? You ain't..."* ***Boom! Boom! Boom!*** Before I could even finish my sentence, my homie Tok started hitting at the dude. The dude took off running back toward the parking lot. I took off running right behind him. By the time I reached the parking lot, all I saw was somebody dressed in ***all black*** standing over the dude—***Boom! Boom! Boom! Boom!***—*putting* four shots in his face and chest. Mr. ***All Black*** stepped off without even looking my way. Whoever that was had just left me standing in a dark parking lot with two dead bodies.

By this time, a lot of people were running to their cars. Just to be on the safe side, I told somebody to give the dude a ride to the hospital. I didn't even see the other body until I heard a female scream. I walked over where she was at and saw a Goodfella from 13th down bad. Dead with both eyes and mouth wide open. He died with a shocked expression on his face.

Toka was charged with two capital murders. The only reason why he got charged was because he was seen shooting at the dude, but none of them bullets actually hit the dude. The dude died from four to the face and chest. The Goodfella died from getting a hit directly in the heart. And Mr. ***All Black Everything*** got away clean. Tok stood tall for the team and kept it silent. His charges were later dropped down to two counts of involuntary manslaughter. He pleaded out to both counts and ended up with only three to five years. *(I'm my brother's keeper... Henchmen love and loyalty.)*

You'd think that with so much mayhem going on, people would be wise enough to stay out of our way. The bottom line was, we weren't out looking for trouble, but we damn sure weren't ducking none either. What they (the Goodfellas) and all them other Northerners failed to realize was that we had home-court advantage.

Shortly after the situation at Club Benjamin, the homie Loco had a run-in with another Upptopper at the liquor spot called J-Butters located in the BO. J-Butters was a late-night liquor or gambling spot that most of the residents of the Port City attended after the club.

On this particular night, it was me, M-l, Loco, and G-Kode. The homie Loco, for the most part, was all about getting money. He had been groomed by big-homie Stace about the streets, so also he knew how to handle a hammer. The thing is, he was so laid-back that if you didn't know him personally, you wouldn't think he was dangerous at all. Nobody except the Henchmen knew why we called him Loco.

The Upptopper was this guy named Ed from somewhere up north. Word was Ed was allegedly a hit man from New York who was once featured on *America's Most Wanted*. At the time, Ed's right-hand man was Faheem (RIP).

Now Faheem was also a well-respected OG in the streets of Port City. However, Faheem was from the Eastside, and them Eastside dudes stick together just like we do on the Southside, which lead to us (the Southsiders) not really getting along with them (the Eastsiders) and vice versa.

The liquor house was jam-packed… I'm talking wall to wall. I was at the counter surrounded by females. The homie Loc was at arm's reach behind me, surrounded by more females. The homies Murder and G-Kode were outside on the porch. The line was long, but I was already at the counter. I dropped 250 dollars on the bar and told J-Butters, *"Just keep 'em coming. Straight shots, Henny and EJ."*

Every time he put some drinks in front of me, I'd pass them back to Loco, and he handed them to some females. I had ordered fifty shots and gave most of them to females. Really, we were just trying to have some fun—you know, flirt, fuck, and wake up with another story to tell…

Too bad Ed didn't know that… *"Ayo, y'all lil niggas need to stop tricking off your re-up money on these hoes and get the fuck out the way!"* yelled Ed from the back of the line.

When I looked back, I saw it was Ed who was now pushing and shoving his way through the crowd up toward the counter. He bumped Loco hard in the shoulder from the blind side, causing him to drop his drink and stumble into a female…

"Yo, watch where the fuck going!" Loco yelled at Ed as he got his balance back.

"Nigga, fuck you. I ain't gotta watch shit. When you see me coming, get the fuck out my way," replied Ed as he stepped aggressively up in the homie's face. I slid from the bar, and as I was walking, I noticed Faheem was still standing in the back of the line, talking to some female. He was about ten feet away from Ed, and in that teen-feet space was about ten to twelve people standing in line.

Loco and Ed were still standing face to face, arguing. Ed had his back to me as I approached him and Loco. I mouthed the words *"Trick bag"* as I came right up on Ed from the blind side and bumped him hard with a shoulder shove.

"Yo, what the f…" said Ed just as he was turning in my direction.

Boom! Boom! Boom!

Was all he was able to say before three hallows penetrated his spine. The homie had literally blown this nigga back out. I watched Faheem closely as he pulled his strap and rushed toward Ed, who was now laying paralyzed on the floor.

"Somebody help me get him to the car!" he yelled.

There were still a lot of people in the liquor house. On our way out, we stepped right over the nigga Ed and left. We watched from our car as they toted him out to Faheem's car. Somebody was holding him up under his shoulders, and somebody was holding him up by his feet.

"That's a dumb nigga," I said to the homies.

"You think his man Faheem know who hit him?"

"Naah, I doubt it. Was too many people and too much space between them. And if he do, then oh well, fuck it. I'm tired of these niggas coming from all over the world and thinking they can run shit on the streets that I grew up on. It don't work like that!" I stated forcefully.

"He brought that shit on his self, so fuck him. I ain't 'bout to lose no sleep over it. It's Henchmen season… War always come before peace."

From there, we rarely ever spoke about that night. Every time we saw Ed in his wheelchair, we just shake our heads and say... *"Stupid is what stupid does."*

Warrior (Henchmen) Bloodline

Once again, I had managed to get my name caught up in the middle of some mayhem and murder. After that night, a lot of us just laid low to see how shit played out. The police had turned up the pressure on us and were hitting everybody spotted. About three weeks later, they surrounded Tok's crib and arrested him. They hit my sis's spot looking for me, but luckily, I was out in the Motherland, lying low.

The Goodfellas had kidnapped one of the Henchmen homies named Uncle Paully. Somehow, he had managed to escape naked after they tortured him and made it to safety. Word was they wanted to know where I stayed at and he told them, but I didn't find that out until later. I gave Gator the heads up to be on high alert, and he was definitely war-ready. He had plenty of guns, ammo, and the surveillance cameras. Wasn't nobody going to be able to creep up on the fam.

The city was on fire. My name was all over the place. ***Extortion, murder, robbery, drugs, gang activity***—I was getting blamed for everything. The Feds had recruited an entire team of snitches, and it was us (Henchmen) against them.

Uncle Paully was the weak link; I guess after getting kidnapped, stripped naked, and barely surviving, he decided to switch sides. He provided the police with a twenty-page detailed report about our organization and agreed to help take me down. I never thought to think that it would be one of my own kind out to get me. I was too busy focused on the Goodfellas. But I started noticing every time Paully came around, the police would swarm the spot.

I had a close call with Hargrove at the pool hall on the Northside. He and D. T. Oaks pulled up, and a lot of my young boys came running inside the pool hall. *"Damn."* I was trying to tell them not to come in because I knew the police was gonna come in fucken with them, but it was a useless argument. So I just went to the back, stashed my gun, and work inside the pool tables' hidden compartment.

After that, I told G-Kode, *"Let's play pool."* We got the first table right by the door. I made sure to keep my back to the door so they couldn't see my face as I racked the balls. I shot and missed, but I heard the police radio behind me. I kept my back to them and moved with them as if I was setting up for my next shot. Once I got halfway 'round the table, I put the pool stick on the table and stepped out the door.

I got past Oaks, but Hargrove was still sitting in the car. We locked eyes. He started opening the door. I took off running! He chased me all the way to the projects while Oaks radioed for backup.

Finally, I was too tired to keep running, so I stopped, turned around, and squared up. *"I ain't going back to jail,"* I said, breathing heavily as he whipped his baton out and told me, *"Get on the ground."*

"Man, I'm not going back to jail!" I yelled more forcefully this time.

By this time, a crowd of people had started gathering around. He pulled his pistol out, cocked it, and told me to get on the ground again. I saw all the backup going to the pool hall, so I knew it was only a matter of minutes before they swarmed the projects. I started backing away from Hargrove. He still had his pistol out. I saw the school bus stop and lil kids getting off. I ran toward the bus screaming, *"Help! Help! He got a gun!"* Mothers went wild, running to grab their kids. I saw G-Kode drive slowly around the bus, looking for me. I started running behind the car, waving my hands. The brake lights came on, and the passenger door opened. I got to the car and jumped in. *"Go, go, go!"* Hargrove was only about fifteen feet behind me. He threw his baton at the car; it bounced harmlessly off the back window as we sped off. We drove about three blocks, and I saw my stepbrother Raymond with Ish. I told G-Code, *"Pull up on them."* I hopped out the car with G-Kode and got in with Raymond and Ish. There were police cars swarming all over the Northside. I laid down in the back seat and told brah what happened and to take me to my pop's house.

Outrunning Hargrove was unheard of. Everybody that hustled knew he was fast and had wind for days, but I had just pulled it off. I knew they were 'bout to hit everywhere looking for me. I knew I was safe at my dad's house because it was outside their jurisdiction.

I stayed at my pop's house long enough to see my lil sis Kesha and for my pops to say a special prayer for me. He put anointing oils on my head and spoke in tongues to cast the evil spirit off me. After he prayed for me, we sat down and had a real man-to-man convo.

"Son, you're a very powerful person, but the devil is trying to destroy you. He's sent some of his strongest warriors at you, and you've defeated them all. So now he's trying to trick you into self-destruction because your spirit is too strong to allow man to destroy you. Every time your name is on the news, the people from the church call my phone, thinking it was me. Son, we share the same name, the same blood, and also the same spirit. I'm not in the church every Sunday because I'm afraid of what's in the streets. I'm in the church every Sunday because I'm afraid of what's inside of me. Don't think I'm unaware of what you're doing in the street because I used to do the same thing. I made a mistake and left a witness behind one time. Luckily, he lived. I only got five years, but that was all I needed to tame this demon."

All I could do was listen as my dad gave me some spiritual insight. I had never thought to look at the World from spiritual point of view, but hearing my dad explain it to me made perfect sense. I had made a lot of enemies, but none were strong enough to defeat me. But here I was, self-destructing. The more money I made, the more shit I got into. After listening to my pops put things in their proper perspective, I saw how reckless I was moving. I was becoming my own worst enemy. It was time to get back, focused.

"I'm glad I came out here. More than likely, I got some warrants, so Ima go ahead and get all this mess behind me. But remember, a long time ago, you told me never trust a rat, snake, or a coward. Well, right now, I gotta be extra careful. They're everywhere. The only people I can trust right now is family. Family always first," I said as I walked out the door back into a world of madness and evil spirits, yet protected by the unseen powers of prayer, positive energy, and the warrior (Henchmen) bloodline…

Uncle Paully

The streets were buzzing once again; word was the Henchmen had killed 2 Goodfellas and that Frank White was in the midst of all the mayhem. To make matters worse, I had just pissed Hargrove off, so I really had to be extra careful; and I still hadn't quite figured out that Paully was a rat. I had my suspicions but no evidential proof.

We'd usually go to Paully's house and hang out because he stayed in Hornet Square, which was directly up the street from Taylor Holmes and around the corner from the Game Room. On the day that I got chased by Hargrove, G-Kode and I had just left Paully's house.

Uncle Paully was originally from the Southside and had stayed in a projects called Houston Moore before moving to the north. His house became a lay-low spot for most of the Henchmen homies once we migrated from Jervay (the Southside) to Taylor Holmes (the Northside). We never did anything out the ordinary over there, so I found it strange when one day, as I was leaving, his neighbor called me over and told me the police had been asking around about me. I found it odd that Paully's neighbor had told me about the police asking around, but Paully never mentioned it to me at all.

I knew I had pissed Grove off, but I didn't think he would reveal his hand. By asking around, he was basically giving me a heads-up, and that didn't make any sense. Something wasn't quite right about that.

One morning as I was leaving Trice's house, I was walking to Paully's because that's where I had left my car parked at. It was really early 'round seven. I had adopted the habit of doing things early to avoid the police who usually switch shift in between six or seven in the morning.

When I got to the car, everything was good. I didn't see no cops or nothing that would raise my suspicion. However, after about five minutes of driving, I looked in my rearview and saw about four police cars with their lights on but sirens off. I didn't know where they came from or how long they'd been behind me. I assumed it wasn't me they were after because I hadn't committed any traffic violation. Plus the car had tinted windows, so there was no way they knew it was me. We had so many different cars (thanks to Ghetto and Polk) the only way that they could've known it was me was if somebody had told them.

I attempted to pull over, hoping they'd go around me and thinking that it wasn't me they were after. Instead of going around, they tried to box me in.

"Oh, hell no!" I said to my myself as I smashed the gas and swerved around the first two cars. *"Catch me if you can, mafuckas!"* I said with the pedal to the metal.

Once I cleared the two cars in front of me, I was in the lead. Since we were in the hood, I really had the advantage. I knew all the cuts, alleys, and back roads like the back of my hand. I knew I couldn't outrun the police radio, so I was just looking to get some distance—enough distance to jump out and run. I was better off on foot.

I came right down 11th Street and shot across Market Street without stopping, leaving the Northside and entering the Southside through the BO. The police had slowed up to get across Market, and that's exactly what I had expected them to do. That was just the distance I needed. I slowed up, open the door, drove up on the curb, got as close as I could to the grass, and jumped. I lost my balance, stumbled a few steps without falling, and came up in a full sprint. All I heard was "Stop! Freeze! Stop now!"

I wasn't trying to hear that shit. I had already hit the cut and started jumping fences. I ran about six blocks, cutting through backyards and jumping fences, and ended up on 17th Street. I walked inside the dry cleaners that used to be right beside Shop&Go then went and politely asked the lady working the counter to call me a cab. When the cab arrived, I instructed him to take me back to the north. My plan was to get another whip, give the homies a rundown 'bout the situation, and go hide out in the Motherland.

I gave the cab driver twenty dollars and told him to keep the change. I got out about four blocks away from the spot. I cut through some yards and came out in the alley behind Hornet Square. I jumped the fence and walked swiftly across the parking lot, and just as I was jogging up the staircase, the homies were coming down. It was Wise, Murder, and G-Kode. I was moving so fast up the stairs that when I turned the first bend, they were reaching on me.

"Maaan, you almost just got yourself shot," said Murder.

Taking his hand off his strap, *"I ain't notice that was you at first. Where you coming from?"*

"I just got in a high-speed chase. I wrecked the whip, but I got away. I ain't have time to grab the guns out the car. They was right on my ass. They looking for me on the south down by the BO. So don't go over there because they probably still swarming. I'm 'bout to go grab some keys and get low. Ima catch up with y'all when I get back in town," I said, walking into the house.

When I walked inside the house, the first thing I saw was Paully, some unknown female, and Cutty (RIP) smoking weed. I briefly told Paully about what had happened and took a few pulls from the blunt. Before I grabbed some keys, I had taken a quick shower and changed clothes. I was on my way out the door, but something told me to look out the window first.

"Oooh, shit!" Police cars were all in the parking lot, both the sheriff and city cops. And as if they weren't enough, the damn patty wagon pulled up, and out jumped the SWAT team with machine guns.

"Ain't this a bitch," I said, walking to the back door and looking out the window. *"Damn."* The spot was surrounded! They had me trapped! There was no way out! *"How the hell did they know I was here?"* was all I kept thinking to myself, but I didn't have time to dissect the thought because I had to clean house fast.

The first thing I did was take all the guns apart and started stashing pieces in each room and flushing the bullets. All the drugs besides the weed went down the toilet right along with the ammunition. The apartment was on the second floor, so I was listening very carefully to hear when and if they had started coming up. By the time I looked back out the window, I saw the news van along with the cameraman reporting live. The police had put out roadblocks, and a crowd had started gathering.

"Don't open that door," I told Paully after hearing footsteps coming up the staircase. *"They can't have no warrant, not that fast."*

Next thing I know, somebody was knocking on the door, calling my name. *"Shawn, I know you're in there. Come out. This is Sheriff Joe McQueen, and I want this to go nice and smooth. Just come out, Shawn. We know you're in there. We don't want anybody to get hurt. Just come out."*

I couldn't believe my ears. Sheriff McQueen was the head honcho. To hear him at the door calling my name let me know the situation was a lot more serious than I first thought, but I still wasn't opening the door.

I needed to relax. *"You got some more weed?"* I asked Cutty (RIP). I just sat there in a daze, smoking the blunt. I kind've felt like I was going back to jail, so I was just stalling for as long as I could.

After about thirty minutes of asking me to come out, Sheriff McQueen left. I only had one option left, and that was the attic. I told Paully I was going in the attic to take a look. My plan was to knock the wall down and go through the apartment next door, so I took a hammer up with me. As soon as I got in the attic, this coward Paully opened the door for the cops. He didn't waste no time.

I jumped back down out the attic and rushed to the front just as the SWAT team was swarming inside the apartment. Paully, Cutty, and the girl were being escorted out. I caught up with them and made it past about five SWATs by pointing behind me and saying, *"He's in the back. He's in the back."* They didn't recognize my face, so I used that to the advantage.

I made it out the house and down the stairs. Next thing I know, I was staring down the barrel of a police addition: AR-15. *"Put your fucken hands up! I got him! I got him! This is him!"* he said, placing the barrel of the machine gun on the bridge of my nose.

It was Sarvis, the same officer that had arrested me years ago for pistol-whipping a dude at school. He still recognized my face. I didn't know who he was until he took off his helmet.

"So we meet again, Mr. Jennings," he said, pushing me face-first against the wall and handcuffing me roughly behind my back.

"Man, fuck you!" I said as I turned back around and tried to spit in his face. I saw the cameraman coming and was hoping to provoke Sarvis so he'd jump on me in front of everybody.

Sheriff McQueen put a stop to it all. He came over and personally escorted me to the cop car. *"Just calm down, son, It's no need to make matters worse,"* he said. You see, Sheriff McQueen was a Black man, and some of his family had married into the Motherland lineage. Although this was my first time actually meeting him in person, I knew that he knew my bloodline, and because of that, I was protected... The people at my father's church were very powerful.

Jail Credit

I was taken to the county jail and charged with multiple felony offences and listed as a person of interest in connection to the double homicide.

Although Tok had already been charged, the investigation was still ongoing. It just so happened they put me in the block with Tok, and it was then that I found out Paully had provided the police with a twenty-three-page detailed report. He told them everything there was to know about Henchmen as well as the double homicide.

The DTs ended up taking a trip out to the Motherland. From what I heard, they wanted to take a look around, but Gator wasn't having it. Word was they were inquiring about some guns that Paully had told them we kept out there. Thank God that Unc was a gangsta. My mom told me that when DTs came out there, Uncle pointed to the Private Property sign and told them, *"If you don't have a warrant, you're trespassing because you're not welcome on my land. Now please leave before I have to report you to your superiors."* All I could do was smile. *"That damn brother of yours is crazy,"* I said.

It was a lot of people in the dorm that I knew—Uncle U, Ghetto, J.V., Thug Luv, and a few faces I had seen around the city. My bond was 800,000 dollars, so I was stuck. I didn't have that type of money, so the only thing I could do was wait and see what Mr. Hicks could find out.

And that didn't take long. When he first came to see me, he told me the exact same thing he said last time he saw me. *"I told you you were public enemy no. 1. Now look at this mess you've made. I'll see what I can do to clean things up, but it would be best if you sat still for a while and let things cool off. Don't discuss nothing over the phone, and if anybody tries to speak with you, give them my card. I'll be back in a few weeks to check on you. You can call the office collect. The best time to catch me is early around eight. Just hang tight and let me do my job, and as a heads-up don't put too much trust in your so-called friends. They're part of the reason you're in here."*

I wasn't slow. I knew exactly who and what he was referring to, but I just kept it to myself.

After Mr. Hicks, my mom was the first person to come see me. I couldn't post bail, but I had a lil nest egg stashed away for times like this. She loaded my commissary account and gave me an update on Unc and how all my lil bros and sisters were doing. She tried her hardest to hold back the tears, but I saw her eyes watering up. I'm pretty sure she saw mine watering up too.

"Mom, Ima be okay. These people nor this place can't break me. I come from a bloodline of warriors, and we never give up. We fight till the end, and it's far from over."

"Son, I just hate seeing you like this. You're so much more. Sometimes I feel like it's my fault."

"It's not, Mom, and I'm not looking to blame you or anybody else. I'm just livin' and learning. And life has a way of teaching us all we need to know."

"Shawn, I've had six kids. I've given birth six times, and I've brought six healthy live into this world. But when I had you, you weren't like the rest. You ripped my insides apart and came out yelling at the top of your lungs, fighting the doctors. Son, I know you a fighter because that how you came out my womb and into the world. But I also know how hard it is to win against these people in this system. I just want you to be safe, son."

"I will, Mom. I love you, and it's family always"... I stopped and waited on her to finish my sentence.

"First, son," she said, blowing me a kiss before getting up to leave.

Jail was hell but wasn't something I couldn't handle. My mom and sis kept minutes on the phone. My wifey (Trice) at the time came to see me almost every week. Every now and then, my BM Steph would write and come see. Even the lil shorty (Queen) I had met at the club that night was showing me love. It was only a matter of seeing how things played out in court.

Almost every day, Uncle U would have me working out with him—push-ups, sit-ups, and curls with the water bag. J.V., Thug Luv (RIP), and I were the youngest dudes in the dorm.

It was around this same time that I found out Needy had helped set me up to get robbed. Jail is a bored place, and if you don't know how to bid, you could easily find yourself in the midst of gossip. Needy had started whispering to people about how he had robbed me. Thing is, he fucked around and whispered my name to the wrong person (Uncle U), not knowing that me and Uncle U had put helluva work in together on the streets.

"Yo, Frank, what this nigga talking 'bout, saying he robbed you?" Uncle U asked me right in front of Needy.

"That nigga ain't never robbed me. He was there the night M-Bells got me but swore up and down he ain't have nothing to do with it. Matter fact, he put his word on it when I asked him 'bout it."

"Well, he was just over there whispering 'bout it. I told him real men don't speak in whispers, and if he had something say about you, he needed to say it to your face."

"So whatsup? You got something you wanna say to me?" I asked him. He went speechless, looked at me, looked at Uncle U, then dropped his head, and walked off.

"Let's eat that nigga," Uncle U suggested, but I wasn't pressed. That shit had happened years ago, and I wasn't concerned about it. However, we did tell him he had to get out the dorm, and when the officer came back 'round, that's exactly what he did...checked off.

It took ten months for Mr. Hicks to work his magic, but finally, I was called to court. I had been waiting in the holding cell all day when eventually Mr. Hicks showed up.

"Hey, Shawn, how's it going? Or is it Frank White? Which do you prefer?" As always, Mr. Hicks had a way with words that always got people to open up. *"How would you like to go home today?"* he said, giving me the I'm-serious look.

"O-kay, Mr. Hicks, my name is Shawn, not Frank White. I don't know who Frank White is besides a mobster in a movie. I'd love to go

home today, but unfortunately, that's not an option because I've officially been labeled as Port City public enemy no. 1—or at least that's what my lawyer says."

"Well, here's what I got for you—really good news. All your charges with the exception of your drug charges and one gun charge had been dismissed. Your first-degree robbery with a dangerous weapon has been dropped down to third-degree common-law robbery. And since you don't have a record and have sat in jail for close to a year, you're eligible for probation. You have a sixteen-to-twenty-months suspended sentence over your head with ten months jail credit towards it. Make sure you contact the probation officer within seventy-two hours. There was no way they could prove that was you driven that car. No way to connect you to any homicides. And all the guns they got out of that house and car could've belonged to anybody. Now the best thing you can do is lay low and stay out of trouble. And yes, you're still officially public enemy no. 1, but I'm also officially the best damn lawyer in the Port City... Be sure to give me a call when you get settled in. I've already spoken with your mother and sister, so they're expecting your call..."

When I got back to the jail, I told all the homies the good news, gave my contact info out, and promised to follow up on a few favors. All they had to do was send the word, and it was done... Ghetto beat his body, J.V. beat his body, and Tok only ended up with three to five... Need I say more? I am my brother's keeper.

Streets Won't Let Me Chill

It felt good to be free. I could move around without worrying about the police. The only problem I had was, I was popped, dead broke. The last of my change was spent paying Mr. Hicks to perform magic.

My homies Wise and Killa Black had come by and took me shopping and afterward gave me some bread, but I was used to having at least five figures to play with.

I wasn't trying to rush back out on the block, but something had to give. I went to the dice game with my last 700 dollars. Big-homie Stace had the bank. It was push pay and trips double.

"All bets good. Put your money under your shoe, and nobody move!" he said, shooting the dice. His point was 4.

"Fifty to a hundred dollars, I 4 or better," I said, grabbing the dice and shaking them.

"Bet good," he replied.

I schooled the dice then rolled… Trip 5s… I had 250 dollars under my shoe. Plus I rolled trips, and my point was better than 4. So on my first roll, I had won 600 dollars, and from there, it was on. I walked away with close to 8,000 dollars that night. Before I left, I spent 3,200 dollars with Big Homie, and just like that, I was back on my grind.

I was still hanging out on the Northside and had run into my old celly Nap from Juvie. He was up and on top of his game. I used to always bump into him at the dice games. I'd always pull him aside and ask him, *"You seen Jesus lately?"* We'd always share a laugh about it, and even till this day, that's still our lil personal joke.

G-Kode, Murder, and I were back hanging tight again. Truthfully, I was just happy to be out of jail. I ended up getting Trice pregnant as soon as I got out. Being in jail had me backed up; and honestly, on the strength that she had held me down, I was more than ready to give her my seed. She earned it.

I wasn't even on the bullshit no more. I was chilling trying to grind my way back to six figures without hitting a lick, but like Jay-Z once said…"The streets won't let you chill."

You see, while I was in jail, G-Kode and Murder had been hitting licks, which wasn't a problem; but they had failed to update me on who they all had gotten, which left me in the blind to who they were beefing with. This one particular cat they Henched was this kid named Carlos from Hillcrest. Los and I were cool because we used to hustle on 10th and Castle together back in the day. But once again, that being-cool shit will only get you but so far in the streets.

One night, it was me and G-Kode just riding 'round the city, going from spot to spot and posting up. We had just left Houston Moore, and as we were leaving out, I was laid back in the passenger seat on my Motorola cell phone talking to Queen when all of a sudden, all I heard was **boom, boom, boom** (gunshots)!

I dropped the phone, sat up, grabbed my .40 off my lap, looked around, and saw they were behind us. *"Go! Go! Go!"* I yelled as G-Kode mashed the gas.

Whoever it was had their lights off. Plus their car was a dark color that blended in perfectly with the night. We came out of Houston Moore from the side parking lot, cut across Greenfield, and shot up toward Mo-town but made a right.

"Slow down some," I said as I let my window down just as we made that right. They were still driving toward us at full speed as I came out the window with the .40 barking. ***Boom! Boom! Boom! Boom! Boom!*** Sheeeeeesh. They hit the brakes hard and backed down. ***Boom! Boom! Boom!*** I sent three more shots at them just so they'd know I had more ammo. *"Who the fuck was that?"* I asked G-Kode, settling back in my seat and throwing a fresh clip in the .40.

"That's that nigga Los and Regus from Hillcrest. We Henched them at a dice game a while ago."

"And you just now telling me this shit? And I been out a month now! I know Los, and he ain't on it like that. But Ima see what he talking 'bout. Y'all niggas is crazy, word!"

I knew G-Kode wasn't no shooter; all he did was hustle. But he was also like my lil brah, so I had to straighten this shit out.

It was about a week later when I caught Los on the North early morning sitting in the car with his head down, rolling a Dutch right on Nixon Street across from the corner store on 6th. I wasn't sure what his reaction to seeing me would be, so I approached with caution. I had the .357 snub cuffed behind my thigh as I tapped on the window with my knuckle. When he looked up, I saw the shocked expression on his face.

"Frank, whatsup? Maaan, when you get out?" he asked. His facial expression looked sincere. My instincts were telling me he honestly didn't know I was in that car.

"Shiit, been out a few weeks now. But whatsup with you though?"

"Just chilling, man. These streets is fucked up."

"Yeah, I know a lot of bullshit going on. Heard you and G-Kode had some issues."

"Man, Frank, them niggas Henched me in my hood in front of everybody. Caught me slipping at the dice game."

"Yeah, I heard, and I was in that car the other night when y'all started shooting. That was me banging out the window."

"Oh, word, I ain't know you was in there. You know we go waaay back."

"Yeah, I know, and that's why instead of all that dumb shit, I'ma ask you to dead that on the strength of me…" And from there, the beef was dead.

However, later, Los would go on to write a book called *Eastcoast Hollywood*, and in this book, he speaks about many things and situations that he wasn't directly involved in. He also speaks about how he spared my life after Big Tim had placed 30,000 dollars on my head. But what he fails to mention is that the same way he spared my life, I spared his. Consider it even. Real men operate off of the Code of Honor, not dollar signs. Somebody had to offer you 30,000 dollars just for you to even think about coming for me. I came at you for free just on the strength of my lil homie. That alone should tell you we're two different type of dudes. I literally do this for fun. And oh yeah, just so you know, that Pretty Tony shit ain't real right. The street don't respect it! The last person that brought that shit back to the Port City didn't make it (RIP, Lil Johnny). If you trying to get real right righteous, then get at me. I'm connected from Carolina to Cali. You know what it is… Family Always First!

•

Big Tim

Now that I was out and back into the swing of things, I realized that shit hadn't changed. Even though I had been proven innocent in the court of law, dudes were still acting funny style and scary toward me. Big-homie Stace, Nap, and Noon were the only dudes in the city that would serve me. Wise and I were together one day, and I was just venting about how hard these bitch niggas make it for a real nigga to eat.

"I'm about to start robbing all these scary niggas. I hate that soft shit! They act like a nigga just spose to starve out here, waiting on them to show up with the work. It don't work like that. That's why I don't respect most them dudes. They scary, soft, and they hidden behind that money. They know they couldn't survive out here with us! That's why they be scared to come through. Acting all nervous and shit when they pull up!"

"We been out here waiting on this nigga for damn near three hours, and he still ain't showed up. I could've been sold half my pack by now."

We were waiting on Big Tim, who was one of Wise's connects. I had to go through Wise to shop with Tim because I guess he didn't trust me. Tim had been told Wise he was on his way to meet us but hadn't showed up yet. I had given Wise 6,500 dollars to get 9 ounces of ready rock, something I really didn't want to do but had to do because I couldn't find no soft. I guess Wise finally realized Tim wasn't gonna come, so he gave me my money back. But I could tell he was just as frustrated as I was.

"Don't even trap, baby boy. Ima take care of this one for you. When dudes don't honor their word, they deserve what they get," he stated as I was getting out the car.

The next morning, I was at Steph's crib when she woke me up by shaking my shoulder and telling me somebody was at the door. The first thing I did was grab my gun.

"It's Wise," she finally said after I was halfway down the stairs.

"Well, why you ain't just let him in?"

"Because that's your company, not mine, and I don't know what the hell you be doing in them streets. So I'm not opening no damn door for nobody because I don't trust none of them niggas!"

The way she said that let me know she had that on her chest, but I wasn't 'bout to argue with Steph's crazy ass this morning. It was early. I just wasn't in the mood. Steph liked to fuss then fuck, and I was down with that; but not right now... I had to see what Uncle Wise wanted.

When I got downstairs and opened the door, the first thing Wise said was *"What's the day mathematics?"*

Quickly, I remembered that yesterday was the fifth power refinement, so that made today the sixth equality. *"Being able to deal equally in all aspect of life. Peace God! Yo, stop playing with me. I know damn well you didn't come wake me up to ask me that shit,"* I said, knowing Uncle Wise well enough to know that if he came by this early, it was a legitimate reason why.

"Naah, pardon self. I was just seeing if you still had it."

"Hell, yeah, I still got it and ain't gone never lose it. I know who I am, but whatsup with you?"

"Ole boy finally came through last night. Called me soons I got home. I thought about all that shit you was saying last night, and you know what? You was right. Them niggas is soft, and that's why I Henched his ass."

"You did what? Stop playing! Not Mr. Wise and all civilized. I know damn well you ain't Hench nobody."

"Shiit, just give me 4,500 dollars for these" he said, dumping nine ounces on the table.

"Word is bond," I said, still not believing Uncle Wise had actually hit a Hench.

"Yeah, word is bond, fool. Fuck him. He shouldn't have kept us waiting, and he should've honored his word. We missed a lot of money last night bullshitting around, waiting on that nigga."

"Shiiit, say no more, my nigga. Let me go grab this money. Ima be right back." Damn, I love my dogs!

117

Uncle Wise had really surprised me with this one. That's mostly because I knew hitting licks wasn't his MO. Wise was wise, feel me? He was more like the mediator of our organization. If somebody had an issue with us and for some reason, felt uncomfortable dealing with or speaking with one of us; they'd usually go to Wise. Now here it was; he just Henched his connect on the strength of me... He was definitely dealing in equality.

However, it would be a week later when I got word that Wise was in the hospital. It was Azalea Festival weekend, and I was at the mall. I had called Wise to see if he wanted me to snatch him a pair of Js that had just dropped. When his mom answered his phone, I knew something wasn't right.

"Hello, yeah, where Wise at, and who this?"

"This is his mother, and he's in the hospital."

"For what? Is he okay? What happened? This Frank."

"Oh, hey, Frank. Yeah, he okay, but he got a concussion and some stitches in his head. They say somebody hit him in the head with a gun, and when he fell, he hit his head again on the pavement."

"Okay. Just let him know I called... Matter fact, what's his room number?"

After I got the number, the first thing I did was call and check on the homie.

"Hello, yeah, whatsup, fool?"

"Whatsup, baby boy?"

"Whats the day's mathematics?" I said, trying to bring some humor to the situation.

I heard him let out a light chuckle before answering, *"Knowledge Cipher All Born Knowledge—to look, listen, learn. Also to respect all aspects of existence."*

"Okay, I was just making sure you still got it. I just spoke with you Old Earth, and she told me you got knocked into the land of the dumb, deaf, and blind. How you feeling?"

*"Yeah, it was **True Islam Master** caught me from the blind side, but I'm good. Gotta couple stitches and major headache. I should be up outta here soons they do these X-rays on my head."*

"Al-ight, homie, I was just checking on you. You know I'm on top of it. I'm 'bout to turn the heat up on him. He might be your roommate before the day out," I said, laughing and hanging up the phone.

And just like that, I was on the prowl. I had my daughter with me, and my plan was to chill out and enjoy the festival. But I just so happened to see Big Tim. I wasn't trying to make a scene about it, but when I saw him, I walked up to him and told him, *"You know you gotta answer for that, right? You know Ima see you."* I wasn't loud or yelling or none of that extra shit. I just wanted him to see my face so he'd know who he was fucken with…but the nigga got loud and tried to grandstand on me in front of everybody. And I had my daughter in my hands.

"Nigga, you ain't gone do shit to me! I don't know who hell you think I am, but I'm not scared of you. Lil nigga, you got me fucked up!" he barked at me.

He was making a scene, and there were a lot of people around. The 10th Street park is always flooded during Azalea Festival day. I had my daughter in my arms but my gun on my hip. When he started talking loud, I shifted my daughter to my right arm so my left hand was free—just in case I needed to grab my gun. Big Tim was a big dude, so fighting him would only give him advantage. Yeah, he was big in size, but he wasn't no lion. My heart was twice the size of his; I saw a bitch all in his eyes.

After he made a scene, I just walked off and left. My plan was to go drop my daughter off; but as I was leaving, I saw where Tim had his car parked at—which was about a half a block away from my car, but on the opposite side of the street—so I just waited.

Call me crazy, but I was actually sitting in the car talking to my daughter about shooting Tim. *"You see, baby, Daddy don't tolerate no disrespect especially not from no soft-ass nigga. And he had the nerve to make a scene. I was gone let the nigga live, but nooo, he just had to get loud. So now Ima sit right here and wait on his ass. Ima see how loud he get when this .357 touch his ass."*

She was too busy making a mess with her animal cookies to pay me any mind. Every now and then, she'd just look at me and smile.

We waited for about an hour when I finally looked in my rear-view and saw Tim walking toward his car. *"Daddy gone be right back, baby,"* I said, leaning over and kissing my daughter on her forehead. She just looked at me and smiled as I got out the car. Big Tim had his back to me, unlocking his car door as I walked in his direction. By the time he got the door unlocked and got in the car, I was standing right at the door, smiling.

"Didn't I tell you I was gone have to answer for that shit?"

Boom! *"That's for Wise!"*

Boom! *"That's for making me wait!"*

Boom, boom! *"That's for disrespecting me in front of my daughter!"*

I put four .357 hollows through the window right in his lap and left him slumped over the steering wheel…but somehow, he survived.

Make It Hurt

I got away clean but later that night, got arrested in the club parking lot for fighting. Club Rio was located right next to the Ramada Inn on Market Street. I really don't know how it all started. I just saw my cousin Kesha fussing with some dude on the dance floor. I couldn't hear nothing because the music was loud. But I did see her snatch her arm away from the dude twice. The third time he reached, I swung and kept swinging till he was sitting on his ass on the middle of the dance floor.

When security came to pick the dude up and kick him out, I was gone. However, once the club ended, as I was walking toward my car, I noticed the window was busted. Once I got inside the car, the first thing I did was check under the seat for my strap. As soon as I grabbed the gun and stuck it on my waist, all I heard was "Freeze! Turn around with your hands up!"

I was scared as hell; I literally still had my gun in my hand. One wrong move, and I was a dead man. I raised my hands nice and slow before turning around. I turned around and saw about five policemen dressed in full SWAT gear, all black everything with *Police* in big bold letters across their vests.

What the fuck was a SWAT team doing in the club parking lot waiting on me to come out the club? Clearly, this was a setup. Somebody had put the police on me. But who?

Just as they were taking my gun off my waist and placing me in the police car, I heard rapid gunshots. ***Blatt! Blatt! Blatt!*** The SWAT that was standing, celebrating my arrest, took off running toward the shots as I was escorted downtown and charged with possession of a firearm by a felon.

As I was waiting on Terry Jackson to come post my bail, They brought Don, Noon's brother, in. I hadn't seen him in years. I thought he was still locked up. I didn't even know he was home.

"Whatsup, nigga?" He looked and saw it was me and just shook his head, smiling. We kicked it for a while, and when Terry came to get me, he was telling Storm he'd have to come back in the morning for him.

"Hit my brother and let him know I got first appearance in the morning and to be ready to post my bail after that."

"Al-ight, I got you. Ima hit him soons I get home, and make sure you come through the North so we can build!"

When I got out, I went by Steph's crib. She told me Wise had come by looking for me. I was glad to hear the homie was okay, but I was also tired as hell. I took a shower, hit Noon up, told him what Storm had said, then fell straight to sleep. I slept all day, and the only reason I woke up was because the damn phone wouldn't stop ringing.

"Hello!" I barked into the phone, mad that I had been woken up from a very peaceful slumber.

"Oh, nigga, you too good to come chill with your big sis on her bday?"

"Oh, damn. My bad, sis. I forgot all about the party. I been in here knocked out all day. I fucked around and went to jail last night, but I'm 'bout to get up. Ima be over there in a few."

"Okay, but somebody wanna speak to you right quick."

"Yoooo."

"Yeah, whatsup? Everything good over here. They got me manning the grill." It was Wise. That was his way of letting me know he was holding the spot down.

"I'm on my way. Had to rest up. I swear these bitch niggas be draining my energy."

When I got to sis's house, it was a nice crowd out there. Everybody was enjoying themselves. Me, Wise, and a few more homies had stepped aside from everybody else to discuss the issue with Big Tim.

After I told Wise what happened, he explained to me how he got caught slipping. *"Talking to some females. Soon as I went to turn* around, the nigga slapped me with the gun. He came out of nowhere. Next thing I know, I was waken up in the hospital getting stitches in my head."

Another one of the homies from Jervay came through and was telling me to be careful because Tim had put 30,000 dollars on my head. Supposedly, it was some dude from OT in town to get at me.

"You know Tim my cousin, but he's a funny-style nigga. So I don't fuck with him like that. Just be careful 'cause it's a lot of disloyal-ass nigga out there that'll line you up for that type of money," the homie said, giving me a heads-up.

After that, we all went back to partying. What I had just heard had me hyped. To me, gunplay was like sex; I got off on catching niggas slipping. I had only been out of jail four months and was already caught up in some more drama…once again, behind a bitch-ass nigga.

As I was going in the house the fix me a plate, I saw Queen sitting in the front room by herself, which surprised me because I didn't even know she was here.

"Why you sitting in here by yourself, and how long you been in here?" I asked, walking over and sitting on the couch beside her.

"I was waiting on you, and I was sitting in here because I really don't know none them other people like that. I been here 'bout a hour."

"You good tho? We got everything—food, smoke, drink. Whatever you want, we got. So enjoy yourself."

"I'm good. I really just came over here to see you. I heard about what happened, and I saw what you did. You crazy," she said, smiling.

"I didn't do nothing for you to see," I said, lying with a straight face. "You want me to fix you a plate?" I said, changing the subject.

"Yeah, I'm kinda hungry."

"Well, come show me what all you want on it."

When she got up, I notice the Kapree pants hugging her ass just right. Queen was short and petite with a nice bubble butt. She was like the perfect mixture of Toni Braxton and Ashanti, caramel complexion with the beauty mole. We already had sex before, but I always held back because she couldn't take no dick. But tonight, her lil ass was in trouble. I was already hyped from hearing about the hit on my head. Plus she came looking for it, so I had to give it to her—Henchmen style!

"You getting fucked hard tonight," I said, handing her the plate and going back outside to join the party.

When we got to the room, first thing she did was hit the shower. I was already 'bout tipsy and feeling good, so I just laid back and rolled the dutches. She came out the shower with just a towel on and sat on the opposite side of the bed.

"Bring your ass over here."

I guess she wanted to play that shy role, or maybe I had scared her by telling her how hard I was gonna fuck her. Either way, it didn't matter. I was bone hard, and she was 'bout to get all ten inches of it.

When she came and stood in front of me, I passed her the blunt, took the towel off, and palmed her ass cheeks—pulling her closer to me while sucking on her bite-size titties. I took her right and cocked it up on the bed beside me while running my middle and index finger up and down the slit of her pussy, stopping briefly to massage her clit and bite gently on the tips of her nipples. She let out a soft moan as I felt her heat and wetness on my fingers.

"Hold up right quick," I said, smacking her ass and standing up to take my shirt off. She untied my shoes as I undid my belt. Next thing I know, I was ass naked and lying on top of her.

I took both her legs and put them on my shoulders. She immediately reached down and grabbed my dick just as I was sliding in her. She squeezed her eyes shut as I entered.

"Look at me," I said while slowly stroking her with only half my dick inside her. When she opened her eyes, *"Do you want this dick?"* I asked, watching her bite her bottom lip and nod.

"Do you want all of it?" I said as I started stroking her a lil more forcefully. Again she nodded, yeah, and said, *"But it's gone hurt."*

"No, it's not. Ima make it feel good," I said, reaching down and removing her hand from around my dick. I placed both my hands on top of hers and slid all the way in. I felt my dick touch the bottom of her box and kept there for a second.

Her eyeballs rolled to the back of her head. All I saw were the whites of her eyes as her mouth formed a perfect O shape. Her walls gripped me tight as I felt her pussy convulge around my dick. Then I started stroking. With each stroke, she'd manage one word.

"Shawn! It hurt! Don't stop!"

"Shut! The! Fuck! Up!" I said, covering her mouth with my hand and continuing to stroke long, deep, and hard... Finally, I pulled out. *"Turn around!"*

At first, I was on my knees, hitting her from the back, but she kept scooting up and making me slip out. So I squatted down, grabbed both her hips, and slid in; there was no more running. Plus she had already scooted all the way up to the headboard. All she could so was bury her face in the pillows and take it.

The night was quiet as I laid back, thinking about the latest turn of events in my life. I was only nineteen with one child and another on the way. Plus even though I didn't know at the moment, I had also just gotten Queen pregnant. I was on probation with ten months hanging over my head that I'd probably have to go do because I had just caught another felony gun charge.

On top of all that, I had turned up the pressure on all the dope boys. They wanted me dead or locked in jail. I had tried to chill, but that chill shit doesn't get you nowhere in the streets. It's always the cool, chill niggas that end up dead over some bullshit. Its either you're a lion or a lamb, and I was definitely in that lion category.

Now as I laid here, listening to Queen snore lightly as she laid across my chest, something she said earlier came back to me. What exactly did she see me do, and would she keep her mouth shut about it? I woke her up by pinching her nostrils together. She sat up and punched me playfully on the chest.

"You trying to kill me in my sleep," she said, smiling.

"Naah, I wouldn't do you like that, shorty. Your pussy too good to waste like that," I said, chuckling to myself.

"I bet that's all you care about too. Is my pussy."

"Naah, you know it ain't like that. You know we good peoples. But look, earlier at my sis party, you said something, and I was wondering what you meant by it. All bullshit aside, what did you see?"

She went on to recap the argument I had with Tim. *"I seen you walk away with your daughter, and I thought you had left. But later on* when I looked down the block, I seen your car still there. I was walking towards where you were parked at when I seen you get out the car with something over your face and follow ole boy to his car. And soons he got in, you shot him."

"And seeing that ain't bother you none?" I said, seeing if I could trust her.

"Hell, no. I been knew your ass was crazy since I met you. Plus I know you wouldn't do me like that."

"And what makes you so sure about that?"

"Because," she said, grabbing my dick and straddling my lap frog-style, "my pussy too good... Now make it hurt."

Red Storm

After getting arrested and hearing about the hit on my head, I figured it would be smart to relocate. I moved across the bridge to Leland and rented out two single wide trailers in a low-budget trailer park. The rent was only 200 dollars a week, so I was only paying 1,600 dollars a month for both spots. One spot was located at the top right by the entrance, and the other was located all the way in the back, surrounded by the woods. Most my neighbors were Mexicans that did a great job at minding their business, so I wasn't worried about much.

I wasn't scared, but at the same time, I wasn't stupid neither. I had too many enemies, and at any time, they could strike. I just didn't want to bring my problems to Steph's doorstep with my daughter in the house.

I still hustled out on the North, but I was just more cautious with how and when I played the block. I started pulling the graveyard shift and would always post up somewhere in the cut so I could see everything without being seen. If I did hustle during the day, I was in a crack house, or either my real clientele had my phone and pager number.

I could feel it in air; even though I couldn't see my enemy, I knew they were out there.

It just so happened, one night as I was leaving off the Eastside, I noticed I was being followed. Whoever it was had waited a while. It was damn near three in the morning, and I had been over at this chick's spot since nine.

One habit I think most dudes that play in the street have is always looking in their rearview. Luckily, for me, that was something I did before I pulled off. When I got in the car, I looked in the rearview and saw some headlights come on just as I was cranking up the car. As soon as I pulled off, they pulled off behind me. I smashed the gas; they gave chase. I was still looking in my rearview to see if I could recognize the car as I sat the .45 on my lap.

I made a right down 17th and headed toward the north. They followed me all the way to Nixon Street. Once I got to 8th and Nixon, I slowed up but didn't stop just to see what they'd do.

They swerved around me, dumping shots—***Boom! Boom! Boom! Boom!***—into the side of the car. I heard the bullets slapping into the door, and the window shattered. I ducked down, slammed on the brakes, and managed to get behind them then went after them with one hand on the wheel the other out the window—watching the .45 spit flames into the night.

They got away, but they also got my message loud and clear; killing me wasn't gonna be no easy task, and I damn sure wasn't going out without a fight. This gunplay shit was becoming second nature to hitting licks and hustling. It was just another part of the game I had chosen to play. The difference between me and all the other players was simply this: I refused to lose. It was a very strong possibility that whoever was gunning for me could end up dead them-damnselves. "Kill or be killed" is the lion's creed. Law of the jungle—any lion that's scared of blood starves to death, and I wasn't 'bout to let these bitch nigga stop me from eating.

When I got the call from Noon telling me he and Storm wanted to holler at me, I figured it was an opportunity to link up with some real niggas that I had literally known my whole life. We met up in the Brooklyn Square parking lot. Noon was money-minded as always and was concerned about why I had fallen off.

"You went from coping a half a joint a week to barely a big. You hustling backwards. I know you a hustler and know how to handle your BI. But you can't be out here risking your life and freedom for nothing. The main objective out here in these streets is get money. All that other shit don't even matter. I use to try and tell this nigga the same shit. He never listened. It took for him to go to prison to see the bigger picture," he said, referring to Storm.

I felt everything he was saying, but he was leaving out something that both me and Storm knew a lot about, which was…

"There has to be consequences for dudes when they cross certain lines. Yeah, getting money is most definitely the main objective, but at the same time, respect is priceless. I came in the game getting money at a young age. Hell, I'm still young, and I'm still getting it. But I had to learn to become a lion in this concrete jungle. Either shed blood or starve to death. I done been robbed by niggas I thought was my homies! I done been shot by niggas I thought was my homies! I done been told on and betrayed by niggas I trusted. And now I'm out here with money on my head. I got niggas trying to kill me, and all I wanna do is get this money. Every nigga that I ever got at brought that shit on they damn self. When a nigga violate me, my family, or somebody I love, it's not about the money no more. It's about the Code of Honor because that what I operate off of."

From there, we basically came to an understanding. Noon and Storm were 'bout to put me on in a major way. Storm had linked up with Hybeeb, and Hybeeb had the plug. What we were about to do would solidify our spots as the first official OGs to ever grace the state of North Carolina.

At the time, Storm was rocking with the Sex, Money, Murda homies. He wanted me and the Henchmen to join his line up, but *"It's too much bad blood between us and them [the Goodfellas] for me to make that move."* Too much blood had already been shed, and there was no overlooking that. I went on to explain how while he was locked up, we had basically painted the city red with Henchmen, and most of the beef we had came from the Sex, Money, Murda niggas on 13th.

"The beef dead now, but it was real hectic out there last year. Niggas was dying, disappearing, getting kidnapped, and deading shit," I explained to him. *"If it was any set besides that, I'd rock with you, but I can't rock with that one."*

There were no hard feelings, and in fact, we went on to discuss making some more major moves.

Hybeeb at the time was pushing Double II, a.k.a. KSBG, and basically still had the plug out west. Even though at the time, he was locked up, he still had clout on the streets. Thanks to his two sons Fresh and Mal G, who, in his absence, had stepped up and continued to push the line. I never knew all the details of what Storm and

Hybeeb had going on at the time. All I knew was that I had finally linked up with some official niggas. Some niggas that were like *me— down to die for theirs—and* I respected that.

Wins and Losses

About two weeks after we had that convo, Storm pulled up on me in the back of the projects (Taylor Holmes).

"Ride with me right quick," he said. We had already discussed the move, but I ain't know if they (him and Noon) were really serious until then...

"You ready for me?" he asked.

"Yeah, I'm ready. Go cross the bridge. I gotta go grab this bread."

Once we got across the bridge, I directed him to the trailer park.

"You good. This my spot," I said, getting out the car and inviting him in. Once inside, I went to the bedroom and removed my life savings from the floor vent. I only had 18k dollars to my name. The deal was I'd pay 13k dollars for half a joint and get fronted the other half. However, once I came back to the front room, he had two bricks laid out for me.

"Ima front you the other one for 28k dollars. I don't feel safe driving back across the bridge with it. Can you handle it?"

"Damn right I can! Matter fact, Ima go ahead and give you 5k dollars more on the bill so we at 35K dollars total. And I should have that within a week, two at the most."

I had just found me a connect, which meant no more having to deal with a middleman or scary-ass dope boys. And not only did I have a connect but I also had the realest niggas in the city on my team, and now we all were about to eat.

Once Storm left, I waited a while before moving all the work from the first trailer to the second one. The purpose of having two spots was just a safety precaution. The first spot was where I took my company. The second was where usually laid my head. I could sit in my front room in the second one and see if anybody came to the first one—just my way of being on point and living up to the motto… *"Frank, pay attention!"*

I went straight to the microwave with it. For every twenty-eight grams of coke, I'd add ten grams of soda. Plus this was that drop-straight ether. Shit was locking up and coming back as soon as the cold water hit it. I turned the first eighteen ounces into twenty-six, and from the looks of things, I did a damn good job.

I called G-Kode and told him to come pick me up. By the time he pulled up, I was back at the first spot. When we got to town, I called Wise and Killa Black and told them I had ounces for 800 dollars. Between the two of them, I sold ten ounces for 8,000 dollars and fronted Wise five more. G-Kode and Doggfaze brought five a piece, and that left me with one. That I broke down in straight grams and fronted to the young hustlers on the block.

I had G-Kode drop me off back at my car in the projects and walked to Steph's spot. When I got to Steph's spot, she was asleep, so I kept quiet. I stayed downstairs and counted up. I had made 16K dollars in three to four hours and still had another 5k dollars floating in the streets with another brick and a half in the stash.

After I counted up and did the math in my head, I knew I was looking at a nice profit. Before I left, I counted out one thousand dollars and left it on the kitchen counter with a .357 bullet on top of it. I used to always tease Steph about pulling out the .357 on Wild Child. Plus she knew those were my favorite guns…she'd figure it out.

Money was no longer a problem. Within the first three months of rocking with Storm, I had stacked over 100K dollars. I hid most of my money at my mother's house in the Motherland. She didn't even know I had hidden a book bag with 50K dollars inside her walk-in closet. I'd always go out there when she was at work and all my lil brothers were at school… I figured if something ever happened to me, at least my fam would be straight. Being in the streets had taught me to always put something aside for rainy days, especially when you're public enemy number 1.

Shit was just going too good to be true. I was eating; my team was eating. No more hitting licks and laying dope boys down. I was just stacking my paper and waiting on Trice to drop my seed. I was happy as hell when we found out she was having a boy. A Lil Frankster, just what I always wanted... Life was good... But as usual, your past always catches up to you sooner or later, and in this case, it was just crazy.

I had just pulled up in the projects and went inside the store to get some dutches. As soon as I left out and walked across the street, I saw about three to four police cars pull up at the store.

"Damn, they looking for somebody," I said to myself while rolling up my dutch. I knew I didn't have any warrants. I had just gone to court yesterday for both my gun charge and probation violation. My probation was modified from unsupervised to supervised, which only meant a monthly piss test, but that was it.

Something told me to leave, and I was about to; but I wanted to wait till they (the police) left. I didn't have no Ls; plus I had another gun and some work in the whip.

I was standing in the Brooklyn Square parking lot, which was directly across from a 6th Street store. It never crossed my mind that they could be looking for me because I had been chilling lately. Next thing I know, they were swarming the parking lot headed my way.

"Oh, shit!" was all I could say when they jumped out and yelled, *"Put your hands up! Run and we'll shoot!"*

I was more shocked than anything. *"What's this about? I don't have any warrants. I was just in court yesterday,"* I said, hoping this was a case of mistaken identity.

"And I just took a warrant out on you two hours ago," said a plain-clothes DT named Oiler. *"You robbed a federal informant, Jennings. You're going down this time. This one isn't afraid to testify."*

"I ain't rob nobody!"

"Does the name Napoleon Sleeper mean anything to you?" the DT said, giving me a stupid look.

"I don't know no damn Napoleon nobody! The fuck is you talking 'bout?"

"Don't worry about it. You're going down this time, Jennings! Cuff him and put him in the car," he said.

After cuffing me, they patted my pockets and pulled out my car keys along with a QT of dro.

I was standing right by my car when they swarmed me, so when the DT hit the car alarm button on my chain, it sounded off. I watched from the back of the police car as they searched my car and found both my gun and thirteen ounces of crack. I was taken downtown and charged with armed robbery with dangerous possession of firearms by a felon and trafficking. My bond was 1.5 mill.

Come to find out Napoleon was this kid from Leland we called Sleepy. I had robbed him around the same time I shot Tim.

Now the story with Sleepy is similar to what happened with Tim. He decided to play the waiting game. I called Killa Black about ten that morning and really stressed the fact that I needed to re-up. *"It's mad money coming though, and I'm fresh out of everything,"* I said.

"I'm 'bout to re-up myself, so we can just go in together and see if he give us a play," Killa responded.

It was damn near eight o'clock that night before this clown showed up. At first, he was acting like he wasn't gonna give it up. One smack across the face with that .357 magnum changed all that tough-guy shit. When it was all over, I was up nine ounces of ready rock, and so was Killa too. I smacked his ass one more time just off G.P.

"That's for keeping me waiting all day." I got no patience, and I hate waiting.

Now come to find out this nigga was a fucken federal informant. And because of that, I had interfered with a federal investigation, which had pissed the DTs off. Even Mr. Hicks couldn't save me this time. It was time to pay the piper. All I could do was hope for the best pleas possible.

Within three weeks, my PO had revoked my probation, and I was on my way to Foothills Correctional Institute located in Morganton, North Carolina. I left jail to serve out the remaining ten months on my suspended sentence. During that time, I was called back to court to face my pending charges.

"The best I can do is eight to ten years. They're willing to dismiss the trafficking and gun charge. If you plea out to the AR and the other gun,

it's really a decent plea considering there's a federal informant involved. I'd advise you take it," said Mr. Hicks.

"That easy for you to say. You're not the one doing the time," I said.

I knew Mr. Hicks wasn't lying, but I just couldn't see myself plea out to eight to ten years.

"Look, can I get some time to think about it? Give me a day or two to think about it. This isn't a easy decision to make."

"Okay, I'll buy us some time. But, Shawn, I'm telling you this as a friend first: you should take this plea. The DA had a hard-on for you, and she's a female. So that says a lot."

After giving it some thought, I figured, ***Fuck it.*** I might as well take the plea. I had gotten away with a lot shit over the years. I knew eventually, this day would come. Eight to ten years was a long time, but it wasn't life. I'd be back out...in due time.

Foothills

The first thing I did after taking my plea was tell my big sis to come see me.

"I might be shipping back out sometime this week, so make sure you come ASAP," I explained with urgency in my voice.

"Ima try to make it tomorrow when I get off work. I get off at five, so it'll be sometime after that."

The next day at exactly 7:00 p.m., they called me out for a visit.

"Whatsup, big sis?" I said, smiling happy that she made it. It's always a good feeling to know your family has got your back.

"Not shit. How you feeling?" she asked.

"Shiit, I'm fucked up, sis. They got me this time. I gotta do damn near ten years."

"You gotta do what? Ten years, you serious?"

"Hell, yeah, these people tire of my shit. They saying I'm a menace to society, threat to the general public, and all type of shit. If I take all this shit to trial, I might never make it home. You see, they gave Polk damn near thirty years. I can't let them get me like that."

"But damn, brah, ten years is a long time."

"I know, sis, but it ain't life. Ima survive this shit and make it out… But look, I need you to go to my crib and clean up."

"Your crib, and what crib is that?"

"Soons you come off the Leland exit, make a right. Drive bout a ½ a mile, and you'll see a bunch of small trailers on the left-hand side. That third trailer on the first row is mine, lot no. 14. It's a fake doorbell on the back door. Just unscrew it, and it's two keys inside. Once you get inside, go to the bedroom and move the bed aside. Lift up the floor vent and get that money. Its two plastic bread bags tied together with 20k dollars apiece in each one… Also that other key is for my other trailer, lot no. 27. It's all

the way in the back by the woods. Walk straight out the back door to the edge of the woods. Keep walking twenty steps into the woods then make a right. Go ten steps. You see a fallen tree with two Coca-Cola bottles filled with dirt at the base of it. Dig about three feet, and you'll see a plastic trash bag with three more sixteen-ounce Coca-Cola bottles each wrapped in certain wrap. Just hold on to everything until I know exactly what I wanna do. And tell mom I said look in closet where she kept all our old school and sports stuff at. That red book bag is hers.

"I'll probably be leaving here within the next couple days. Ima hit you when I get back to the dorm sometime later tonight. Just hold it down and give my love to the fam."

I arrived at Foothills with ten more years overhead. The place was infested with racist redneck COs. They had a habit of addressing me as *son* or *boy.* I'd always be sure to enlighten them. *"I'm not your son. My daddy is a Black man that hates rats, snakes, and cowards. And the only boys I know are cowboys and White boys, and I'm neither."* I became known as a smart-ass to the staff, but I could care less. I wasn't used to dealing with or being around rednecks. Where I come from (Wilmington, North Carolina) is located on the beach. All the White people I knew where chill and relaxed. Hell, all my uncles with the exception of one had White wives. I had a lot of mixed cousins, so I definitely wasn't racist; but being at that place made me grow a special kind of hate toward rednecks.

It was a few homies from my hood there. Lil Dave, Flames, Lil Illy, Double-O, Khaos, Smoke, Nate, Trey-O, Wild Child, Dez, Big-B, and (RIP) Mike Williams. Wild and I deaded our beef. I mean, at the end of the day, no matter how you looked at it, we were beefing over a chick; and that shit is corny.

"We in here together, and we gone need each other before we need her. Yeah, that's my B.M. and all that, but she grown. Y'all business is y'all business."

Wild and I basically took over Foothills. He had his squad called Dogg Pound Soldiers, and of course, I had The Henchmen. We formed an alliance under the Code of Honor and merged our squad together. The Bloods were our only allies, and at the time, Dirty from

Durham was the top dog. Most of the homies from Port City were either DPS or Henchmen. Flame was my second in command.

Once the administration caught wind of what we were doing, they shipped and separated us. But it was already too late; we had already built solid teams. Shipping us to different prisons only helped expand our reach—which, in turn, helped us recruit more people... The movement was unstoppable...

Morrison Only Made Me Stronger

At the time, there were only four prisons in the state of North Carolina that housed adolescents: High Rise, Polk Youth Institution, Foothills Correctional, and Morrison.

I was transferred to Morrison, which is located right outside Rockingham, North Carolina. At the time, it was a medium-custody facility, a cash camp with plenty of Black people working there. The entire atmosphere was different. It had been eighteen months since I had actually been around my people.

As soon as I stepped off the bus, I saw my cousin Diesel Bomb and some more Port City homies waiting at the gate. The homies grabbed my bags and helped me tote my property to the dorm. It smelled like straight weed inside the dorm. I couldn't believe this shit. The spot was sweet, and I could already tell that I was gonna fit right in.

Diesel Bomb was DPS, and on top of that, he was family; so we basically became inseparable. He was the first one to actually put me up on getting money in prison. And trust me, it's a lot of money to be made behind these walls.

The first eighteen months of my bid were the hardest. Foothills was damn near six hours away from Wilmington, which meant I didn't get any visits. Trice had given birth to my son Shy'ion. We were still communicating through phone calls and letters, but she was gradually falling off. By the time I got to Morrison, our relationship was pretty much over.

When she finally came to see me, I knew something wasn't right. I could feel it. For the first half of the visit, I just acted like my usual self. I didn't mention anything about the decrease in letters or unanswered phone calls, which were both starting to become noticeable. I was just glad to finally be able to hold my son. He looked just like me.

So anyway, as Trice was talking, I started staring at her in a real intense kind of way, looking deep into her eyes. Trice had cat eyes, and I used to always tell her they made her look sneaky. In fact, Cateyes was one of her nicknames.

"I can always tell when you done did something because your eyes give you away."

"What are you talking about?" she said. *"What have I done?"*

"I don't know what you've done because I'm in here and you're out there. All I know is what you tell me. But sitting here looking at you, I can just tell it's something you're not telling me."

"Well, I haven't done anything with anybody, if that's what you're getting at."

I sat forward in my seat and reached my hand out to take hers. She dropped her head as I held her hand in mine.

"Look at me, Trice. Look at me real good. You see anything about me that says I'm stupid?" I asked softly, giving her a real intense stare.

Instead of answering, she pulled her hand back, dropped her head again, and started crying. I was crushed. I knew those were the tears of betrayal. I knew that whatever she was about to say next was gonna hurt. I guess seeing his mom cry sparked something in my son because he started crying too, reaching for his mom. It took everything in me not to cry as I handed my son back to his mom.

Sitting there seeing my child and his mother crying was all my fault. It was my fault because I didn't think this far ahead. I got caught up in the moment, and because of that, I had unintentionally hurt my family. For me, that is the worst feeling in the world. But still, I had to be strong. I had to show strength. I had to let go of my weakness. I still had years of this prison shit to do, and I was determined to survive.

"Stop crying. It's not your fault. I'm the one that left you out there. I'm not mad at you," I said, reaching for her hand. *"We good, Cateyes. I'm hurt, not mad, but I need to feel this pain. This is all my fault."*

From there, she went on to explain who the dude was and what took place. And honestly, all I could do was laugh to keep from crying.

"What's so funny, and why is you laughing?" she asked, somewhat irritated.

"Nothing really. I'd just rather laugh than cry. Just live your life, and don't let my fuck-up stop you from living to the fullest. I ain't mad at you," I said, getting up and hugging both her and my son goodbye.

The situation with Trice was just an add-on to what I went through with Steph and Queen. Steph was mad about Trice and therefore had switched sides. She was writing Wild and sending him pics of my daughter, a clear violation, but I knew the motive. She was just trying to even the score. But hey, I guess I deserved it. I had gotten two females pregnant, and even though we were never a couple, I know she felt a way about it.

Queen, on the other hand, had delivered a stillborn. I kept having dreams about a lil baby crying for help. I had the same dream for damn near two months. You know they say when a man sleeps a lot, he got somebody pregnant. All I did was eat, sleep, and shower. The homies thought I was homesick and stressed out about my time, but that wasn't it. The dream just kept coming back, and no matter how hard I tried to help the baby in my dream, it wouldn't stop crying. Trice had already had Shy'ion, so I knew it wasn't about him. Plus the baby in my dream was a girl.

Right before I got locked up, I was at Queen's house, and she told me she was pregnant but it could possibly be somebody else's. I let her know that it was a strong chance I'd have to do some time because I had caught a case while I was on probation.

"You gone hold me down or what?" I asked.

"Yeah, Ima hold you down," she replied.

"You say that now, but we gone see when the time comes." I knew I was gonna get locked up, but I thought it would only be for ten months, not ten years.

"For real, Shawn, I think I love you," she said, looking at me seriously.

I didn't mean to start laughing, but how she said it sounded funny. Plus she knew I had a girl, a BM, and on top of that, she was dealing with another dude. As I was laughing, I turned my head in the opposite direction to keep from laughing in her face.

Whack! Whack! She hit me hard as hell with a big-ass stick.

"Oh, you think that shit funny!" she said, stomping her feet and watching me haul ass to my whip and holding my aching arm.

"Yo, you fucken crazy. I should shoot your lil ass!" I said through the window.

"You think this shit funny, Shawn, but I'm serious!"

"Well, put that damn stick down and get in so we can talk."

From there, she got in and basically told me her life story, and I felt shorty's pain. Her pops was doing life, mom had her when she was fifteen, and the other nigga she was dealing with was soft.

"I feel safe around you. These dudes don't even try to talk to me when you're around…" And now I was listening to her tell me she lost my seed. She kept crying and telling me she was sorry. She was seven months pregnant when the baby passed away. So she still had to go through with the delivery. The dreams were real. Once again, I had received a sign from the spiritual world, and that shit was real.

I think every hustler's dream is to buy his mom a crib and make sure his family straight. It's just a lot of us lose focus along the way. The 50k dollars wasn't enough to buy a house, but it was enough to help get started.

My mom had used the money I left her to move from Wilmington to Raleigh. I was glad she had moved because that was one less problem, and plus I had left a lot of unfinished business behind. Even though Gator still had all my guns and was keeping a close eye on everything, I still didn't like the idea of my people being there with me not out there to protect them. When Paully got kidnapped, he gave up my location to both the Goodfellas and the police.

For the most part, everything was good; my family was straight, and I was straight. It was just a matter of making it home…and staying out of trouble…which I would soon learn was easier said than done.

With all the shit I had went through during that first eighteen months, I was somewhat stressing. I had picked up the habit of smoking cigarettes, which was something I never did in the real world. At the time, they had just passed a new rule saying we weren't allowed to smoke inside the dorms. We could smoke, just not inside the dorms. Most staff smoked their damn selves, so they rarely enforced the rule; but it's always an asshole CO that just wanna nitpick about pointless shit.

So one day, it was raining outside, and I wasn't about to go stand in the rain to smoke. I went to the bathroom sat on the toilet and fired up a CI. I heard the CO keys jingling and put my CI. out. I had only taken two pulls but didn't wanna waste my cig, so I kept it in my hand. Usually, if a CO smells smoke and sees you in the stall, they'll just yell for you to *"put it out."* This dickhead actually came and looked in the stall. Even though I wasn't actually using the toilet, it was just the point he had violated my privacy. Cigarette or not, he was dead wrong and completely out of pocket.

"The fuck is wrong with you, man? You gay or something?" I said, standing up and ice-grilling him.

"This is a nonsmoking facility, and you're no longer allowed to smoke inside the dormitory area. It creates both a safety and health hazard. Now give me the cigarette," he said, extending his hand for the CI.

"I don't give a damn what kind of facility it is. Don't come looking in the stall when you see somebody using the bathroom. I'm not giving you shit. You want it that bad, get your damn self!" I said, tossing the CI in the toilet.

I went to step past him and walk out the stall, but he stepped in front of me.

"Oh, must think you some kind of a tuff guy or something?" he said then pushed me hard on my chest.

The second his hands touched me, I snapped. I grabbed him by the collar, spun his ass around, pushed him into the stall, and went in for the kill. By the time I realized what I was doing, he was balled up beside the toilet, trying to block blows. I had totally snapped.

"Don't! You! Ever! Put! Your! Fucken! Hands! On! Me!" With each blow I swung, I managed one word. There was no video camera

inside the bathroom, so I knew it would be his word against mine. And I knew damn well they weren't gonna believe me. I knew they were gonna put some bullshit in the game; they always do. But fuck it; at least I got my shit off.

Once I left out the bathroom, I went and told Diesel Bomb and the homies what happened.

"Man, I just beat Horn's ass. I know they 'bout to come get me. Might as well enjoy this fresh air while I can."

We all went out to the yard under the workout tent and rolled up. I was nice and high by the time I made it back to the dorm. The Serg was at the officer station talking to Horn. Horn had speed knots all over his face. I went to my locker, grabbed a picture of Shaunte and Shy'ion, and kicked it with the homies.

"Hold me down if these fool try some slick shit," I told the homies.

"You know I got you, fam," replied Diesel Bomb.

To our surprise, they didn't make a big deal about it. That's mainly because Horn never radioed for backup. Plus we both knew he ain't having no business putting his hand on me, and on top of that, the homies had my back. When they came and got me, all they said was, *"Cuff up,"* and took me to the hole. The cuffs were tight, but other than that, I was good… Morrison only made me stronger.

Soul City

I spent the next eighteen months on lockup for assault on staff. I was transferred back to Foothills for the first six months to complete an M-Con (Maximum Control) then placed on I-Con (Intensive Control) and then transferred to... Soul City, a.k.a. Warrenton County.

Now Warren County is located in Mason, North Carolina, a.k.a. Soul City. They call it Soul City because it's predominantly populated with Black people. The prison itself is a medium-custody facility, but they have a special housing unit specifically designed to house inmates that have been deemed a threat to the general prison population. I-Con is a step down from M-Con, but both are control statuses, which basically means 23/1 confinement. The degrees of control statuses confinement go in this order: H-Con (high-security control status—the worst), M-Con (maximum-security control status—very bad), and I-Con (intensive-security control status—not good).

The prison is notoriously known for having the most beautiful COs in all of North Carolina and a real down-to-earth atmosphere. Morrison was sweet, but Warren County is hands down the best place to be if you love women as much as I do.

On I-Con, you're basically locked down all day with the exception of one hour for Rec and shower. The staff that work these control-status housing units have to have some type of special training. I guess because it's a hostile environment. The benefit of having to deal with the same staff on a day-to-day basis is that eventually, over an extended period of time, you'll form some type of relationship. Whether good or bad, that's just human nature.

After getting processed in, I was walking to my cell. I heard somebody yell, *"War before peace! Frank, pay attention!"*

"I'm my brother's keeper. These mafuckas is Henchmen!" I yelled back over my shoulder, going up the stairs to my cell. Come to find out it was Doggfaze and Killa Black. Before I could even unpack my shit, I heard them yelling through the door.

"Yo, brah, what cell you in?"

"Ion know. I'm up here by the shower in the corner."

"He in 235!" somebody else yelled.

"Yo, Frank, whatsup, nigga? War before peace."

"Whatsup, who that?" I said, not recognizing the voice.

"This that ku-ku-kat Killa Black."

"Oh, word, my nigga. What's good?" I said excitedly. *"What the fuck y'all niggas doing here?"*

"Yo, make sure when they come 'round for Rec in the morning, you come out. Can't really talk loud 'round here. It's a lot of clowns with big ears in this block."

"Al-ight, Ima make sure I'm up. Let me unpack my shit and clean this cell up. Ima holla at y'all later. Yo, send me something to read too!"

Later that night as the CO was making rounds, I heard something slide under my door. As I was getting up to get it, I heard Doggfaze yell, *"Book em Dano? [**code for:** You get that?]"*

*"Dano book em! [**code for:** Yeah, I got that!)"* I yelled as I picked up a large envelope with assorted magazines and two white regular-size envelopes inside.

The first thing I did was flip through some girly mags and open up one of the envelopes.

"Oh, shit, brah shaking the building," I said to myself once I saw what was inside. It was about a quarter of weed with a pack of tops tobacco and a kyte.

> *Frank,*
>   *War b/4 peace fool! This shit don't stop brah.*
> *It don't matter where they put us at we always gone*
> *make it happen. Highly educated style, feel me!*
> *They gave me 8 years for that chase, I got 5½ left.*

This shit flying by fast as hell. I been here about 4 months. Fucked around and blew some nigga, hit em up Henchmen style. Its mad hoes here and they chosen you just cant let these lames and snitch niggas know your B.I. im upstairs in cell #212 Killa downstairs in #107. And you r'member J-love from Houston Moore? He downstairs too. Just make sure you come out in the morning so we can build... love u fool, im ur keeper... P.s don't run my battery dead, we only get 2 packs a week.

"*Don't run what battery dead?*" I said to myself, opening up the other envelope and looking inside. At first, I thought it was a radio, but when I turned the envelope upside down and dumped it in my hand, I realized it was a small-size flip cell phone.

"*My mafucken nigga,*" I said to myself aloud as I got off the bed, walked to the door, and yelled, "*Dano mafucken book em!*"

"*I already know 4.5.6 [**code for:** Holla back]. My nigga, we gone build in the a.m.*"

"*Al-ight, Firstblood [**code for:** I love you].*"

The first person I called was big sis.

"*Hello?*"

"*Yeah, whatsup, sis?*"

"*What, who is this?*"

"*Oh, now you don't know your own brother.*"

"*This Shawn? Boy, how is you calling me? You home?*"

"*Hell, no. I wish I'm on a cell phone.*"

"*Oh, I was 'bout to say. How the hell you get a cell phone in there?*"

"*Stop asking so many damn questions, sis... Whatsup though? Everything good out there?*"

Big sis went on to give me an update about the streets—who all had gotten locked up, shot, killed, and all that. Come to find out damn near my whole team was cased up. Ghetto had beat the body but got ten years for trafficking. J.V. was out and applying major pressure to the streets. All the homies from the Motherland were laying low and doing their thing. Face-Off wasn't doing too well finan-

147

cially but was doing good at what he did best, which was holding the family down. Murda was hanging with Ty-Dow, the same nigga that shot me. Wise and big-homie Stace had both got picked up by the Feds. Word was Cousin D, Bo-Lodge, and Boo Rock had gotten 5K1 for snitching on Stace. Big homie blew trial and got thirty years Feds. G-code had caught seven to nine years for trafficking. Illy caught eight years for attempted murder on a government official. Killa Black was serving two years for possession with intent to sell and deliver. J-Love had caught sixteen to twenty years for a body. What fucked me up the most was when she told me about Uncle U getting killed.

I half listened as my sis continued to talk about what was taking place on the streets. I was still stuck on what happened with Uncle U. For somebody to have caught him slipping like that was rather odd. My mind drifted back to our last mission together. We had caught both Black Zak and his Jamaican connect in the middle of making a transaction.

I was the first one through the door, masked up and waving my burner…" *Get the fuck down! Anybody move, and I'm popping you!*"

Just as I was stepping through the door and sweeping my burner across the room, I felt a presence before I actually saw the person. As I was turning around in the direction of the presence, something soft hit me in my face. The nigga Black Zak had literally just thrown a box full of money at me. It took my mind about five seconds to compute what was actually in the air…money! By that time, he had hit the light switch off and took off running through the house. Uncle U and Killa Black had already laid both the Jamaican and this other kid named K-Brown down. I didn't know the layout of the house, so I had to cut the light back on before going after Zak. I went through the house searching room for room. Once I got to the kitchen, I saw the back door swinging and heard the dogs out back barking. I got back to the front room just as Uncle U and Killa Black were stuffing all the money and drugs inside pillowcases…a brick of cocaine, twenty pounds of weed, and ninety-something thousand dollars. That's was the last mission we had went on together. Word was the Jamaican had put out a hit on us. Even though we were all masked up, it was no secret among the citizens of the Port City who The Henchmen were and what type of work we put in.

Now I had been locked up for almost two years before my sis told me Uncle U had gotten killed. After finding out how he had gotten killed, I made it my BI to further investigate the matter. What I found out was pretty much what I had expected.

Uncle U had befriended this guy named Jamaican Mike. Jamaican Mike, along with this other guy, had turned Uncle U to a lick. The lick went sweet because the lick was supposedly bait for Jamaican Mike and the other guy to kill Uncle U. However, during the lick, Jamaican Mike and the other guy froze up; so instead of the Jamaicans getting revenge, they just ended up getting robbed all over again. Three weeks later, the other guy car was seen parked on the side of the highway. Police found him chopped up and completely dismembered, stuffed inside a trash bag in the trunk of the car.

Around that same time, June 26, 2001, two days after his Bornday, the Jamaican caught my dogg slipping. The first shot dropped him and hit him in the neck. The second one was up close and personal, a face shot—right in front of his wife... In fear for his life, Jamaican Mike turned himself in to the authorities for some unrelated outstanding warrants. The Jamaicans posted his bail, but when he got to the lobby and saw them, he refused to leave the jail. That was probably the smartest decision he ever made... It saved his life.

Of course, the streets speculated about it because nobody was ever charged with either body. Nobody knew exactly what happened besides those involved, and out of the three that were involved, two ended up dead. And the third was too scared to speak on it.

When I heard about what happened, I just laid back on my bunk and thought about all the shit Uncle U had taught me. *Never speak in whispers among people you trust. Always wear a mask and glove when on a mission. The weak fear the strong, and the strong rule the weak; but the wise rule the strong.*

I thought about all these things as I felt the coolness of a tear slide down my face. It was right then and there that I decided: "*Ima rep for you until I'm dead and gone, my nigga. Ima keep your name alive out here on these streets,"* I said to myself, sitting up and grabbing my cell phone. *"all Henchmen will be required to pay homage to Uncle U a.k.a. Steven Sideberry on both Born and Death dates; by way of feasting in his honor,"* I hit Send, delivering a group message to multiple Henchmen homies.

The message was sent, the message was received, and the H-Team as well as the streets respected it... In his honor, I would later appoint Badass, his older daughter, as The Henchmen first lady. RIP to the OG Henchmen. Love and loyalty... I am my brother's keeper.

"Whatsup with Storm and Noon?" I asked, snapping back into the present moment.

"Oh, they good. I barely see them, but they still around. It just crazy out here, brah. You can't really trust nobody. That why I just stick to my thing."

"And how shit looking with that?" I asked, referring to the money and work I left her with.

"Shit, everything good. You straight in there, or you need something?"

"Nah, I'm good, Money-wise, I'm still strapped from that first drop."

When I first got popped, I left my sis with 40k dollars and lil over a brick of coke. My first two weeks back on the yard, I received a red envelope every day with 1,000-dollar money order deposited in my account. We could only spend forty dollars a week, so I was straight. Plus my homie Holiday from the Motherland sent me a nice check every month. I had sis give most of the work to E-boogie, who was a real laid-back, low-key, get-money type.

"But Ima probably need you to make some moves for me. I'm here with Doggfaze and Killa Black. They got they hands in some of everything, so you know I gotta get in where I fit in. What's Boogie number, and see if you can get Storm number for me too."

"Al-ight, I'll just text 'em to you."

The next person I hit was E-Boogie.

"Hello."

"Heey, whatsup, baby boy? Sis just told me you was 'bout to call what's good with you?"

"Shit, I'm cooling, brah. Doing this shit one day at a time, feel me? And I appreciate you handling that for me too."

"It's all good, baby boy. We day ones, from the sandbox to the streets."

"I already know. Whatsup though? You straight, or you still trying to do something?"

"Shiit, I'm straight, but a nigga can't never have too much money."

"Bet, that's what I like to hear. Let hit my people and see if they can press play. Give me a few days. If you don't hear from me, just hit sis up. And oh yeah, tell Holiday I said whatsup. He been holding me down with the letters and pictures."

"Al-ight, baby boy, I got you. You good though? You need anything?"

"Naah, I'm good. Just need you to keep doing what you already doing."

"Consider it done then," he said, ending the call.

I didn't get to sleep till 'bout three in the morning. I had rolled up a couple joints the next morning and smoked after they picked up the breakfast trays. I had to scoop all the water out the toilet and blow the weed smoke down the commode drain. I was still new to this spot; plus I still had the phone in my cell, so I didn't want to bring any unwanted attention to myself.

By the time they came around for Rec, I had everything squared away and stashed.

Time-out; okay, I need you to c'here right quick. Yeah, you, the person reading this book. Put your ear to the paper because I can't say this loud, okay. Can you hear me?... Well, good. Listen closely... This book is the truth, the whole truth, and nothing but the truth. I hate phony, fake, fraudulent people; so I wrote this book for the real hitters only. However, I'm quite sure there will be a few fake phony-type individuals who'll end up reading this book, which is why I gotta give my real readers a heads-up. It's some things I can't discuss—such as my inside prison connections and how I managed to receive contraband inside of every close-custody facility across the state of North Carolina. Even after doing ten years, I came home under federal investigation, but I'll explain all that later... For now, just enjoy the read, and here's a lil secret for all my real right readers. People in positions of power are nat-

urally attracted to stand-up guys, especially if they know you can keep your mouth shut under pressure... But sssshhh, that's a real hitter secret for real hitters only! Time in!

I'm back. Okay, now where was I at? The next morning, we all went out for Rec. It was Doggfaze to my right, Killa Black across from me, and J-Love beside Killa. We each were in separate Rec cages close enough to hear one another without yelling.

As we were talking, they all kept mentioning Dmoe. Killa was telling me he was Henchmen material. Both J-Love and Doggfaze agreed. I was telling them about Flames and come to find out Dmoe and Flames were best friends. I told them about the alliance we had with Wild Child and DPS. After that, they told me what I had to do to get it in, what COs were cool, and who were assholes.

"So you telling me we can sell thirty-dollar phones for three hundred dollars, grams of coke for four hundred dollars, and all I need to do is get it and drop it off to somebody? Well, look, Ima handle that ASAP. Just line shit up on your end and let me know when you ready. Ima go ahead and get a hundred phones. If this shit sweet as y'all say, we can't lose. It's a win-win."

And it definitely was. Doggfaze and I stayed at Warren County locked up for a year. By the time we got off, we had flooded the yard with everything from crack to cell phone. All parties involved saw a major profit and prospered.

Right before I left the lockup, the homie Wayne Burch came through, and I was helping him with his law work. When he sent me the paperwork, that's when I saw with my own eyes that Double O had dry-snitched on him. They both had gone to hit a lick, and somebody (the victim) ended up getting shot. It just so happened they get pulled over and arrested a few blocks from the crime scene. When questioned by the police, Double O said, *"Yeah, I was there, but I didn't shoot no body."* So if it was two people involved and you're saying *"Yeah, I was there, but I didn't pull the trigger,"* that only leaves one person who could've done it, which was Wayne. I wrote Wild and told him his man Double O wasn't all he was pretending to be. Hell, I even told how I made him suck the barrel of my gun, but I guess he ain't believe me because he kept rocking with Double O.

Luckily for my homie Wayne, the victim never came to court, and since he never admitted to anything, he beat the case. Double O, on the other hand, had to do three years because he admitted he was involved… I saw it with my own eyes.

It took a while for me to get in touch with Storm, but when I did, it was worth the wait. I plugged him into E-Boogie and had Sis invest a majority of what I had in the stash into a power move. I couldn't lose. They had locked me up physically, which only sharpened me mentally. I was using Henchmen as my platform to remain relevant in the streets and on the yard. I had been gone a little over four years, and I had grown a lot wiser.

I was using the prison system as a recruiting warehouse. Every time one of my homies went home, I sent the streets a message… *"Get phat while you can. I'll be back."*

Lanesboro

Once I got off I-Con, I was transferred to Lanesboro Correctional Institution, which was located in Anson County, right outside Charlotte.

When I got to Lanesboro, I was actually able to stay out of trouble. I earned my basic electro-mechanical skill certificate, qualified for my associates degree in business administration, and had started back-kicking it with Queen.

Then once again, it went bad, all behind a bitch-ass nigga… Okay, now being that Lanesboro is right outside Charlotte, quite naturally, there are a lot of dudes from Charlotte there. Now the thing about *a lot* (but not all) dudes from Charlotte is they're full of shit. Charlotte, North Carolina, is the biggest city in the state (population-wise) and one of the fastest growing cities in the world, but for some reason, dudes from Charlotte seem kinda slow. Don't get me wrong; I know some solid dudes from Charlotte, but for the most part, they're all cutthroats.

The CO's name was Ms. D, and she was real cool peoples that respected the struggle. Almost every day, dudes would line up just to talk to Ms. D. Me personally, I always thought that was kinda lame, but people say I tend to take myself too serious, so I just learned to live with it and look at it as just another part of prison life. Even with that being said, I still never stood in line. I just spoke and kept it movin'. Word was Ms. D was from Charlotte too.

So on this particular day, I'm playing poker. They had just converted all close-custody prisons into no-cash facilities, so instead of playing for cash, we were playing for joints of weed. Each joint was valued at five dollars. It was mostly dope boys at the card game, and I was up about fifty joints.

My Port City homie B-Row was in the dorm with me. I had seen him out there talking to Ms. D but ain't paying him no mind. However, when he came back in the dorm, he went straight to my cell, which really wasn't unusual because I had an open-door policy with the homie which was...

If you need something out my cell, just get it, but let me know you got it.

But as soon as B-Row got to my cell, another dude from another dorm came in the block and was heading to my cell also.

"I fold," I said, laying my cards on the table and walking to my cell. I didn't recognize the dude's face, so it shocked me when he said my name.

"You Frank? I need to holla at your homie," he said, standing outside my door.

"Al-ight," I said, stepping inside and closing the door in his face. *"Ayo, you know that nigga out there?"* I asked B-Row while covering the window to my cell so the dude couldn't see in.

"Naah, not really. Not like that."

"Well, what he want?" I asked.

"I'on know," he replied.

"Well, here, take this," I said, digging in my mattress and pulling my banger out. *"His demeanor don't seen too friendly."*

"Naah, I'm good. I'on need that."

"You sure?"

"Yeah, I'm sure. Fuck that nigga!"

"Al-ight then," I said, tucking my banger on my waste and step-ping back out of my cell.

I went back to the card game but was keeping a close eye on B-Row. I saw the dude was talking loud and being aggressive.

"Well, we can go to your cell and fight!" I heard the dude say.

At that point, I made eye contact with B-Row. *"You good?"* I mouthed slow so he could read my lips. He nodded, but his body language was saying *"**I really don't want to fight this nigga.**"* For one, he should've taken the banger when I first offered it to him. Two, he should've set it off on the dude as soon as he got loud; and three, when the dude told him to go to the room so they could fight, he was walking slow as hell.

I made eye contact with him again as he was going to his room. *"You good?"* This time, I said it loud so he'd know I had his back, and this time, he didn't answer me at all.

"I fold," I said, mad as hell. I had a 6-5-3-2-1 in a game of low-ball, and I was up almost seventy joints; but I had to hold my homie down.

By the time I got to the room, the dude was just closing the door. I stuck my foot out to keep the door from closing completely. *"Yo, look, whatsup with you, my nigga?* I asked, the dude stepping into the cell. They both started talking at the same time. Come to find out the dude was mad because B-Row was talking to Ms. D. *"Aye, look, both of y'all out of pocket. That bitch a nut rag,"* I said, hoping that they'd both see the bigger picture.

But not only was the dude dumb but he was death stuck also; because instead of seeing the bigger picture, he swung on B-Row. Next thing I know, my banger was off my waist and in his stomach. He folded, grabbed his stomach, and ran for the door—which I just happened to be standing in front of. I sidestepped, aimed for his neck, but missed and hit him directly in his collarbone.

"Dumb-ass nigga, I tried to warn your stupid ass!" I said, mad that my banger had bent on his collarbone.

"Ima be back," he said, running out the dorm swollen and leaking blood.

"Get your dumb ass up outta here, nigga!" I yelled after him, walking back to the card game.

I was too mad to focus on playing cards, so I just cashed out sixty-three joints. I went to B-Row's cell and fired up three back to back. I was pissed at everybody involved in this situation, myself included.

I was pissed at B-Row for being in that bitch's face just like the rest of them clown-ass dudes desperate for some damn attention. I was pissed at the dude for coming over here, talking that dumb shit and thinking shit sweet. I was even pissed at Ms. D just off of GP when she really hadn't done anything wrong (yet). And I was mostly pissed at myself more than anything. I was finally focused and staying out of trouble, and I let this stupid-ass dude knock me off my square.

"Man, this shit crazy," I said, breaking the silence and passing B-Row the joint.

"It seems like no matter how hard I try to stay away from lames, they always seem to find me some kind of way."

It was a few dudes from Charlotte in the dorm that I was cool with, and they had told me to be on point because the dude I had stabbed had a lil crew. B-Row and I were the only dudes from Port City in the dorm, so it was just us.

Usually when they call chow, it's in the alphabetical order. The dude was in A-Dorm, and we were in C-Dorm; but Ms. D was now working the control booth. Instead of doing A-B-C first, she popped A. I was still in the back of the dorm standing in the B-row doorway, watching him clean up the dude's blood. When I looked up, I saw about twelve to fifteen niggas from Charlotte standing in front of our dorm...then the door popped open.

"Oh, shit, that cutthroat bitch," I said aloud. *"She trying to line us up."* She just let like twelve to fifteen niggas slide in on us. *"Look at this shit,"* I said, stepping out the doorway so B-Row could see for himself what we were up against.

I had to think fast and move quick for the both of us. The first thing I did was pull my banger. The second thing I did was start chanting *"Coward run, snakes hide, real men stand up and fight"* to myself. The third thing I did was tell B-Row, *"If we don't make it out of here, we gone die trying. Just follow my lead."*

We only had one banger, and that shit was gonna bend and probably break on the first person I hit with it. I was scared as hell, but I wasn't afraid. I had already accepted death as a possible outcome, and by doing that, I lost all fear. Like I said, I was definitely scared but not scared as in frightened or afraid in a cowardly manner... But scared as in... I walked right up to them niggas crouched low, legs spread, shoulder length apart, and knife in my left hand and aimed high, pivoting on my right foot, *"Whatsup? Let's get it popping! Somebody gone die in this bitch today, believe that!"* I yelled, hyping myself up.

The only thing I was focused on was the door. My goal was simply for me and my homie to make it out alive. For some reason, Ms. D never shut the door. I think they all thought that they'd be able to slide in, catch us slipping, and slide right back out... Frank, pay attention... These mafuckas is Henchmen!

They spread out and surrounded us in a semicircle. Out of all them niggas, only six had bangers. I started jabbing my knife at the dudes directly in front of me. Every time I jabbed, I'd take a small step forward, and they back up. B-Row was right behind me with his guard up. Every time I stepped forward, I'd feel him behind me back to back, touching shoulders. These niggas kept backing up; they were just scared as I was. Nobody wanted to be the first person to get stabbed. Even though they had a lot more man power, they had given me the advantage by allowing me to become the aggressor.

Once we got about ten feet from the door, I took a jab again, but instead of a small step, I took a huge leap, swinging my knife high and wide. They cleared the doorway while ducking from my knife. I reached behind me grabbed B-Row's T-shirt, and we were out... We made it out alive.

Once we cleared the doorway, I spun around and blocked the door. Every time somebody tried to get out, I'd jab my knife at them.

"Hey! Hey! Whats going on?" the CO yelled.

I took my eyes off the door for one second to look in the CO's direction and felt a sharp pain in my right shoulder. The momentum from the blow had knocked me out of the doorway, and dudes had started coming out.

"Code 4! Code 4! Code 4! Green unit!" The CO was yelling for backup. *"Close the damn doors!"* he said, waving his hands to get Ms. D's attention.

I saw dudes dropping their knives and running back to their dorms. I looked around for B-Row, but he had disappeared; so I tucked my knife and went back inside the dorm. When I got to my cell, I looked at my wounds. I had two stab wounds on my right shoulder and one on my right side. I had enough time to get my cell together before the goon squared came. When it was all and done, me and the dude were the only two people they got. They came around and made everybody take their shirt off and looked at everybody's knuckles. Dude's face was swollen, and he had two stab wounds. I had three stab wounds, but I was alive.

Once we got on lockup, I was determined to get the dude again. He kept flying kites, saying "Don't say nothing." I sent word back to him. *"Stop sending me these bitch-ass messages. I'm from the street for real. We keep shit silent to the grave. Me telling these people anything should be your least concern."*

What he didn't know was, while we were on lockup, I had already found me a friend by the name of Ms. G., who was already in the process of finding another job—which meant she was willing to do exactly what I needed done to *line his dumb ass up.*

Ms. G was gangster; I swear, she reminded me of my big sis. I think that's why we got along so well. A lot of dudes thought it was more to it than that, but it wasn't. She had already heard about the situation and knew I wanted the dude's head. It just so happened on the day I went to see the committee to be placed back on M-Con, she was my escort. After they sentenced me, she was asking me, *"Why they give you M-Con and it was you that got stabbed?"*

"Because I won't cooperate and tell them what happened. They always talking 'bout you have the right to remain silent, but yet they punish you when you keep your mouth shut."

"Yeah, I see that's one reason I'm quitting because don't none of this shit make any sense. They say the system is supposedly designed to rehabilitate people, but that's a damn lie. Half the people in this place don't give a damn about nothing but a paycheck. Every time I try to help a inmate, they tell me I'm being too nice. They want us to treat y'all like animals but expect y'all to respect them. Well, this my last day, so you behave yourself," she said as we arrived to my cell.

"Ima try to," I said. *"But before you go, I need one last favor."*

"And what's that?" she asked.

"Bring that clown over here for Rec."

She never said yeah or no. She just walked off, but she never said nothing about me jamming my door so it wouldn't lock. Once she left, I slid my door back open and crept to the Rec cage. I waited for like thirty minutes. When I heard the slider open and saw her escorting the dude with handcuffs behind his back, I stood up and walked to the cage door and waited on the dude to go in the cage beside me. As soon as he stepped in his cage, I stepped in behind him. He was still cuffed behind his back with his hands extended backward, waiting to be uncuffed. I guess he felt my presence because he was in the process of turning around when I sliced his face. I had a toothbrush with razors melted in it. He hollered like a bitch, but besides that, there was nothing he could do. He tried to drop his head and bull-rush me, but I sidestepped, grabbed his shirt collar, and just started slicing.

I snapped out; the only thing that brought me back was when Ms. G started screaming. *"Shawn, stop! Stop! That's enough! You gone kill him! Stop!"*

It was blood everywhere. See, the thing about razors is, when you cut somebody, it's a slow bleed; but once the blood starts flowing, it doesn't stop.

Another dumb nigga laying in a pool of his own blood, I thought to myself. This shit wasn't even exciting anymore… However, there has to be consequences for stupid niggas, or else they'll never learn…

Scotland

I ended up back on M-Con and was transferred to Scotland Correctional Institution. I spent the next twenty-seven months on lockup. Now Scotland, a.k.a. Hotland, is located in Laurinburg, North Carolina, which is in the same area as Lumberton, North Carolina—home of the Lumbee Native Americans.

Most of the COs and staff are all members of the same tribe. If you know anything about American history, you know the Native Americans have been through just as much, if not more oppression, than Black people. For a long time, the United States refuses to even recognize the Lumbee Tribe as Native Americans. That was mainly because the Lumbee Tribe never allowed the American government to steal their land. Laurinburg, Lumberton, Scotland, Marion, Hope Mills, and even Fayetteville, North Carolina, all have a heavy Lumbee population… And I'm saying all that just to say this… I was at a prison that was being run by a people who really didn't give a damn about the American government… And neither did I, and I had a ball.

Sex, cell phones, drugs, and gangster shit. At the time, being Blood was becoming real big. I was still pushing Henchmen, but the administration had my labels as STG level 1 and listed as Blood Associate—which meant wherever I went, I was usually housed in the Blood Block, a.k.a. The Dogg House. Which also meant that I got to promote Henchmen among the people that wanted to know about my movement.

I had gotten word that Storm had just hit the yard with twelve years for trafficking. I sent him a cell phone as a welcoming present so he'd know I was still up and on top of my game.

"What's popping, nigga? I can't believe they got you, homie," I said, letting him know I felt his pain.

"Man, it is what it is, brah. I'm here now, so you know what time it is. I'm 'bout to paint this bitch red from wall to wall."

"Make 'em feel your pain, homie. That's the only thing they gone respect. This spot sweet too, a lot of paper to be made. All you gotta do is keep theses clowns out your BI, and you good," I said, giving him the same advice that Doggfaze had given me.

We went on to discuss forming an alliance… *"I'm in the process of making a power move. It's a lot of shit with these East Coast niggas. Everybody isn't who and what they claim to be,"* he explained.

"I feel you. You know if you make a move, I'm rocking with you. I'm trying to do the same thing Pete did with Henchmen."

Pistol Pete was the only person in the entire UBN who had already established in his own set prior to becoming Blood. Sex, Money, Murder was established before the UBN was formed, just like how Henchmen was established way before Blood even migrated from New York to North Carolina. The same way Pete had put his team under the UBN as an official Bloodset. I was aiming to be the first person from the state of North Carolina to have an official Bloodset also.

The only problem was nobody in the state of North Carolina had the proper authority to sanction a set.

It was then that we started researching and trying to find out who could sanction a set. It was also then that we discovered that the entire UBN had never been properly sanctioned. The founding fathers had never given their blessings for any Bloodset on the East Coast with the exception of one set: ***the First Family.***

At the time, Storm knew some elite members within the First Family. After reaching out and explaining our vision, we were accepted as official OG's among the family.

Of course, we had to set plenty of examples along the way. For one, we weren't a dominant set behind the prison walls, but we were, all the way, official. Two, a lot of the sets in the state of North Carolina weren't real right, such as pretty Tony, BGB, and E-Ricket Hunter. These were all renegade sets without sanction. So even though we weren't a dominant set, we still presented a huge threat because we were connected to the founding fathers (***the elite minds that control movements within the entire organization.***) A lot of dudes became envious and feared being exposed, and it was because of that that we orchestrated one of the biggest Blood wars in all of North Carolina history... But I'll share that story with you later... For now, peep this.

Bertie, a.k.a. Gangster Paradise

After doing twenty-seven months on the 23/1, I had worked my way back to normal population. I was transferred to another close-custody facility: Bertie, a.k.a. Gangster Paradise.

When I tell you that the Bloods ran the yard, I mean that literally. There was nothing moving without Blood saying so. The homie J-Love was there and was already shaking the building upside down. When we linked up, I told him about the First Family and how we were all pushing the same line. As we were talking, I heard my name being called over the loudspeaker.

"Inmate Shawnee Jennings, report to the unit manager officer. Inmate Jennings out of E-block, report to the unit manager office immediately."

"The fuck is that about?" I asked, somewhat confused.

"Man, that's probably Sled bitch ass. He the unit manager. He more of a comedian than anything, so don't pay him no mind. He just like to hear himself talk." And man, was he right.

When I first walked into the office, I saw a Black man that had that ex-military look, tight fade, serious facial expression with a Masonic ring on his finger.

"Jennings, I'm unit manager Sled, and I called you in here…(you can have a seat if you want)…to let you know I'm aware of who you are." As I sat down, I noticed he was twisting his ring back and forth, clearly a sign.

"And exactly who am I?"

"Well, for one, you're a mob boss. For two, you're affiliated with Bloods in some kind of way. And for three, you have a history of violence, manipulation, and getting drugs inside of prisons."

I just stared at him and smiled. *"Definitely a damn comedian,"* I thought to myself, not realizing that I had said it out loud.

"Excuse me?" he said, looking somewhat confused.

"Look, Mr. Sled. I hate to disappoint you, but you really don't know a damn thing about me. So let me tell you exactly who I am... I am a descendant of the almighty alpha male from continent of Kush, also known as Africa. I am the dominate, most-feared species to ever walk the planet Earth. I am a Black man with proper knowledge of self, and my affiliation with Blood is based solemnly around the fact that my ancestors showed resistance in the face of their oppressors and were willing to shed blood for their freedom. Blood is life, and life is blood. And I advise you get to know me personally before passing judgment."

"Well-put and point taken, Mr. Jennings. Just consider this a formal introduction or warning, for that matter. Do not bring any crack to my unit and leave my female staff alone. And know that I'll be watching you very closely."

"Yeah, likewise to you too, Mr. Sled," I said before standing up and walking out.

From there, Love and I proceeded to flood the yard with crack and get friendly with all the female COs.

"Fuck Sled" was our motto. Every time somebody would bring his name up around us, we'd both look at one another and then shout, ***"Fuck Sled!"*** at the same time. Before you knew it, everybody was saying it.

We had so many people smoking crack it was like the street. This one white guy named Hammer was responsible for bringing our operation down. He had spent close to 20K dollars with us over a period of three months. He spent so much that both me and Love decided to fall back from him. He was good money, but we noticed he was getting slower and slower with making payments. We turned some lil homies onto him so they could come up, but the problem with that was, they didn't have the same level of finesse as me and Love did.

One day, the homie had hit my phone and told me they had Hammer hog-tied to a cell with his father on the phone demanding that he pay them the money his son owed.

"Damn, how much he owe?" I asked the homie.

"Five hundred dollars," he replied. *"But it's been two weeks."*

"Brah, he good for it. His pops old as hell. He only go to the bank once a week. If he ain't paid you by the end of this week, Ima pay you myself. Don't trip."

But it was already too late. Hammer's pops had already called the prison and informed the administration.

The first hit came during count time. It was Sled, Lt. Byger, and the STG (Security Threat Group) gang unit. They tore me and Love's cells apart but didn't find anything. Byger was asking around, trying to find out who Frank White was. The second hit was a headshot. Hammer's father had mailed the MoneyGram receipts to the prison. Both me and Love had been sending most of our money to family members. These same family members were listed on our visitation list, which is how they connected us to Hammer. However, since there wasn't a disciplinary infraction for somebody to send someone in your family money, Sled and Byger made up some bullshit story about us running an extortion ring. This was even after Hammer admitted that nobody never forced him to do drugs.

And just like that, I was back on M-Con, me and Love. Then as if that wasn't enough, Sled bitch ass took charges out on me for misdemeanor communicating threats.

When you're on lockup for over thirty days, the psychologist has to do a mental health assessment on you, which consists of coming around and asking a host of stupid questions. So when they came to my door and asked me how I was feeling, I told them the truth.

"I feel like killing Sled bitch ass!" I yelled then punched the door as hard as I could, which made a real loud ***doom***! sound. The psyche lady jumped back, dropped her folders, and damn near had a heart attack *"Fuck Sled, and make sure you tell him I said it!* (***Doom, doom!***)*"* I yelled—this time, kicking the door just to emphasize my message.

I scared the shit out that lady. I swear, I laughed about that shit all day.

About three days later, the CO came to my cell and told me, *"Cuff up. It's somebody here to see you."*

"Why you telling me to go see them if they here to see me? If they here to see me, then they know where am at. They better bring they ass in here because I'm not cuffing up."

About a minute later, Sled and the sheriff deputy came and slid a warrant under my door and officially notified me of my court date.

My lawyer ate that shit... For one, there's no such thing as a third-party misdemeanor communicating threat. I had never spoken directly to Sled. I had only spoken directly to the Psyche, which made the entire conversation fall into the category of privilege information—which is also inadmissible in the court of law. Two, I never actually said I was going to kill him. What I said was I felt like killing him, and that was only after I had been asked to express my state of mind during a mental health assessment. Three, when Sled took the stand, he kept trying to speak about me running an extortion ring inside the prison, but that was also inadmissible because the extortion ring played no part to me allegedly communicating a threat...
NOT GUILTY.

"OKAY, Shawn, no more BS. Don't go screwing up. You only got about three years left. Stay clean." I hadn't seen Mr. Hicks in years, but he always showed up when I called. *"And no more threats. You can't be scaring these people. They think you're some type of hit man,"* he said.

"Okay, Ima chill out, and I looking forward to that dinner invite. I've never been to Figure 8 Island," I said, referring to the neighborhood Mr. Hicks stayed in. It was located on an island; and he used to always invite me to dinner, but I never went. You literally had to catch a ferry just to get to the island, and you had to have a special ID to get past security just to get inside the neighborhood. Plus, according to hometown gossip both Michael Jordan and Trot Nixion own property on the island. I was always kind've hesitant to go, but after ten years away, I knew I'd be ready to explore new grounds...

Tabor City

Now you would think that after me and J-Love had flooded the yard, they'd separate us. I mean, that's just common sense, right? Well, I guess it's safe to say that whoever was responsible for shipping us both to Tabor City didn't have any common sense, that is…because we did the same thing all over again.

Now Tabor city is a small town located right outside Whiteville, North Carolina. The prison itself is a reflection of the town: "kind've slow." There really isn't much going on there because it's a medium or close-custody facility. You see, in close custody, the staff are all very mindful of the fact that there's a lot of people who are never going home. So with that in mind, they know not to cross certain lines because a lot of dudes don't have nothing to lose.

In medium custody, staff tend to nitpick a lot about nonsense. So when you have a prison with both medium and close-custody inmates, it creates an imbalance. That leaves most or the average inmate arguing with staff about some stupid shit, not realizing that sometimes, it's good to have small-minded people in charge of a situation because you can easily capitalize off of their ignorance. Keep them focused on the small, minute things while simultaneously shipping in the mother lode—which was exactly what we did. We literally had pounds of weed, tobacco, and cell phones hidden in plain sight.

When we first got to Tabor City, the Pretty Tony Big-Homie Blake was in the building. Now Blake, in his own right, was master manipulator with the gift of gab. Pretty Tony, at the time, was the largest, most violent Bloodset behind the G-wall. At first, Blake and I were cool. He slept directly across from me, and we would go on to do business together. But there's this saying that goes like this: **"*Good*** *business breeds good blood, and bad business breeds bad blood,"* and homie was bad business, which created bad blood. None of the moves he made never turned out right. Half of the time, shit came up short, late, or incorrect. I had paid for some phones, but somehow they never got through. Then when it was time for the refund, this nigga was moving too slow for my liking. When I mentioned something to his homie and right-hand man Day-Ly, he basically told me, *"Man, that nigga don't know how to manage money, and he don't got no money because he giving it all to some girl he just met."* Day-Ly was different from Blake, but I could tell that a lot of the bullshit ways Blake had was starting to rub off on him.

I had already told J-Love, *"We gotta watch these niggas. They full of that up-top shit, thinking niggas from the south slow."*

"Gotta play a sucker to catch a sucker," replied Love, quoting number 21—my favorite tactic from the *48 Laws of Power*...

And that's exactly what we did. We played stupid long enough just to see how far they would carry us. We let them weave themselves in a web there was no way out of.

When I finally stepped to Blake about the phones, I knew it was gonna go one or two ways—either he give me my money back or come up with some phones. He gave me some bullshit about the Indians stealing our package.

"Well, we 'bout go scalp their ass. I responded knowing damn well he was lying." We ended up in a riot with the Indians, and they locked up a total of about twenty of us up. Jo-Love, Blake, and I beat the charges, but Blake never came back to the yard. He had fourteen months and chose to stay on lockup... There's more to the story, but let me tell you this first...

After we beat the charges, we conquered the yard. When people in positions of power know that they can trust you to keep your mouth shut under pressure, it opens up doors...and the door that had just opened was one that allowed us to do what we were known to do: **make shit happen**. Unfortunately, there was a lot unseen forces working behind the scenes trying stop our shine. I only had about two years left before I went home, and a lot of strange shit started happening.

The first sign was when Queen was mysteriously denied a visit.

"I guess now that you getting close to coming home, you don't wanna see me anymore," she said.

"Naah, actually, I was hoping you would come see me this weekend."

"Well, I was planning on coming this weekend, but when I called, they said you can only get visits from your immediately family."

"What, they tripping? That sound like that gang shit, but I'm only labeled level 1 as a associate. They usually only take your contact visits as a level 3... Ima have to check into that."

On our way to lunch, I was telling J-Love, *"I think they leveled 3 me with that STG [Security Threat Group] shit. Queen was saying they won't let her come see me. We beat that riot charge, and ain't nobody say shit to me about it."*

"They might just be mad that we beat them charges, so they putting some shit in the game. I bet that's what it is," replied Love.

"Well, I'm damn sure 'bout to find out."

And what I found out was this… Blake got caught with a phone that had pictures of me, him, and J-Love in it. We had taken those pictures when we had first gotten to Tabor City. I had asked Blake if he erased them afterward. He said, *"Yeah."* But here it was, almost a year later, and he still had the pics in the phone. Not only did they level 3 both me and Love because of the pics but they also labeled us as members of Pretty Tony, which, in itself, was a complete insult. We were First Family; our bloodline was 100 percent official. Our roots could be traced all the way back to the founding fathers of Inglewood, California.

Pretty Tony was never officially sanctioned. It was founded by a renegade named Chuck, who was one of the first unofficial OG. in the state of North Carolina. Notice I said *unofficial*, and I say that because Chuck was false, claiming a rank and status that he never officially earned. He was a self-appointed, unofficial OG from New York who came to Durham, North Carolina, and gave birth to Blood by way of 9trey. At the time, nobody thought to do a background check to confirm his actual status. So for a long time, he managed to play the role of an official OG, and it was during that time that he gave birth to Pretty Tony, by way of Blake and Cash… Now here

I was being labeled as a member of some bullshit set, all behind a clown-ass nigga. And it gets worse than that. Not only did he leave the pictures in the phone but he also recorded a three-way convo that me, him, and the connect had! Yeah, that's right. I said it. He recorded a three-way convo that me, him, and the connect had.

Now what type of gangster would do some dumb shit like that? That's some police shit. Then to top it all off, around this time, the Feds came to pay Blake a visit. Next thing I know, Blake mysteriously received an early release from prison while on I-Con status... The fuck outta here.

But here's the funny shit: when I told the big homies about the shit he did, nobody believed me. Nigga was so busy dick riding that ain't nobody wanna accept the fact that nigga was a rat. Word was that I was hating on the homie because he was from New York... The fuck outta here. He was a rat, and I was raised not to trust those types; but obviously, everybody didn't get the memo.

Now not only was my name ringing bells on the prison yard but also on the streets. 'Round this same time, I was dealing with my Henchmen homie J.V. We had started loan sharking with mostly dope boys and small business owners. J.V.'s right-hand man at the time was Snake Eyes, a dude that I naturally just never trusted. I used to always ask J.V., *"Why you got that snake around you? You know he subject to bite you at even given moment,"* which is exactly what he did. But only did he bite J.V.; he bit me too.

Snake Eyes got pulled over out of state with an illegal firearm in his possession. From there, he told the Feds everything he knew about both me and J.V. He also told them that I was involved with female COs who were bringing work inside the prison and about my status in the Bloods. Basically, he told everything that he knew or thought to be truth. Next thing I know, J.V. is mysteriously snatched up by the Feds; and guess who the star witness for the government was? *Snake Eyes.* And guess who the Feds now had their eyes on after they gave my homie J.V. twenty YEARS? *Frank White, a.k.a. the Head Henchmen, who was currently still incarcerated but on the ass end of a ten-year bid.*

Not only was I dealing with the bullshit with Blake, Snake Eyes, and the prison administration. In the latest turn of events, I had just gotten word that the homie Merk Piddy had gotten killed. To make matters worse, Fresh was locked up, and it was as if his entire line was hesitant to handle the situation. It was as if without Fresh, they couldn't think logically enough to retaliate and apply the pressure to whoever had killed the homie.

I called the homie Face-off and explained the situation… *"Look, brah, these young niggas ain't really hip to how we get down when it comes to the fam. It's ASAP situation, and they hesitating. I need you to show them how we play when niggas violate the fam,"* I explained.

"I got you, fam. Don't trip. Ima send the streets a message. Just be easy and get home so we can get shit in order," replied Face-off.

"Bet," I said, ending the call and laying back on my bunk and just thinking. I got introduced to the street life at age thirteen; by age twenty-eight, I was official OG status. Now here I was at age thirty, on the ass end of a ten-year bid, and still heavily connected to the streets.

As I laid on my bunk, I replayed the last conversation I had with Merk. I had turned him on to a sweet lick, so sweet that all he had to do was walk in and get it.

"Listen, brah. The door gone be unlocked. All you gotta do is go in and grab it. Ain't nobody going to be in the house. You don't need no gun. It's easy as 1-2-3," I explained.

"Yeah, I hear you, brah, but Ima still strap up just in case something go wrong. You know they don't call me Merk for nothing, fooly."

"Trills, I feel you. Just make sure you be safe and keep your eyes wide open. If you have to take somebody with you, make sure they rock solid and know how to keep their mouth shut. You know the motto: 'Real hitters remain…"

"Silent," he said, finishing my sentence for me and ending the call.

The lick went sweet just as I knew it would. What I couldn't understand was how homie got killed. Word was a fight popped off in the club, and he ended up getting stabbed in the heart. I could never understand how the homies that were out with him that night even let somebody (especially an opp) get that close to brah. With both me and Fresh behind the G-wall, it was Merk Piddy who pretty much had the streets under pressure. Hearing how the homie got killed never sat well with me. Even though we never met personally, our bond was built on two things: **the Code of Honor and a killer's instincts.**

Later that night after lockdown... Face-off texted me, *"Greenlight."*

I texted back, *"Means go."*

"Already gone, bout to circle the block. Meet me at the movies," he responded.

"Pulling up now," I texted then dialed his number.

"War before peace. What's wood?" I greeted.

"I'm your keeper 2s, 3s, and 5s, fooly. Breathe easy right quick. I got the kids with me. We 'bout to go play in the park. Ima leave the phone on speaker."

From there, all I heard was shots for about a good minute straight. I knew fam had ASAP that situation. I hung up the phone during all the commotion and sent him a text. *"Family Always First."*

About five minutes later, he texted back... *"Henchmen Shit!!"*

From there, there was no more to be said. Even though I never found out exactly who was responsible for killing the homie, I made sure that everybody I heard was involved got touched in some kind of way... RIP to the homie Merk Piddy. Trust and believe you were really one of a kind... Us, never them...

Bloodbath

For me, it was business as usual. Despite all the bullshit, Love and I were still rocking the beat.

One morning, we were on our way to breakfast and just got a fresh pack. We had stayed up all night making sure everything went according to plan. We had a routine that we usually followed, which was **"Safety always first and secure the product second,"** but I guess Love was too tired to stay up and secure the product.

They usually search the cells during count time, so I always made sure not to have any contraband in my cell during count time...

That same morning, during the ten o'clock count, I saw like 5 COs coming and rushing in the dorm.

"Block hot! Block hot! They in here five deep! It's a hit!" I yelled out.

After the first five COs came in rushing in, about ten seconds later, another seven more came rushing in right behind them.

"Block hot! Block hot! It's a hit! She on fire!" I yelled out again as they stopped directly in front of my cell and opened my door.

"Step back so we can strip-search you and your cell," said the CO.

"How many times must we go through this shit before you'll give up?" I replied. *"It's nothing on me or in my cell besides what I'm allowed to have."*

"Well, Jennings, as much as we want to believe you, I can't because it's a lot of people saying something completely different."

"Well, I'm starting to think y'all just like seeing me naked," I said, stepping back and handing them my clothes piece by piece. By the time they were finished, I saw them taking J-Love out in handcuffs. *"Yo, you good, brah?"* I asked.

He just looked at me and shook his head. Damn, I knew it was bad. They had caught my dogg slipping. They ended up finding four ounces of weed and a pound of tobacco in his cell. I was hurt. They had just bagged my dogg, and now it was all eyes on me.

I only had about ten months left and had decided it was time to fall back. I had already done everything there was to do besides get caught red-handed. Little did I know that because of Blake and Snake Eyes, the Feds were already aiming for me.

Once I fell back, I had started rocking with the homie Jack-Boy from out of Charlotte. Jack-Boy was in the process of forming his own line called *Karolina Red.* I told Jack-Boy that I'd back him on that because I felt like the state of North Carolina didn't have their own identity when it came to being Blood, which is why a lot of dudes from North Carolina or the South period don't really know the true history of Blood. My plan was to help Jack-Boy get in position and then merge Karolina Red with Henchmen under the First Family banner.

However, being that a large majority of the UBN is from New York, they felt threatened by the idea of Carolina having their own set. Now mind you—at the time, my status was officially OG, and I wasn't under the UBN; and if you remember correctly, I told you that the entire East Coast UBN itself was never properly sanctioned by the founding fathers. This is why West Coast Bloods at one point didn't respect East Coast Bloods because they never had permission to bring Blood to the East Coast—once again with the exception of one set: *the First Family;* which is why they call us the First Family because we were the first official set on the East Coast with proper sanctions from the founding fathers out west... All facts!

Now once Jack-Boy started doing his thing, a lot of dudes were curious to know about Karolina Red. Being that I was backing him, a lot of dudes started whispering that I was Karolina Red myself, which was never the case. I was just giving the UBN a taste of their own medicine. The same way they stole Blood from the west, I was helping the homie steal it from the north.

When the higher-ups of the UBN sent word that Jack-Boy was food, my response was this...

"If he food, then the entire UBN is food! So is Pretty Tony! So is BGB! So is a lot of them bullshit sets y'all pushing! Nobody never sanctioned none of that shit! Chuck ain't real right! Blake ain't real right! Franky Boo ain't real right, but y'all ain't saying shit 'bout them niggas because they all from NY! So how y'all gone say he food and he doing the same shit they doing, but since he from Carolina, he wrong? Naah, I'm not stamping that green light."

"It's eat food or be food, Frank. Ain't nobody bigger than the B," they explained.

"I said all Ima say. If y'all ain't gone eat all them other niggas, then y'all not gone eat the homie. That's dead. At least while I'm here, that ain't happening."

By me being the highest-ranking Blood on the yard, I was considered the shot caller, and I wasn't about to let no foul play pop off. Right is right, and wrong is wrong; and the homie wasn't in the wrong.

So when I got word that Blake and Franky Boo had merged both Pretty Tony and Black Gorilla Gangster together, I knew what they were trying to do, which was create an uprising of renegades. Come to find out even the UBN had disowned them both. They were combining their teams in a desperate attempt to get some type recognition. I guess they both thought they could bully their way into being recognized as official Blood sets.

I already knew they would try to get at me simply because I never green-lighted Jack-Boy. So I did what I was always taught to do: I bombed first. Fuck that. I wasn't 'bout to sit back and let them rock me to sleep. Yeah, I'm from the South, but I damn sure ain't slow. I sent some Henchmen homies to handle some cleanup work just to make a statement, which was *"**War before peace**"* and *"**Welcome to the bloody South!**"*

Once the administration put two and two together, they came and locked me up. They assumed I was responsible for the hits, but they couldn't charge me with shit because I wasn't around when it popped off. I was in the library studying **The Art of War** by **Sun Tzu,** one of my favorite books. They still kept me in the hole for three months just off GP. Word was that the UBN had put a hit on my head by way of the Pretty Tony and Black Gorilla Gangster. The truth was that PT and BGG had put the hit out because I had exposed the fact that they weren't official, and because of that, they had been disowned by the UBN. So in order to avoid further exposure, they had to silence me because I was the only person at the time who wasn't afraid to speak out.

After ninety days, I was transferred back to Scotland and placed in regular population. When I got there, the gang LT, Ms. Hampton, tried to offer me PC.

"You only got four months left. You sure you wanna go to the yard? You know there's a hit out on you."

"Look, lady, I been banging waay before this Blood shit became popular. You think I survived all that shit in the streets by being scared? Just to come to prison and let theses play-play gangsters kill me? This isn't the first time I've had a hit on my head, and that shit usually doesn't play out the way people think it will." And it didn't.

The first thing I did when I got to the yard was get a banger. I could feel the bullshit in the air. The yard was mostly PT and BGG, and word had spread like wildfire once I stepped out to the yard. I was just waiting on them to make their move. It took a month, but they finally did… They just sent the wrong type at me… Weak niggas!

The first thing that gave them away was, they kept cutting their eyes at me while they were in the chow line (Strike one—Frank, pay attention!).

The second thing that gave them away were the ice grills (strike two—These mafuckas is Henchmen). Now I'm discreetly reaching for my banger.

The third thing that gave them away was when they started walking in my direction and all the seats were taken (strike three—Renegades, if I die, they still get paid), banger in my hand.

When the first dude stopped, he hesitated then swung his tray at my face. I was already coming up, swinging my banger. We hit each other almost at the same time. I wrapped his head in forward-facing headlock and took him down before he could even pull his banger. We landed, and I was on top. I felt his man stab me dead center in the back. I rolled over but kept his partner in the cross face and wrapped my legs around him using his body as a shield. All his man could do was stab me in my legs. All this took place in a matter of 'bout thirty seconds.

The COs came running with their sticks out. Once I saw ole boy drop his banger, I let his man go. When I let him go, he scooted back. *Boop!* I kicked him dead in his face. He slipped and tried to get up again. *Boop, boop!* Every time he tried to get up, he put his hands on the floor to push himself up and left his face exposed. And every time, I'd kick him dead in his shit.

I was still on the ground myself. I had to backpedal to get up. When I did, one of my legs went weak, but I kept my balance. I had about three stab wounds in my legs and one in my back. It's funny because even though I got stabbed four times, I still managed to blow one and outsmart the other. Everybody was clowning both of them, but I wasn't tripping on them. I wanted whoever it was that had sent them…

After that shit popped off, I sent word to Storm to press play, but the truth of the matter was Pretty Tony and BGG had way more man power than we did.

"Listen, brah. If we go at these dudes now, we stand a chance of losing. We've gotta think strategically. That way we win the war before it even starts. If we go at these dudes without a plan, we lose. Let me reach out and do some research. Ima find out who all was involved. That way, we don't hit no innocent bystanders… We hit who need to get hit, Henchmen style!"

Home Sweet Home

The day of my release had finally arrived. I was being released on nine-months post release, and because of that, I had to wait on my PO to come pick me up. Plus due to the incident in the chow hall, I had been placed on disciplinary segregation with a pending M-Con recommendation.

The prison officials had briefed my PO about me and my gang affiliations in advance, which, in turn, made my PO (Ms. White) try to act a lil extra with me. She didn't come pick me up until 2:30 in the afternoon, and when she finally did arrive, she brought extra man and firepower.

Normally, when an I/M is released from prison, they leave early in the morning in-between 8:00–10:00 a.m. and are free from all physical restraints such as handcuffs and shackles...but not in my case.

When I was finally escorted up to R&D, I knew something wasn't right. I had six officers as escorts, and there seemed to be some type of nervous energy in the air, as if they knew something I didn't. And whatever it was that they knew had them all acting extra tough as if I was a threat. The funny part was for one, I was shackled from head to toe. That alone made me completely harmless. Two, I was happy as hell to be going home, so I ignored all that silly-ass tough-guy talk they were spitting. And three, I had Queen waiting on me oiled and ass naked in a pair of all-red six-inch stiletto heels.

As soon as I walked through the door and laid eyes on Ms. White, *"What took you so long to get here?"* I asked, somewhat irritated as she attempted to formally introduce herself

"Mr. Jennings, you're being released on nine-months post-release supervision. I'll be your post-release officer. My name is Ms. White, and

you'll address me as such. Here are the terms and conditions of your release. Please read and sign..."

"*Hello, Ms. White, it's a pleasure to finally meet you,*" I said, signing the papers. "*I've been waiting ten years to leave this place, so I was hoping you could speed this process up a little seeming as though I've been waiting so long to leave and all day for you to get here,*" I said as the officers started removing my restraints.

"*You can blame my supervisor for the delay. Seeming as though you're such a notorious gangster, I was advised to bring extra man and firepower to protect the public... I'm sure you understand,*" she responded.

During the back and forth with Ms. White, I noticed a White guy in plain clothes coming out of the lieutenant's office with more restraints. As he approached, my subconscious mind was screaming **cop.** He looked like a cop and walked like a cop, and like most cops, ***he was a man without a mustache.***

He brought my gate check and had me sign for my funds in my personal account. I had 30k in my prison account, mostly money I had stacked during my time in incarceration. When Ms. White inquired as to how and where I'd gotten so much money, I simply responded...*"Public services. I'm sure you understand,"* as the mysterious man without a mustache placed me back in full restraints.

On the ride home, I mostly laid back and relaxed. After ten years, I was on my way home. I had to build and maintain my empire from behind prison walls. The Henchmen had not only expanded in prison but on the streets also. I was now in a real mastermind position.

The ride home was almost two hours, and all I did was think. When we were about five minutes away, Ms. White called my mom and told her we'd be pulling up shortly. When we arrived, my entire family were standing out front. My son was the first one to rush up to the car as we pulled up. When I got out, I had to wait for No Mustache to remove the restraints before hugging my son and daughter. My mother started crying as I gave her a hug. *"Don't cry. I'm here now, Mom. I'm home."*

I heard Ms. White clearing her throat in an attempt to get my attention. I made her wait until I had greeted and hugged all my brothers and sisters before giving her my attention. It's family always first, and my PO ain't fam.

"Oh, I almost forgot about you that fast," I said, walking back in her direction.

"Here's my card. And you have seventy-two hours to report, and it'll be in your best interest not to forget."

I chilled and got reacquainted with my family for the entire day. By nightfall, I had set up a meeting with the homies. Murda and Face came to pick me up, and truthfully, it was as if I had never left. I called the homie Doggfaze and told him I was en route from Raleigh to Wilmington and to meet me at Club Endzone.

When we got to Wilmington, I had Murda drop me off at Queen's house. *"Give me a couple hours, and Ima meet y'all at the club."* I called Queen as I started walking through the parking lot.

"Hello," she answered.

"You said apt 357, right? What side of the complex is that?" I asked.

"It's on the far right, the second building by the pool..."

"Okay, I see it. I'm en route right now."

When I got to the apt, the door was already cracked. As soon as I stepped through the door, I saw her standing there naked with some red heels on. I started taking my clothes off right at the door.

Before I knew it, my dick was sliding in and out of her mouth. *"Damn, I miss you,"* she said, holding my dick as if she was talking in a microphone. *"I miss you so damn much."* She continued licking all over my dick and dipping low to suck on my balls. No lie, she was literally holding a conversation with my dick.

Just for sport, I grabbed her hair, pulled her head back, raised up on my tippy toes, and aimed my dick down her throat. She kept putting her hand on my stomach, trying to push me back so she could breath. I was literally choking her with my dick. I eased up and pulled out as I saw her eyes watering up.

"I miss you too," I said, pulling her up and kissing her as hard as I could and lifting her up and sitting her on the back of the couch.

"I told you I was gone ride till the end with you," she said as I stood between her legs, just staring at her.

"Ssshhh," I said, placing my finger to her lips.

From there, I took my time—kissing her from her head to her juice box and stopping to suck gently on each nipple. My tongue trailed down her stomach. As I took my fingers and spread her lips apart, I rubbed my entire face directly on her clit before sucking it in-between my lips and teasing it with my tongue.

"Sha, Shaw, shhhaawwn. Pleazzzz fuck meee!" she whined as I felt her legs shaking on my shoulders. She came all over my face as I stood up with her still sitting on my face and my tongue still teasing her clit.

I had worked out damn near every day for ten years straight visualizing this moment. Now here I was standing tall with my shorty on my shoulders riding my face and me enjoying every moment of it. The more she pulled my hair for balance, the deeper my tongue went.

After about ten minutes of her riding my face, I squatted back down and sat her on the edge of the couch.

"Turn around," I said as I was rubbing my dick in circles around the lips of her box. When she turned around, I continued to rub my dick up and down her pussy lips. As I slid inside her, I cocked my hand all the way back and slapped her ass cheek as hard as I could. I grabbed a fistful of hair and started stroking her. Her pussy was super wet, and I could feel my dick stretching her walls and touching the bottom of her box.

At first, my strokes were slow and powerful, but with each stroke, I picked up the pace. Queen is short, but the heels had that ass sitting high. Just right for me to put my pound game down real proper. The only sounds in the room were her moans, my growls, and the smacking sound of her ass clapping against my pelvis. I felt my nut coming. The closer I came to release, the louder I growled. I was fucking her so hard, as if I was taking ten years' worth of stress out on her pussy. I was in full-fledged beast mode. Part man, part lion!

When I finally came, I roared like a lion, *"Arrrrhhhhhhhhhhllll!"* as I released my seed deep inside her womb and collapsed on her back..." *Damn, I miss you, shorty,"* I said, out of breath.

"I miss you too. Welcome home, daddy. I love you."

From there, we rolled up, smoked, and conversated for a while. She surprised when she brought me my welcome-home gifts because I wasn't expecting it.

"I know how much you hate depending on other people, so I took the initiative to make sure you wouldn't have to ask nobody for nothing. So I got you some gifts," she said while walking ass naked to the closet and retrieving a gift-wrapped box. *"But first, before opening your present, I have something very serious to ask you,"* she said while standing directly in front of me and giving me her full attention.

"Well, spit it out because you are making me nervous, shorty."

"Shawn, do you really love me? I mean like are you really in love with me?"

"That's a silly-ass and rather stupid-ass question! You just trooped a ten-year bid with a nigga, and now you standing here asking him, or me rather, do I love you. Hell, yeah, I love you. I'm in love with you, or however you wanna word it. And please, don't ask me no silly shit like that again," I said, reaching for the box.

Inside the box were two brand-new burners and a nice-size stack of money. The first gun case I opened held a chrome and black snub-noses Smith and Wesson .357.

"Hell-fucken-yeah!" I yelled excitedly. *"And this why I love your lil ass so much,"* I said, referring to the gun.

"Remember we were talking about me getting my gun license. Well, I went ahead and got it, so you good. They clean. I told you I was gone hold you down to the fullest" she said as I counted the money.

The other burner was a 17-shot compact .40 cal with a beam, and the stack of money totaled at 10,000 dollars.

"Set a wedding date, shorty," I said while palming her ass and pulling her close to me.

Our next hour was spent talking, and it was then when she came clean and confessed.

"Ima tell you this before you hear it in the streets. While you were away, I dealt with a few dudes. I never slept with none of your homies or dudes I know you're cool with."

After that, she told me who was who and what was what. From there, we both agreed to a five-month grace period in which I was entitled to sleep with other females. But only under three conditions: (1) always wear a condom; (2) all her friends were off-limits; and (3) no catching feelings… Once we finished that conversation, I long stroked her back to sleep, got dressed, and called the homie Murda to come get me.

Peace Almighty

When Murda pulled up, he was three cars deep with Doggfaze and O-Dog.

It had been years since I've seen either of the homies. We embraced one another with brotherly hugs and bonds that could only be built in the struggle. We had all done bids and dreamed of doing big things once released… It was our time.

"Damn, I can't believe we all here now," I said, still hyped from just being free.

"It's definitely time to press play and put everything we planned in motion," stated Murda.

"Most definitely," I agreed.

"We can talk about this in VIP? I'm riding dirty, and I got two hittas riding in the car with me," stated Doggfaze.

We all swerved out the parking lot, racing to the club. Once inside the car, Murda handed me a small Coach bag filled with money. *"That's from the homies, something for you to get on your feet with. Just kick back and relax. We gone make sure you good."*

Shit was looking real nice. Everything was falling in place. I hadn't even been out a whole twenty-four hours and already touched 20K.

The biggest moment of that first day out was when we pulled up at the club. *"Yo, why is all these dudes wearing army fatigue?"* I asked Murda as he searched for a parking lot.

"Because they warriors," he said as we pulled up and parked.

As we stepped out the car and made our way through the parking lot, Doggfaze was already standing out in front of the club. As I approached him, he stepped directly in front of me, saluted me, then yelled, *"Peace Almighty!"*

It was then that I realized all the dudes that had on army fatigues had on *"War b/4 Peaze"*T-shirts also. As they all yelled *"Peaze Blood,"* all I could do was smile as I watched and listened to homies paint the night red with the roll call. I was introduced to so many homies that night. I couldn't remember nobody's name. All I remember was somebody passing me a bottle of Henny while some chick was giving me lap dance.

The next morning, I woke and had no idea where I was at. I peeped two dudes in the room with me; they were playing the game station. *"Yo, where the bathroom at?"* I asked, feeling my mouth watering up.

"It's round the corner and straight down the hall."

I ended up standing over the toilet, calling earl. The mixture of white and brown liquor didn't sit well on my stomach. After rinsing my mouth out and splashing some cold water on my face, I was feeling a lot better.

Once I stepped back in the front room, both homies introduced themselves *"War before peace, big brah. They call me Puff. I been pushing the H-Team for four years now. It's all I know. I eat, sleep, and breathe this Henchmen shit."*

"Likewise, big brah," stated the other homie. *"I'm Mafiano, and all I know is Henchmen and hittin' shit. This Doggfaze spot. He should be pulling up back up soon."*

I had to admit, the homies definitely had shit in order. From what I had seen so far, we were at least 200 deep, and I still hadn't met everybody yet.

My thoughts were interrupted by Doggfaze and O-Dog walking through the door. As soon as they saw me, they started clowning me. *"Your ass can't handle that Henny, homie. We had to tote your ass in here last night. You threw up everywhere, all in the whip. I just went and got my shit detailed this morning,"* stated Doggfaze.

"Yo, damn all that. Who was that brown-skinned chick that was all on my dick last night? She told me her name, but I forgot. I was gone hit her with the Henny dick but fucked around and blacked out. Where my phone at? I put her number in my shit."

"You talking 'bout ole girl Model Meek. She be stripping and shit, but she 'bout her B&B."

"The fuck is B&B, brah? Some kind of new slang word?"

"Naah, brah, it mean bread and business. Most these chicks out here fucken for crab legs and a bag of weed, so when you get one that's 'bout her B&B, it's a win-win situation... And your phone in the car, fool."

From there, we chopped it up, about a few things concerning the fam. The three homies John, Puff, and Mafiano were hittas—young loyal lions that stayed close by my side. The third hitta was John, who was legally registered to tote firearms, so he also served as my driver. He mentioned something about us having a beef with the Billy homies. The Billy homie Lil G had the streets for 9-Trey, so I made a mental note to reach out to him and see if we could have a sit-down. Even though I didn't stay in Wilmington, when I came through, the homies always rolled out the red carpet.

Doggfaze was in the middle of telling me about setting up an official welcome party when my phone rang.

"Whatsup, shorty?" I said, answering the phone.

"You and that dick. I need you to come fuck me good before I go to work."

"Damn, ain't we mannish this morning," I said, laughing at how hard shorty had come at me. *"You know I love it when you pop that gangster shit. Give me a second. Ima pull up on you in 'bout thirty minutes."*

"Okay. I love you, Shawnee baby."

"Yeah, I love you too, but don't start that Shawnee shit," I said seriously.

"Whatever, Shawnee. Bye."

All I could do was laugh once I realized she had hung up on me.

I finished chopping it up with Doggfaze about the party, called my mom, and checked in on my kids. I let her know I'd be back in Raleigh later that evening. I pulled up on Queen and fucked her until she called me Frank. Man, I'm telling you, it felt damn good to be free.

Once I got back to Raleigh, I chilled with my kids for the weekend. I swear, they both had my personality. My daughter Shaunte had my "I don't give a fuck" attitude. She always spoke her mind and kept it a hundred on all levels at all times. *At just twelve years old,* I could see she was gonna be a real heartbreaker and hell-raiser.

My son Shy'ion was me all day, the silent, strong type. He appeared innocent on the surface, but beneath the mask was a monster in the making. I knew he'd do big things, but I also knew he'd be tried and tested because of his laid-back personality. I laugh at the thought of those who'd underestimate him…

Highly Educated Negro

As for me, I was enjoying my freedom. It felt good to come home and see how the movement had grown. The First Family had become the most dominant set in the city. The only thing we lacked was direction. Due to the fact that a lot of the homies were young and still learning, the actual concept of BLOOD it was on me to enlighten and elevate their minds.

The first thing I did was give history lessons about the actual birth and true purpose of BLOOD.

"The term gangster was never what the forefathers intended for us to he labeled as. BLOOD was started as a means to protect Blacks against oppressive forces such as corrupt cops, Crips, and White supremacist. Some of the original breakdowns of BLOOD were **Black Liberation Order of Defense, Black Leaders of Our Day, Blood Lines of Our Descendants, and Brotherly Love Overrides Oppression and Destruction and the first official blood set ever were to L.A. BRIMS. Black Revolutionary Intellectually Minded Soldiers.** *It's very important that you know who you are and where you come from... That way, you will always properly represent what it is you stand for."*

Once I noticed the conditions within the Black community, I immediately started promoting HENCHMEN as an independent nonprofit community outreach program. What I didn't know was that Blake and Snake Eyes had already pointed the Feds in my direction. The Feds, in turn, had employed an entire team of confidential informants to track my every move.

My main concern was that I didn't want to see none of my lil homies go through what I did. I figured that because of my status as a well-respected OG, they'd listened to me, and for the most part, they did.

"I use to be just like y'all, but I don't want y'all to be just like me. I want y'all to be better and smarter than me. I need y'all to learn from my mistakes by not getting caught up in the system. Don't fall victim to the system because all that shit they talk about helping rehabilitate you for society is complete bullshit. The criminal justice system was designed to do one thing and thats destroy the Black community. We're God's chosen people, but as long as we allow these devils to control our lives, we'll never know our rightful place as the Original Man and God's children. If any of you'll ever need me, just call me…and I'm coming."

I then started reaching out to local businesses and influential members within the Black community. I explained to them my vision, which was to uplift and elevate the minds of our youth by installing the importance of family structure back into the Black community.

My message was simple: *"We have to set a higher standard. We out here killing each other over nothing while these foreigners and White folks is buying up all the property. We the number 1 consumers in the world, but yet we rank last amongst all other races when it comes to ownership. It's time we put all the BS aside, do some bigger-picture thinking."*

I was able to do a lot of things to help a lot of people, but I was paying for it all out of my own pocket, which put me in a jam. Not really a jam; it's just that I was still hustling. I was basically using drug money to finance everything I was doing. I know that wasn't right, but I looked at it like this; every time I was able to help one of my people in need, I was doing a public service.

Even when the Feds finally arrested me, one of the first things they asked me was "How the hell did you manage to stop so much violence?"

Time-out! Cut!

Okay, I had to call a time-out and talk directly to my real readers. I need your full and undivided attention because the shit I'm 'bout to tell you could get me killed, so pay close attention.

Now you'd think that stopping violence in the Black community would be well received by all, right? But it's not, and let me explain to you why; because crime pays! How? Because of federal funding, that's how! It's all political. Every year, the government

spends billions of dollars on defense funding, and guess who and what falls under the category of the defense funding bill? Your local gang members, that's who. Every year, the government distributes millions and millions of dollars in federal funding for things such as gang prevention programs and special gang unit task force. However, in order to receive this federal funding, the said city, county, or state must show and prove the existence of gang-related criminal activity. This is why most of the time you hear about violence in the Black community, it's labeled as gang related. As of 9/11/01, Homeland Security labeled all local gang members as a domestic terrorist. That label was given to us as a means to justify the millions of dollars your local politicians receive every year in defense funding. This is also why the media will promote gang violence in the Black community more than they'll promote corrupt cops or child molesters. It's all political; the millions and millions of dollars these politicians receive go straight to their pockets. They don't want to stop the violence; they just want somebody to blame for it. The more they promote gang violence, the bigger their federal funding check will be... Deep shit, right? Yeah, I know! That's why it's important to educate and elevate your mental...

And here is some more food for thought...

"Know for certain that for 400 years your descendants will be strangers in country not their own and that they will be enslaved and mistreated there. But I will punish the nation they serve as slaves and afterward they will come out with great possessions. In the fourth generation, your descendants will come back here [Africa], for the sin of Amorite [Americans] has not yet reached its full measure..." then said the Lord (Genesis Chapter 15, verse 13–16).

So for all those who still don't understand what's going on in the world, let me enlighten you. Historical documents report that the first slave ships arrived in America on or around 1619. So 1619 + 400 = 2019—which means the four hundred years of enslavement of the Black race has expired. We are now living in the fourth generation.

The only thing that these politicians can hope for is that we remain asleep, lost, and without knowledge of self. They've tried everything from mass incarceration, the Jim Crow laws, the counter-intelligence program, and even flooding our neighborhoods with drugs and guns... Why? Because we are God's chosen people, the true descendants of Abraham. They can't destroy us (no matter how hard they try), so all they can hope for is that we self-destruct... But the head <u>H</u>ighly <u>E</u>ducated <u>N</u>egro <u>C</u>eeing <u>H</u>is <u>M</u>ind <u>E</u>levate <u>N</u>obly ain't falling for it. I'm wide awoke with eyes wide open.

Time in, annnnnnd action. Now let me get back to the good shit, but if they kill me, you better ride for me. Word!

Club Endzone

It was the night of the official First Family party. Big sis had put it all together. Both my real and street fam were in attendance. I had been home almost three months now but had really been playing it low-key—out of sight and out of mind. But that still didn't keep my name out of the snitches' mouth. After tonight, they'd definitely have something to talk about.

My phone rang as I was in traffic, and I recognized the number on the screen. *"War before peace,"* I answered, always happy to hear from my homies behind the G-wall.

"I'm your keeper. What's wood?"

"Not shit. Just cruising through the city, collecting this rent money. I been meaning to check on those buildings. Last time I spoke with shorty, she said something about the ordinance code. We should be good though. The lady that owns the building is in good standings with whoever in charge of the ordinance code, so it's all looking good. I put some bread on all the bros' books, so everybody should be good. Yo, when the hell is you coming home?"

"Shit, I got 'bout eighteen months left. Matter fact, all us come home around the same time—me, Ghetto, Flames, Dmoe. I think J-Love gone be the last one out... But yo, you know they locking all the homies in the hole because of the war."

"Yeah, I know. Trust me that's why I went ahead and sent everybody some money. Real shit, brah. These streets is sour! I come through, but I don't sit still. I pick up, drop off, and I'm gone. Big sis throwing the official welcome home party tonight, so Ima cut up. But after that, I'm back on my B&B."

"The fuck is B&B, brah?"

I let out a light chuckle, still remembering when I had asked Doggfaze that same question. *"It's short bread and business. Out here, you either on B&B or you on straight B, which is short for bullshit,"* I explained as I pulled up at Model Meek's spot and parked.

"B&B, huh? Yeah, I like the way that sound. Ima most definitely add that to my lingo. Well, yo, *Ima let you handle your BI. Send my salutes to the fam and make sure you flic it up for me."*

"I got you, fooly. Eyes wide open."

"Know that…eyes everywhere," I said as Storm ended the call.

Within the first three months of my release, I had managed to get a strong grip on the streets. I also managed to unite the First Family and the Billys both on the streets and behind prison walls. As a result, on January 26, 2012, one of the biggest prison Blood wars of all North Carolina history was sparked off—from Scotland, Pertie, Maury, Pasquotank, and Lanesboro. *Greenlight* meant "go," and aided with the assistance of the Billys, the First Family had orchestrated a bloodbath against both Pretty Tony and Black Gorilla Gangsters.

Word was both Blake and Franky Boo were bragging about the hit, saying they had sent two dudes at me in the chow hall… So I returned the favor. Blake ended up shot up in an alleged drug deal gone bad in Charlotte, North Carolina. Poor Franky Boo—we officially labeled him a Westside (eat-on-sight) plate. He would also go on to be federally indicted for a separate situation…

It was during this time that the big-homie Storm had plugged me directly in with the First Family's founding father… True God. We never met in person and only spoke several times very briefly over the phone. I was amazed at how humble he was. It was during one of our brief conversations in which he dropped a priceless jewel on me. *"Only those who doubt their power feel the need to prove it. Your character is what determined your legacy. A solid and strong character will leave a solid and strong legacy. Always uphold the Code of Honor. Never compromise your morals, principles, or values, and legacy will be written in stone."*

It was then that I came to understand what real power was. What True God had spoken had opened my eyes. I knew it was time for me to step back from the streets and solidify the Henchmen Legacy.

Model Meek never failed to live up to her name. When she answered the door, I just stood there taking in her beauty—hair, face, titties, red nails, and wardrobe. The ass wasn't all that phat, but she had enough to please a nigga from the back.

"Why is you just standing there staring at me?" she asked while still standing in the doorway.

"Because I'm really thinking about saying 'Fuck that party' and just fucken you instead."

"We got all night for that. Plus that liquor make me wet, so Ima make it worth your wait," she said, pulling me in the house by my collar and licking all over my face.

Not only was she a bad chick but she was a boss chick too. Shorty knew a lot of get-money niggas, so I used a lot of her resources to do some networking. We were currently in the process of renting some buildings. The building would be used as the headquarters for an independent nonprofit community-outreach HENCHMEN program. This was one of the many ways for me to solidify my legacy— by giving back to my community. I was still in the streets, but I didn't plan on staying there long. I had made some nice investments in clubs and clothing and was strategically plotting my exit. According to my calculation, all I needed was a nice two-year run, and I was done with the streets.

I waited as Model Meek went and grabbed my book bag.

"I told him to stop by the club tonight just so you can see him. Ima meet him there, but I'm not leaving with him. I just want you to see his face for future reference."

She was referring to a guy named Sykes who had been spending a nice amount. In fact, the book bag she just gave me was a filled with about 50k dollars from our last transaction.

"Meet me at Retha's spot," I texted the homie John as I head for the door. *"Ima catch you at the club,"* I said as I stopped to open the door, with her walking behind me.

"Them panties match your nails and toes?" I asked as I turned around.

She just smiled, turned around, pulled her tights down to her ankles, looked back at me, and twerked her ass so I could see the red G-string thong buried between her butt cheeks.

I gave it to her right there in the hallway—facedown, ass-up style with my book bag still on my back. We weren't trying to make love; we were fucking. She got her nut, I got mine, and it was over.

"Ima catch your ass later," I said, laughing on my way out the door. *"Ima need you to keep that same energy for after the club."*

"You know I will. Only real niggas make me cum."

I bent the block coming off 14th and Castle and spotted all three of my young lions in the cut right in front of Retha's spot. I stopped and yelled, *"War before peace!"* as they all turned and came and got in the truck.

"Take that book bag and put it up at the spot. And whatsup with these Billys? Why I keep hearing we s'posely beefing with them? What's that about?"

"One of they homies got rolled, so they sending shots. Ain't really nothing we can't handle. It's just they on some TV gangster shit. Shooting in broad daylight. All in traffic and ain't hitting shit," stated Puff.

"It wouldn't be hard to pull out that all black and put something to sleep, big brah. Just give me the word..." replied Maff.

"Ima see if I can bark at G 'bout it and dead that shit. It's too much money out here for niggas to be making the streets hot behind bullshit. Either we gone dead the beef or clean it all the way up... Where y'all parked at?"

After I dropped the brahs off, I headed home. Queen and I had moved to another spot farther on the outskirts of the city in a quiet neighborhood called Northchase. We still had the apt in The Creek, which we used occasionally to entertain our company, but we mostly stayed in Northchase.

I got home, showered, ate, and got dressed for the party. As I got dressed, I listened to Queen fill me in on what the Facebookers were commenting about in regards to the party. It was some haters online popping that "fuck Frank" shit. When Queen showed me their profile names and pics, *"I don't even know none of them niggas. Never heard of them,"* I said while standing up and ducking the compact .40 in my waist. The ladies, of course, were shouting out the First Fam and showing mad love. Big sis had themed the party First Family Reunion and posted it on her page.

"Log on my page and post: Free drinks and entrance all night for my ladies in red. Eat your heart out, haters… Franky's home!"

The club was packed, the party was jumping, and at the present moment, we had the picture booth on lock. Bands, bottles, and bitches were everywhere.

I was sipping some roozay straight from the bottle when I felt somebody tap me on my shoulder. When I turned, I noticed my man Tone Harris from back in the day, the same nigga from the incident in which I was left with two dead bodies in Club Benjamin's parking lot. He was now part owner of Club Endzone.

"What's good?" I said, dapping him up and showing some love. What he said next fucked my entire night up.

"The marshals in here, so y'all gotta put them bottles in brown bags," he said, handing me a bag.

I initially thought he was talking 'bout the fire marshals because the club was packed. But when I looked in the direction he nodded toward, I saw him—again! It was **No Mustache,** and for the second time, my subconscious mind screamed, *Cop!* Then it all hit me. This was the same guy who had made me ride home from prison in handcuffs and shackles. The reason why my PO had picked me up so late was because her supervisor had advised her to bring extra man and firepower. That extra man and firepower was **No Mustache,** who I had just found out was also a US marshal. All this could only mean one thing…the Feds were on me.

I stuck around just long enough to watch them watch me. During this time, I spotted Model Meek with ole boy Sykes and file his face away in my photographic memory. After I grew tired of playing the cat-and-mouse game with the marshals, I slid out the side door unnoticed…

Confidential Informants

It had been a month since the official welcome-home party. After that night, I made it a top priority to be on point at all times. I knew I was being watched by the Feds, and I knew they were waiting on me to slip. I never stepped a foot back inside Club Endzone again.

When I inquired and asked Tone why the marshals were in the club, he stated that most of the security detail were all on federal probation. So the marshals usually showed up to confirm their proof and place of employment. It made sense, but still, just to be on the safe side, I decided never to return.

I had also found out that *No Mustache* was not only a US marshal but was also a special agent by the name of S. Taylor, who was assigned as the head officer of a joint task force of local and federal officers called The Safe Street Gang Prevention Task Force.

After J.V. got chased up, his co-D who was Snake Eyes agreed to cooperate as a confidential informant, and it was then that Snake Eyes informed *No Mustache* about the Henchmen and First Family organization. This explains why prior to my release, the prison officials had labeled me as level 3 STG (Security Threat Group) risk factor. Both Snake Eyes and Blake had provided the Feds with information, labeling me as the Head Henchmen.

Now that I knew who my enemies were, I knew they'd be trying to send people at me. I downsized my circle to consist of people I felt I could trust. For the most part, I did a damn good job, but sometimes doing good just isn't good enough.

In my attempt to squash the beef with the Billys, I had set up a powwow so we could get down to the bottom of it. Just so they'd feel comfortable, I agreed to meet up on their territory. Of course, I had my young lions with me and my no. 1 hitta Face-Off close, but out of sight just in case shit went sour.

When we walked in, I spotted the homie B and Wild Child. B was Billy too, and Wild Child was still pushing Dogg Pound Soldiers but was aligned with the Billys. Wild and I had history, and this was our first time seeing each other since I came home. We had bided together and had made plans to put the streets on lock upon our release.

Lil G had a nervous energy about him that I couldn't quite place. His eyes kept shifting around the room and to the door. I ain't really thinking much of it, but just to ease the tension in the air, I pulled out some Sour D and started rolling up.

"I don't know about y'all, but me personally, I done did too much time and put in too much work in to be out here beefing over bitches. That shit is lame," I said as I split the dutch and filled it with weed. *"We got the strongest sets in the city. If we were to dead the dumb shit and put our heads together, we could literally take over,"* I continued.

"All that sounds good, but you gotta understand my homie dead. And I feel you (not you personally), but your lil homies played a role in him getting killed. If I was to tell my homies to stand down, it'll be like spitting on his grave, and I can't do that," stated Lil G.

"I feel and I respect what you're saying, but you gotta look at it like this. So far, only one life was lost. If we keep up with all this pistol popping, more than likely, it'll be another dead nigga in the dirt soon. And guess who the White folks down at city hall gone blame for it? Me and you," I said, taking a deep pull from the dutch and then passing it to him. *"I just feel like niggas need to dead all the dumb shit, focus on getting money, and pointing our lil homies in the right direction,"* I stated as I sat back and blew smoke to the sky.

"I say we do it like this: if niggas got issues with each other, they can take it to the backyard and get it off their chest," stated Wild Child. *"Let niggas get their issue one on one,"* continued Wild.

"Anybody gotta issue they wanna get off their chest?" I asked, looking around the room.

Nobody said nothing at first, then Lil G spoke up. *"Yo, any of y'all know what happen to my brother?"* he asked, looking directly at my young lions.

Lil G had two brothers, Sonny and Alkwon. Sonny was a rat but was dangerous with a gun. Alkwon was laid back and really wasn't into much but had somehow come up missing. Nobody had seen or heard from him. He disappeared around the same time Merk Piddy got killed.

"Naah, homie. We don't know nothing 'bout that," stated Puff as Maff and John nodded in agreement.

From there, we deaded the beef, called up our squads, and let all the homies know.

"If any of y'all not feeling each other, take that shit to the backyard and fade it out," I said, addressing both the First Fam and the Billys.

"If anymore shots get fired without the proper greenlight, those responsible will be dealt with," added G.

We then turned and faced one another. *"Peazzze Al-mighty!"* I yelled while saluting the young gangster and staring dead in his eyes.

"Peaze blood!" he yelled back with a sinister smirk on his face.

"Now let's get this money!" I said as me, him, Wild Child, and B all sat down and discussed making some power moves.

Are You Still Down?

With all the madness going on, I figured it'd be wise to pay my pops a visit at the church.

During the service, I discreetly made my way next to my sister Kesha. As I was sitting down, the preacher spoke of the apostle Paul and how while in prison, Paul was consumed by the Holy Spirit. Then suddenly, and as if in a trance, he pointed at me, gave me a stern look, and prophesied, *"You, my son, are a child of God and have been chosen by the heavenly council to do great things. Embedded inside of you are the powers of the Apostle Paul. You will suffer many mishaps and great misfortune, but you will prevail for destiny has chosen you!"* He shouted loudly as he wiped the sweat from his forehead, stared silently out into the congregation, gave an *Amen,* then continued on with the sermon.

I was completely awestruck when I looked at my sister. She simply shrugged her shoulders, as if to say *"I'm just as lost as you, brah."* I had been called a lot of things in life, but never in my wildest dreams did I ever imagine being called a child of God who was destined for greatness.

After the service was over, I stayed behind and spoke with my dad about *No Mustache* and the Feds investigating me. I also told my dad about the community outreach program I was in the process of starting. After hearing me out, my father introduced me to a city councilman by the name of Cynthia Baker, who was also a member of the church. I again explained my vision to Ms. Baker about the Family Always First Foundation.

"My goal is simply to restore the family structure back into the Black community by way of uplifting and elevating the minds of the youth. The Family Always First Foundation will be the banner for my

HENCHMEN program. My first project will be called Intelligence over Ignorance, aka the Double II project. With this project, I plan to be hands-on with some of the most rebellious youths. I'm going to every hood, trap house, project, and street corner to recruit students."

"I think your plan sounds great and is much needed. If there's anything we (meaning us here, the church) can do to assist you, we will."

"Actually, there is. I'm in the process of purchasing a commercial property. This process is being delayed by the ordinance code. If you could, I'd like you to run the likes of Family Always First Foundation by whomever responsible to see if you could help speed things up."

"I most certainly will, and I know exactly who to call," she replied.

Within two weeks, I was sitting inside the lobby of the Registry of Deed lobby waiting on my big sis and Model Meek to emerge with the title to the building. I had decided not to have my name legally linked to anything. My sister was listed as sole owner and operator, while Model Meek had adopted the title as executive manager and business consultant.

They both were all smiles as we emerged from the town hall building with our mission completed. Before going our separate ways, my sis stopped at the bottom of the steps and looked me up and down while smiling and shaking her head in approval.

"Brah, you gotta stay focus and leave them streets behind you. You done did everything it is to do out there in them streets. With what we doing now, Ima need you to give the foundation your full attention."

"I got you, big sis. Trust me, I'm focused..." I said before walking off with Model Meek...

Model Meek saw them before I did... *"It's a Chrysler 300 and a Ford Focus that's been following us since we left from downtown."*

We were riding in my latest toy, a black tricked out 4.6 Range with both front and rear surveillance monitors. I hit bottom for the rear surveillance monitors. Sure as shit stinks, we were definitely being followed. They were two cars back. With every turn Model Meek made, they followed.

"Don't lose 'em. We gon sleepwalk 'em. Pull up at the next gas station," I said while handing her my phone. *"Throw that phone away.*

Get me two prepaid straight talks and put twenty dollars on pump 5," I said, stepping out to pump the gas.

The Feds had pulled on the opposite side of the gas pump. I knew they were watching, so I played it off as if I was rapping a song.

> ♫If I shoot you, I'm brainless♫
> ♫But if you shot me, then you're famous♪
> ♪What's a nigga to do…when the streets is watch-
> ing♫
> ♫Blocks keep clocking♪
> ♪Waiting on you to break♫
> ♪and make your first mistake♪ (**Jay-Z,** "Streets Is Watching")

I was bobbing my head, but the entire time, I was watching them watch me. After pumping the gas, I hopped back in the passenger side and leaned the seat back and told Model Meek, *"Drop me off at the mall,"* as I programmed the phones.

The first person I hit was Queen. *"Clean the house up and take the trash out."*

"What's is you tal…oh yeah, okay. You hungry?" she asked.

"Yeah, actually I'm starved… Pick me up some pizza from that spot in the mall."

"Okay, Ima clean up first though. I love you, Shawnee."

"I love you too…" I said, ending the call.

"Make sure you call me and let me know you good," said Model Meek as she pulled up at the mall.

"I got you. Ima hit you up ASAP. I'll probably send one of the homies to get the truck sometime tonight."

"Al-ight, but you need to be safe, Frank. For real. If you trying to go out of town, I know some people in Florida. You can lay low there until all this shit blow over."

"I'll give it some thought and get back at you on it," I said as I shut the door and blended into the crowd. I walked aimlessly around the

mall for about an hour just to see if I was being followed. Once I knew the coast was clear, I headed to the pizza shop.

"No pepperonis, just turkey sausage with extra cheese and banana peppers," I said, surprising Queen as she stood at the corner, about to place an order. *"And make that a extra large, please."*

She turned around all smiles and gave me a big hug.

"Whatsup, lil lady? I guess you must really miss me," I said, hugging her back and making sure to squeeze her ass cheeks in the process.

"Shawn, please tell me everything is okay. I'm not trying to lose you again. I need you here with me not dead, not in jail, not with the next chick, but right here with me and our child."

I wanted to tell her everything was all good but couldn't. The only way our relationship had survived so many storms was because we always kept it real with each other, even when the truth hurt.

Once seated inside the booth, I gave her the rundown about the Feds.

"I don't know what they know exactly, what or who exactly telling it to them. All I know is that I'm on their radar, thanks to some clowns that can't keep their mouth shut. They been watching me since before I left prison. That's why they stopped allowing you to visit me and put me on level 3 STG... And did you just say something about being pregnant?"

"Yes, I did, which is exactly why I need you to be safe. I mean, damn, Shawn, you just did ten years! You can't come home and expect to fix everything for everybody. Them niggas is gone be your downfall, can't you see that?"

"How far along are we with the pregnancy?" I asked, changing the subject to a more positive note.

"Five to seven weeks. I missed my cycle, but the pregnancy test was positive. I set a doctor appointment for next week."

"So why is we sitting here stressing when we supposed to be out celebrating? Fuck the Feds! They may or may not come get me, but until they got me, it's 'fuck em!' Feel me?... Will you box that up to go for me, please?" I asked the waitress while handing her a ten-dollar tip.

"Yes, sir, no problem," she said while walking back to the kitchen.

I pulled up at the very same place we were at twelve years ago, when Queen first told me she loved me. The same place where she had told me she was pregnant and had made a promise to ride till the end with me.

"Yo, you remember this spot?" I asked, killing the lights but leaving the car on. We were in the same parking lot directly behind her mother's house in Rankin Terrace.

"How could I forget? I told you I loved you, and you laughed at me."

"It was the way you said it. It just sounded funny...and your crazy ass almost broke my damn shoulder hitting me with that damn stick."

"'Cause you hurt my feelings. I was mad at you."

"Damn, them was good old days. We were young, dumb, and swore we knew it all. I can't believe we still kicking it...and you pregnant again."

"And your hardheaded ass about to leave me out here by myself again."

"I like Spiritual, Shaquan, or Success as first names. The last name isn't even up for discussion. You thought of any names yet?"

"I haven't given it much thought."

"We talked about this before I came home. Part of the reason our bond is so strong is because we wanted to have another child... I like Spiritual the most... But anyway, is you still down for me or what, shorty?"

"Till the end. And you know that, so don't ask me no silly shit like that again," she stated, using my own words against me. I had told her the same thing when she had asked me if I was **really in love with her.** She had just thrown my own words right back at me, and I had to admit that shit made my dick hard.

"And that's why I love your lil ass so much 'cause you a real rider," I said, leaning over and kissing her with every ounce of passion my body possessed.

The Double II Project

The marquee in front of the building read **_Intelligence over Ignorance,_** a.k.a. **_The Double ii Project_** sponsored by the **_Family Always First Foundation._** We had dubbed the building as club MYA (Minority Youth Achievements), and today was the grand opening. Not only had we secured the purchase of the building, but thanks to city council woman Mrs. Baker, we were also listed as a privately owned establishment—which meant that whatever functions we sponsored would not be regulated by the 2:00 a.m. curfew enforced upon normal establishments by the city ordinance. In other words, we could party all night long without any marshals shutting us down.

The lobby was neatly decorated with faces of Black greatness: 2Pac Shakur, Huey P. Newton, Nelson Mandela, Jay-Z, Rick Ross, Meek Mill, Harriet Tubman, Rosa Parks, Assata Shakur, and Iyana Vincent. Above the bar draped a huge banner with **H**ighly **E**ducated **N**egro **C**ee **H**is/**H**er **M**ind **E**levate **N**obly, The Henchmen acronym.

The atmosphere was all positive vibes. The Billys as well as the GD (Gangster Disciples) were both in attendance. The First Family was definitely swarming the building. Ms. Baker, the city council woman, along with my father and the pastor from the church showed up to support. And of course, all my family came out.

As I walked through the marquee into the lobby, I stopped briefly to admire the faces of Black greatness. It was then that I remembered the words of both True God and my father's pastor. True God had motivated me to transcend from the streets and solidify my legacy. _"A solid and strong character will leave a solid and strong legacy."_ The pastor had further motivated me by informing me that I had been chosen by the heavenly council to do great things.

As I exited the lobby and stepped into the main opening, I knew right then and there that I had successfully bridged a gap. Church folks, gangsters, and kids all in the same building at the same time for the same cause all thanks to one man…me.

I walked around and acknowledged everybody that I knew before grabbing the mic and signaling for the DJ (P. Money) to cut the music. The crowd noise suddenly got silent enough for me to speak.

"First of all, I'd like to thank each and every one of y'all for coming out today and supporting this grand opening. The Family Always First Foundation is a independent nonprofit community outreach program. Our first two projects will be HENCHMEN along with Intelligence over Ignorance, a.k.a. The Double II Project. What we're aiming to do is restore a sense of unity back into the Black community by way of uplifting and elevating the minds of young, at-risk youths. We can't keep allowing the judicial system, streets, and prisons to destroy our kids' future nor dictate how we govern our communities. With the Family Always First Foundation, I'm making it my personal mission to be on call 24-7 to help assist any and all these young men and women in whatever way I can… starting right here and right now. For the first half of the grand opening, we'll be giving away free school supplies and gift certificates. We also have monetary prices for our first, second, and third place winners of our spelling bee. For all my grown-ups, we'll be reopening tonight at ten and partying till the sun comes up… Have fun, enjoy yourself, and know it's family always…" I paused and pointed the mic toward the crowd…

"First!" they all yelled…

After my speech, I made my way through the crowd. I saw Queen sitting with Shaunteona and Shy'ion and made my way over to them, flopping down and playfully leaning on Shaunte.

"Dad, you're heavy, and you embarrassing me. Please sit up." I immediately sat up and playfully pinched her cheeks. *"Daad, stop!"* she said harshly through clinched teeth. My son Shy'ion edged me on while both Queen and Shaunte double-teamed me with girl power.

"Okay, okay, I see you two divas aren't in a playing mood, so me and my roll Dog 'bout to roll out. Come on, man. Let's go and enjoy ourselves," I said as me and Shy'ion stepped off.

As we made our way to the outside patio, which had been converted to large lounge-type area equipped with an industrial-size grill, I figured now would be the perfect time to tell my son the same thing my father had told me.

"What's your plans for when you get older?" I asked while fixing us both a plate.

"Well, I like computers, so I been thinking about computer engineering."

"You serious?" I asked, completely shocked by his answer.

"Yeah, I wanna do web designs, computer programming, and stuff like that. I figure I'll make a mill before I turn thirty-five. That way, I can take care of my mom and hold the family down."

"I like the way that sound. And speaking of holding the family down, I got something I need to tell you, but you gotta keep it between us for now," I said while passing him his plate. I waited until we were both seated before telling him. *"It's a possibility I might be going back to jail."*

"For what? What did you do? I thought you said you were chilling out."

"I am chilling out, and truthfully, it's not about what I did nor what I'm doing. It's more so about who and what I am. No matter how much good I do for myself, my family, or the Black community, Ima always be considered a threat. Because for one, I'm HENCHMEN. For two, I represent the true meaning and purpose of BLOOD, which is brotherly love. And for three, the morals, principles, and values that I swore to live by require that I stay dedicated to the cause no matter what."

"But if you're not doing anything and you're chilling, then how can you go back to jail?" he asked me, seeming slightly confused.

"Take a look around you," I replied, spreading my arms around in the air for emphasis... *"I'm paying for all this out of my own pocket. Bringing people together is something I'm good at doing, but you gotta understand that a lot of people are afraid of unity amongst Black people. So just by me being able to bring my people together, that alone makes me a threat. Add that to the fact Ima convicted felon who just spent the last ten years studying the Black Panther party and how systematic oppression was specific designed to keep Blacks in bondage. I come home*

and start awaken the minds of those they wish to stay sleep. I give a voice to those they wish to remain silent. I speak of our ancestor as being kings and queens and us being of royal warrior bloodlines… This type of talk scares people, especially those who know it's the truth. So now I have the Feds investigating me because these cowards can't keep my name out their mouth, and it's only a matter of time before they strike."

"Damn, pops. Man, we need you out here. It ain't the same when you're gone. It's like the fam fall apart, and the streets lose hope when you're not around."

All I could do was nod in agreement. I just had my first grown man with my thirteen-year-old boy who seemed to understand everything I had said.

"Ima need you to stay focus on that computer stuff. Hopefully, this shit blow over, but if not, you already know it's family always…"

"*First,*" he said, finishing my sentence for me as we pounded our fist together.

All Eyes on Me

After the grand opening of club MYA, it was as if, the Feds were no longer trying to conceal their interest in me.

The first sign of shit hitting the fan was when Doggfaze got locked up. I got the call from Maff letting me know brah had got bagged. Doggfaze called me two days later and gave me the full scoop.

"They pulled me over and got the slammer out the car. My hail 75k dollars, but my PO put a hold on me. They mention your name, saying some shit about we extorting the town."

"Man, fuck them people! Whatsup with this hold your PO put on you? How that shit work?"

"They can only hold me for five business days. They can't violate me unless I get found guilty, so I should be good in three days. I already talk to a bondsman. Ima give 'em your number so you can holla at 'em."

"Al-ight. Bet Ima swing by your mom's and wifey spot and drop something off."

"Okay, do that... Love you, brah."

"I got you, fooly. I'm your keeper..." I said, ending the call

The next piece of bad news involved my cousin Murda. Somehow, the police had got word that he was on his way back from OT. Next thing I know, I see his picture on the news... *"Today, a joint task force of local and federal agents attempted to apprehend suspected drug trafficker Don Davis, a.k.a. Murda 1, who fled the scene in all-gray Acura, taking police on a high-speed pursuit through several counties, reaching speeds of up to over 100 mph. After wrecking the car, Mr. Davis fled on foot inside this wooded area located behind me. Mr. Davis is considered armed and dangerous. Police are asking anybody with information to contact crime stoppers."*

"Run, Murda, run!" I said, hoping the homie would get away. I stayed up all night waiting on my phone to ring, smoking blunt after blunt. The next morning, I got a call from Murda's wifey. They caught the homie hiding in a shed in somebody's backyard. Luckily, he was able to get rid of the work, so he was only charged with felony eluding arrest; but truth be told, we lost 280K dollars on that one.

When Doggfaze called me back with the bondman number, I made the mistake of going against my gut feeling. The bondswoman was a female named Tammy; and Tammy, according to Doggfaze, would post his bond for 5K dollars instead of 7K dollars because Doggfaze was cool with Fonz, who was Tammy's boyfriend. My gut instinct told me not to trust Fonz simply because he had been catching cases sense the nineties and had never done any serious time.

So Doggfaze called me and said, *"Just give the money to Fonz. Ole girl gone look out on the strength of him."*

"You know, I don't fuck with that dude like that. He suspect," I said, sounding somewhat frustrated by the suggestion.

"I know, but damn, brah. I'm trying to get the hell up outta here ASAP."

"I got you, brah. Ima call this nigga… Matter fact, what's his number? Ima hit him three-way right now."

Little did I know Fonz was a confidential informant. He had been assigned by **No Mustache** to get close to me but never could because like I said, I never trusted him.

On the day I gave him the money to get Doggfaze out, I had made the mistake of calling him to one of the trap spots to collect the money. Although I wasn't the one who made the transaction, by me even being present was enough to get **No Mustache** and the Safe Street Gang Prevention Task Force excited. Plus with the way he reported the story back to the Feds, he made it seem like a movie scene. I did what any real homie should've done and posted my man bail. But by doing so, I had also just given the Feds some more ammunition to shoot at me with.

Meanwhile, Murda 1's bond was set at 1.5 mil. There was no way we could post that without bringing more heat to myself. His charges weren't that serious. It was just the fact that he had embarrassed a lot of law enforcement agencies with his driving skills. He outdrove and eluded the state troopers, city cops, and FBI. Hell, had it not been for a noisy neighbor, they would've never known he was hiding inside the shed.

Then the last person I expected to turn sour ended up being a rat. One night as I laid in bed, I heard a knock on the door. As a precaution, I'd usually chill at the apt in the Creek until around 9:00–10:00 p.m. When I had moved back to Wilmington from Raleigh, that was the address I had given my PO.

When I got to the door, I looked through the peephole and saw my parole officer. I knew something wasn't right because I only had about three weeks left on parole. Up until this point, I had passed all piss test and paid all my fines, so my new PO (Mr. Taylor) never gave me no problems. Just to be on the safe side, I tiptoed back and double-checked the room, making sure everything was straight. However, when I went back and opened the door, it was no longer just my PO; it was the entire Street Gang Prevention Task Force. **No Mustache** was now standing directly beside my PO.

"What's popping, big-homie Frank White? Mind if we search?" he asked while smiling at me as if this was a joke.

"Under the terms and conditions of your release, you're subject to warrantless searches. Please place your hands behind your back so I can cuff you while they search," added my PO.

"Yeah, I understand I'm subjected to warrantless searches, but that's only at the discretion of my parole officer, not the fucken FBI," I said angrily. *"Matter fact, fuck it! Go ahead and search. Ain't shit in here,"* I said, placing my hands behind my back.

"You know, Frank, I been hearing your name in a lot of different places from a lot of different people. Oh yeah, and congratulations on your Family Always First Foundation. You really surprised us with that one. Who'd think a gangster such as yourself would have such a big heart?"

"Man, what the fuck do y'all want? Why are you'll here? Is this a random routine search or a interrogation? I haven't broken any law. Your flunkies haven't found anything illegal in my place of residence. So again, why are you'll here, and what is it that you really want?"

"I want you to tell me something, big homie," said **No Mustache.** *"Around five months ago, the biggest Blood war in all of NC state prison history sparked off, and word is your responsible."*

"The fuck outta here. Ima free man now. I don't concern myself with prison politics. How the hell could I possibly be responsible for such a thing?"

"Because you're big-homie Frank White, and here's how..." he said, pulling out his phone and playing a sound clip from a recorded conversation.

I listened as a muffled voice on the sound clip told everything they knew. Whoever it was was saying how not only had the First Fam and Billys united on the streets but had also united behind the G-wall and that I had gotten the greenlight for Pretty Tony and BGGB to get cleaned up due to the fact they weren't properly sanctioned sets. They also mentioned that both Blake and FB had been bragging about the hit they put on me prior to me leaving prison, and because of that, they were both now labeled Westside plates. Blake ended up getting shot in an alleged drug deal gone bad in Charlotte, North Carolina, while FB got blew off the yard. Both were now labeled as food.

I continued to listen as he told police that both me and Wild Child were running an extortion ring and that we were extorting gambling houses, local businesses, and big-time drug dealers. He even mentioned the power moves we had discussed making and the meeting we had.

It then hit me that the only people that knew this type of info were the homies...and as if on cue, I heard the muffled voice say, *"I think they kidnapped my brother."*

I knew right then and there who it was. I also now knew how they had gotten the tip on Murda 1 from and why they had started following me. They had added an additional rat to their roster, one that I had never suspected... The big-homie Billy... Lil G.

NO MUSTACHE had confused his arrogance for authority, and by doing so, he had just revealed his hand...

Fuck the Police

Due to the fact they had never found nothing illegal in my crib, they had to uncuff me after the search.

My main focus from that point was the Family Always First Foundation. I spent most of my time in the hood being actively hands-on with helping anybody who needed my help. Buying groceries. Settling simple disputes that could've easily turned violent and just cooling with my young lions. Leading my lil homies in the right direction.

I had successfully completed my parole, and as a celebration, I went and got "Family Always First" T-shirts made and passed out to all my people.

Queen was about six months pregnant with Skai (Sky), and I was loving every minute of it. I know all parents think kids are special, but I knew this lil girl would be something special. I could just feel it all in my soul.

Word was some videos had surfaced of Alkwon (Lil G's brother) begging for his life. Somebody had supposedly sent the videos to Lil G's phone. It was fucked up that he had to suffer like that, but when I thought about both Lil G and Sonny being rats, I didn't feel no sympathy. Karma was definitely a heartless bitch.

And then it happened... They struck!

I was brushing my teeth as I stepped on the porch and scanned the block. I made a mental note of an all-white van parked up the block. *"Go check that van out up the block,"* I told Face-off as I texted Queen and told her I had spent the night at the trap and to meet me there.

When Face returned, he told me, *"That van ain't got no side windows, so I couldn't see inside. But I shook it, and ain't nothing happen."*

214

I figured it was them boys, but right as the thought registered in my brain, my phone rung... It was Queen.

"Get everything up out of here," I told Face as I stepped in the backyard to take the call. *"I think that's them boys down the block."*

"Whatsup, lil lady?" I said, answering my phone.

"Where exactly do you want me to meet you at, and why is you there in the first place instead of at home?"

I listened while Queen pretty much bit my damn head off for not coming home last night. As she was talking, a black cat had come in the backyard and brushed against my legs. Suddenly, the cat just took off, running at full speed; jumped on the privacy fence; looked back at me; then disappeared into the woods... *"Follow that cat,"* my intuition told me.

"I'm on the south side. Meet me at 14th," I told Queen, but even as I ended the phone call and was walking back inside the house, my intuition was telling me to go follow that cat.

"Yo, we gotta get the hell out of here. Something ain't right," I said as Face was placing everything in some book bags.

"Ima head out to the Motherland and lay low until nightfall. Just hit me up when you surface," replied Face as we walked out the front door.

As soon as I got in the car with Queen, I flipped the sun visor down and looked in the mirror. We made it about four blocks before they swarmed the car from every angle.

"Lock the door, keep the windows up, and don't say nothing."

"Freeze! Put your hands up, and step out the car!" They all yelled as they approached and surrounded the car with guns drawn. *"Unlock the doors now!"* they yelled while slapping their hands against the windows.

I looked at Queen; she looked back at me. The moment had finally come. I leaned over and kissed her stomach. *"Daddy loves you, Skai,"* I said, talking directly to her stomach and hoping by some miracle, my unborn seed could hear me.

As I sat up, I saw a tear slide down Queen's face. *"Till the end, Shawnee baby. Till the very end."*

My face was dotted with pieces of glass as the agents shattered then burst the passenger side windows with the butts of their guns. I threw my hand up in surrender as they unlocked the door and pulled me out the car with guns aimed, pointed and ready, directly at my face. Once they pulled me out the car, we all somehow lost our balance and fell to the ground. From my position on the ground, I could see they also had Face-Off pulled over farther down the block. Within minutes, backup arrived and secured the entire block, including the trap house.

I saw them place Queen in handcuffs. *"That's all my shit! Everything in the house, the car—that's all mine. She don't know nothing, and y'all just seen her pick me up. That's all my shit. Y'all not here for her. Y'all here for me, so let's get it over with."*

From there, I was taken to jail and charged with two counts of drug trafficking. My bail was set at a million dollars… I was stuck.

Queen got out that same night. Out of spite, they had charged her with a roach of weed in the ashtray. Face-Off's bond was set at 150k dollars; we had him out within three days.

Now here's how the story of my life unfolded… First of all, the confidential informants twisted the entire story up. They made it seem like some shit of a movie. They (informants) told the Feds that I had started extorting local businesses, gambling houses, and high-level drug dealers. They also informed the authorities that I was one of the most dangerous dudes in Wilmington, North Carolina, and that I had united all the Bloods under my command.

In my attempt to unify the Black community, I had reached out to Lil G. Lil G was the big homie of the Billys, and I had shared my vision with him; but what I didn't know was that Lil G was as rat. It was through him, Snake Eyes, Blake, and Fonz that the Feds knew my every move. I was being watched by local, federal, and confidential sources.

On the day of my arrest, I was allegedly pulled over as a passenger in a vehicle for not having on my seat belt. I was pulled over by the Safe Street Gang Prevention Task Force. There were about ten officers involved in my arrest, and not one of them ever wrote me a ticket for seat belt violation, which was supposedly their probable cause. On top of that, I had tinted windows, which would've made it damn near impossible for one to even see inside the car. Period. However, when I raised the illegal search and seizure issue during my suppression hearing, it was denied. I took the magistrate judge seven months to make the ruling.

Upon my arrest, I told the officers that the female driver had no knowledge of any drugs being in the car. *"All the drugs found in the car belong to me. I take full responsibility for everything."*

When interviewed by the Feds, the first thing they asked me was *"Do you want to help yourself?"*

"Yes, but this isn't about me. It's about my community," I replied.

"What do you mean?"

"What I mean is that if you guys really are who and what you claim to be, which is the Safe Street Gang Prevention Task Force, then keeping the streets safe should be your number one priority."

"And what's that s'pose to mean?" they all asked simultaneously.

"It means that if you want to help me, then help my community by sponsoring a gun drive and granting immunity to all convicted felons and gang members who show up with guns to turn in... Surely, that will help keep the streets safe."

"But it doesn't work like that, Jennings," they replied.

"Well, how exactly does it work?" I asked, already knowing the answer to my question.

"C'mon, Frank, you know how this game gets played."

"Yeah, you right. I do know how the game gets played, but I don't play those types of games! What I'm seeing here is that none of you really give a damn about my community or keeping the streets safe. You're more concerned with me snitching on somebody than actually solving the real problem..."

The very same night of my arrest, September 20, 2013, Jose, a member of the First Fam, was killed. In my absence, there was no order on the streets. All the work that I had done to help unify my people was destroyed in a matter of days. In retaliation to the murder of Jose, the First Family had literally set the city on fire.

"Jennings, attorney visit!" yelled the CQ.

I had been expecting Mr. Hicks to visit me. He had already represented me during my first appearance and was scheduled to pay me a visit. However, once I went inside the attorney room, Mr. Hicks wasn't inside. Instead, I was greeted by Hargrove, who was now the head homicide detective.

"I don't know nothing, and I damn sure haven't killed nobody," I said while still standing.

"I'm not here for that, Jennings. Just relax. I need you to tell your boys to calm down. It's getting out of control. It's like the damn Wild-Wild West out there right now. We need you to help calm things down," he replied.

"Y'all wanted me off the streets. So now that I'm gone and things are out of control, I'm spose to help y'all calm things down? Every time these kids get somebody to look up to, y'all label us gang leaders then lock us up. Leaving them completely lost and at the mercy of the streets... That kid that got killed was one of mine, and my father always taught me to protect my family. So it's not the Wild-Wild West out there right now. It's the First Family, and they're only doing what they been told and taught to do, which is protect each other."

Now here I was back, locked up with my seed on the way, two counts of trafficking, a million-dollar bond, and both the Feds and locals watching my every move. To make matters worse, about three weeks after my arrest, one of the task force officers that assisted in my arrest was shot by a real good friend of mine.

Word was, I had put out the hit on the task force officer in retaliation for my arrest. Truth is, I had nothing whatsoever to do with that situation. The homie Bloody B was my man, and they tried to use the fact that we were communicating and corresponding as grounds to support their conspiracy theory.

I can't say 100 percent what actually took place, but from what I heard, the same task force that arrested me tried to arrest Blood B. In the exact same fashion, they swarmed his vehicle in unmarked cars. I guess the homie thought it was a hit, so he hopped out busting shots and ended up shooting two task force officers. One got hit in the chest but had a vest on.

The other got hit in the leg.

I started noticing a lot of dudes in the dorm going out on lawyer visits. They started assigning more officers to work my housing unit. And I could literally hear the recording device recording my phone conversations. A lot of weird stuff started happening, and once again, it was all eyes on me.

Three days later, after the officers got shot, they (the Safe Street Task Force) killed Bloody B. Somebody had given up his location, and when the police tried to pull him over, he hopped out (unarmed) and ran in the woods. They (the police) literally hunted him down and killed him.

After that, it was basically us against them, and *them* being the police. We all knew it was a no-win situation. However, at this point, it wasn't about winning or losing. It was about making a statement; and we made one which was *"Fuck the police..."* On the day of the funeral, all the homies showed in all red Dickies suits with *"Fuck The Police"* sewn in big red letters.

Maaan, matter FACT, TIME OUT!

Let me give you the TRUTH, the whole TRUTH, and nothing but the TRUTH! First of all, RIP to the homie BLOODY B; and for those of who don't know, this is why we scream "Fuck the police!" They're killing us every day and getting away with it. According to Mapping Police Violence, a research group that tracks deadly police encounters, US law enforcement officers killed 6,800 civilians from 2013 to 2018. Officers were charged with a crime in only 1.7% of those cases AND/BUT less than 1% of those officers charged are actually found guilty.

And for those of you who still doubt or disbelieve that the US judicial system isn't systematically oppressing the people, explain this: How come the US has only 5% of the world's population but over 25% of the worlds incarcerated?? How come more than 2.1 million people (almost 1% of the US population and the highest percentage in the world) are in jail or prison? And guess who makes up the largest percentage of those incarcerated? Blacks constitute 60% of those in state prisons and 42% of those in federal prisons.

And dig this: in the US, five times more money is spent on building new prisons than building new schools. The War on Drugs, aka the War on US, was really just another form of systematic oppression used as justification for mass incarceration of young Black males. The US spends 19 billion dollars annually on the War on Drugs, aka the War on US. And this all goes back to FEDERAL FUNDING and the DEFENCE BILL because this is how the politicians profit.

It's all politics. And Blacks are always systematically disregarded throughout the political process; why? Because we lack equal political representation. White men account for only about a third of the US population but dominate our political system... This is why Blacks have very little political leverage.

And no, this isn't some racist shit I'm telling you. This is some real shit I'm telling you. You see, without a geographical nationalitly there is no cultural ethnicity. You have no way of identifying yourself, knowing who you are nor where you come from. When you destroy a people's culture, you also destroy their identity... WE were robbed of our LAND, LAW, and LANGUAGE; enslaved and subjected to a foreign land with foreign laws; and forced to speak a foreign language. OUR true identity was lost—the knowledge, wisdom, and understandings of our ancestors stolen and forgotten!... THIS WHY IN THE TRENCHES, IT'S ALWAYS UNDERSTOOD THAT IT'S US AGAINST THEM. RIP TO ALL MY HOMIES THAT DIDN'T MAKE IT... BLOOD IS LIFE, AND LIFE IS BLOOD... BLOOD IN, BLOOD OUT!

That was my last and final time-out. Its late fourth quarter, and the game is almost over. So kick back and enjoy the rest of the book, and if they kill me, Ima live forever within the pages of this book. And like what Uncle 2Pac once said, "Only my real highly educated Negros know this be the realest shit I ever wrote." Now time in, and let's get it!

When my mail arrived, it was missing my pictures of the funeral. About two hours later, the gang unit officers called me out of the dorm. When I walked in the room, I saw they had photocopies of my pics laid across the desk.

"Do you know these people?" they asked.

"Why is you'll asking me these dumb-ass questions? Get to the point. What do you'll want? And why you'll call me out here for?" I replied.

"Because we wanted to know how you feel about the situation."

*"How the fuck would you feel if somebody you knew got hunted and gunned down, huh? You'd probably feel like '**fuck you**' towards whoever did it, right? Okay, so theres your answer, and that's how I feel. I feel like fuck the police because they just kilt my friend! Anymore dumb-ass questions, or can I go now?"*

You see, where I come from, there's no such thing as freedom and justice for all. Every day, dudes are dying, catching court cases, and getting locked or killed by the very same people (the police) that swore to protect them.

My vision was similar to that of the late great Huey P. Newton, Malcolm X, and Martin Luther King Jr. All I wanted to do was let freedom ring by any means necessary—freedom from mental, economic, and social slavery.

Unfortunately, there's no happy end to my story. When it was all said and done, I was sentenced to 188 months for one-count distribution Federal Indictment. No conspiracy, no codefendants—just me, myself, and I. I was labeled a career offender and, on top of that, received an 851 **kingpin or gang-leader enhancement** for a nonviolent offence. I never cooperated or offered any assistance to the government, which is really why they enhanced my sentence.

Yet despite the stiff sentence, I'm good! Remember how I once told you about how people in positions of power are naturally attracted to stand-up guys...? I'm now an elite mentor within the First Family. My duty and responsibility is to assure that the ideas of our forefathers such as Black Liberation and Brotherly Love remain relevant. I'm currently working on creating the **B**uilding **R**esponsible **I**ndividuals **D**efining **G**enerational **E**mpowerment of **S**elf (**BRIDGES**), a nonprofit community outreach program. I'm also a devoted follower of the *Ifa.*

Yoruba African Culture

A lot of people have given up hope on today's youth.
They've been labeled lost and hopeless.
I strongly disagree!
You see, because in our world…hope is everything.
It's all a lot of us will ever have. Hope for a better tomorrow.
Because that's how we survive today…hoping things get better.

The whole, entire purpose of me writing this book and sharing my story was to get three things across to my readers:

1) Always keep your family first no matter what you go through in life.
2) Never trust a rat, snake, or a coward. They don't deserve to live.
3) Always follows that small voice in your head. It's the voice of greatness. It's the voice of Ifa/God, and we are God's chosen people.

In closing, I gotta give an RIP salute to all my fallen Port City, First Family, Henchmen soldiers. The spirits of the real rights will forever live through me… Family always first… I am my brother's keeper!…

Epilogue

Gone, Not Forgotten

Face-Off... Wealth in the form of wisdom. It took me a while to really grasp the concept of what you meant by that, but now I know. I'm seeing life through the eyes of true understanding. I'm wide awake and completely in tune with the spiritual world, trust me. I feel your presence and hear your voice every time the wind whispers. For my wisdom has now become my wealth, and with that said, we'll never be departed... Our spirits will live on forever. Even after our death...eternally your keeper...

Lil Poppa... The day we lost your physical presence here on earth was a day when we all questioned God and asked him, "Why?" Nobody could make any sense of that situation, myself included. In search for answers, I visited your makeshift memorial site and bowed my head in prayer. It would be a couple of years before I see the answers to my prayer take shape. Within two years after your death, the city of Wilmington began to evacuate all the residents of Jervay. The public outcry for help was heard only in honor of your name. Jervay was eventually torn down and rebuilt... All the old-school Southsiders still cross their hearts and whisper, *"RIP Lil Poppa,"* when they pass by your spot on 10 Street.

Uncle U... "War before peace" is the HENCHMEN motto. We took an oath and swore to be each other's keeper. I'm still right here, dogg! Still holding it down with my *H*s held high. We built a solid team, and you left a solid legacy. You'll never be forgotten...the H remains!

Bloody B... Fuck the police! That's what I told them when they asked me how I felt about your passing, and truth is... I still feel the same way about it. What them cops did was dead wrong, and they need to be held accountable. The sad shit is, you got more people working with the law to help kill and lock us up. Then you got helping make sure we receive fair trials and equal justice... I'm still trying to unite the homies in the hood and wake the sleepwalkers up. It's a full-time job, but I love it.

Merk Piddy... First Fam salutes, homie, and that's with the upmost respect. The legacy you left behind speaks for itself. I see so many that attempt to mimic your style, but they all fall short. Trust and believe you were truly one of a kind. May your walk with spirits lead you to a gangster party in heaven. The First Fam was well as the streets still honor your name... Piddy Gang, stand up! #us never them.

Jose... I knew you were different the first time we met. Unlike a lot of others, you saw the vision before I even showed it to you. You knew which direction we were going, where we came from, and what we needed to do in order to stay on track. The streets took us both down on the same day because we believed in the same thing. We shared the same vision. My mind has been reawakened to an enhanced level of spiritual awareness. I feel the presence of all the departed. The streets speak for the spirits of the dead, and I'm their voice. You might be gone, but Jose Gang live on! #us never them.

Killa Black... That Ku-ku kat Killa Black! Damn, dogg, I can't believe you gone. Life is crazy like that. Here one minute, gone the next. One thing about it, we had enough fun to last three lifetimes. What we did will never be done again. The world just ain't the same—cameras everywhere, everybody snitching, and that's why I changed directions. Writing books and promoting my nonprofit (BRIDGES) organization. Striving to become a successful, legitimate member of society... *Highly educated style.*

Kenny Hall... Before all the street shit, you showed me what the true meaning of Brotherly Love was. A lot of times, people speculate without knowing the facts about what they're speaking on. Fact is... I had nothing whatsoever to do with your demise. We lost a Goodman, and I personally lost a good friend. However, I think life is designed so that we learn the most from our mistakes and losses... RIP OG. I ain't forgetting about you.

Uncle Harold... Having you around was like having two fathers. You showed me what being a man and holding the fam down was all about. Family was really always first in your eyes. And I'm thankful to have witnessed that... Tell Lil Harold I said whatsup as well as Grandma and Granddad too. I'm making plans for a family reunion. Hopefully, I can pull it off... Much love, Unc, and First Fam salutes.

To my readers: I hope you have enjoyed reading this book just as much as I've enjoyed writing it. This book was specifically written to expose my trials and tribulation in life while also expressing growth.

I'm currently working on my next novel entitled *The Code of Honor*, a book of morals, principles, and values. For more info on or about the author, you can contact me at 602-314-3439. Text messages only.

Thanks for your support and stay tuned for *The Code of Honor...*
Revelations of Blackpride

Epilogue

Always Us

1) Moms—A warrior goddess as soft and strong as the wind… Mother Oya… I love you.
2) Pops—Prayer and positive energy is most definitely the greatest form of protection… No weapon shall prosper.
3) Redstorm—The only blueprint for success is ambition. I put all my pain in the gas tank and drove out. Page after page with my pen on cruise control… All gas, no brakes.
4) Maff—Don't worry about the race. Just focus on the finish line… Marathon mentality.
5) Los—The real OG of Club Myas. Much love and respect.
6) Queen—I couldn't tell my story without you being a part of it. Things change, but the love remains. I ain't mad at cha, shorty.
7) Model Meek—It's hard to put into words, but we both know what it is…very special.
8) Black Angel—Your name speaks for itself… Heaven-sent.
9) Shyion—The future of our bloodline is in your hands… Stay awake.
10) Holiday—From the sandbox to the street… Boro bonded.
11) E-boogie—Keep doing it just how you doing it… It can't be done any better.
12) J-luv—Like cooked food…need I say more?
13) Polk—The Henchmen history could not and would not be properly told without mentioning your name.
14) Puff—My young thunder cat is now a full-fledged lion… my pride and joy.

15) <u>Badass</u>—Solid and strong men leaving solid and strong legacies. WB4P, sis. His held high… I'm your keeper.

16) <u>Kelly</u>—Lady Sidberry, Henchmen love and loyalty. I ain't forget you, sis… Keep the Sidberry legacy alive.

17) <u>Flames</u>—My shadow and silent assistant since day one. We been standing side by side… That'll never change.

18) <u>Ghetto</u>—You play crazy, but for those of us that really know you…we know you got plenty of sense.

19) <u>Kawada</u>—Had to pay due homage to you, homie. When it came to hitting licks, you were the best to ever do it.

20) <u>G-code</u>—We all grew up, but we (you and me) never grew apart… Straight Franken!

21) <u>Noon</u>—You gave me the game on a different level. Getting money is most definitely the main objective.

22) <u>Mr. Utley</u>—You inspired me to learn the history of Black greatness. And more importantly, you encouraged me to write… Thanks for the motivation.

23) <u>Shauteona</u>—My firstborn and first lady. The love will always remain unconditional. No matter what, I've always got your back!

24) Mother Africa—In my time of weakness, it was you who provided me with strength and aligned me with destiny. I salute and honor you for making me the man I am—a proud Black man with knowledge of self. Here to spread the vision of Black pride!

Paperwork Party

1

1

2   UNITED STATES DISTRICT COURT
              EASTERN DISTRICT OF NORTH CAROLINA
3   SOUTHERN DIVISION
                        7:14-cr-00097-H-1
4
   UNITED STATES OF AMERICA,   .
5   .   DECEMBER 6, 2016
                                  .   GREENVILLE, NORTH CAROLINA
6 VS.   .
                                  .
7 SHAWNEE OTTO JENNINGS,   .
                                  .
8   .
            DEFENDANT.   .
9 . . . .

10 *
                        SENTENCING HEARING
11   BEFORE THE HONORABLE
             UNITED STATES SENIOR JUDGE PRESIDING
12
   APPEARANCES OF COUNSEL:
13
   FOR THE GOVERNMENT   -
14   ASSISTANT UNITED STATES ATTORNEY
                            310 NEW BERN STREET, SUITE 800
15   RALEIGH, NORTH CAROLINA 276011

16 FOR THE DEFENDANT   -
                            THE EDMISTEN & WEBB LAW FIRM
17   THE PROFESSIONAL BUILDING
                            127 WEST HARGETT STREET, SUITE 104
18   RALEIGH, NORTH CAROLINA 27601

19 COURT REPORTER   -
                            CAROLINA COURT REPORTERS, INC.
20   105 OAKMONT DRIVE, SUITE A
                            GREENVILLE, NORTH CAROLINA 27858
21   (252 355-4700

22 Proceedings recorded by stenomask, transcript produced from
   dictation.
23

24

25

2

1   (ON THE RECORD AT 1:40 P.M.)

2   THE COURT: In the case of United States versus

3   Shawnee Otto Jennings, let the record reflect Mr. Jennings is

4   present with his counsel, Mr. William Webb; Counsel for the

5   United States, Mr. Lathan, is present. I begin by inquiring

6   of Mr. Webb, counsel for the defendant, are there any

7   remaining legal objections to the revised presentence report,

8   Mr. Webb?

9   MR. WEBB: No, Your Honor. I would like to make

10   a statement for the record, that this is a little bit of a

11   unique case in that the initial final presentence report

12   indicated there were no objections on the part of either

13   party, either the defendant or The Government. Since then

14   there's been a revised presentence report, which we received

15   this morning. As a matter of fact, the revised presentence

16   report is in fact accurate so long as the 851 information is

17   in effect. But Mr. Jennings has requested that I lodge his

18   objection to the fact that this revised presentence report is

19   the one that we're dealing with today, and that The

20   Government has not been wed to the original initial final

21   presentence report.

22   THE COURT: In fact you just received that

23   report, I assume today, did you not?

24   MR. WEBB: This morning.

25   THE COURT: This morning. The difference was

1　the career offender status remained. It was the difference

2　of adding some points that impacted the --

3　　　　　　MR. WEBB: The base offense level went from 32

4　to 34, if Your Honor please.

5　　　　　　THE COURT: Two points.

6　　　　　　MR. WEBB: We're going to be asking --

7　　　　　　THE COURT: Goes from 151 to 188.

8　　　　　　MR. WEBB: Right. And then went from 188 to

9　235. We're going to be asking for a variance down to the

10　range that was initially sent forth in the final presentence

11　report of 151 to 188.

12　　　　　　THE COURT: All right.

13　　　　　　MR. LATHAN: May I speak to that, Your Honor?

14　　　　　　THE COURT: You may.

15　　　　　　MR. LATHAN: Your Honor, the 851 Enhancement and

16　its impact on the guideline comes as no surprise to either

17　party. We've had discussions about the 851 Enhancement from

18　day 1, and we both contemplated that the guideline range

19　would be 188 to 235. I recognize that that was not included

20　in the original PSR, but to act as though it came as a

21　surprise going into sentencing is simply not the case. Mr.

22　Webb and I have talked about this on multiple occasions

23　throughout the history of this case.

24　　　　　　THE COURT: All right, thank you. I understand.

25　Now, no remaining objections to the presentence report other

4

1 than the -- what I think is basically what defense counsel is

2 pointing out is that it was unusual to get on the day of the

3 sentencing hearing the written report showing the

4 differences, even though there may have been discussions

5 about it; and I agree with him, it does come as a little bit

6 of a shock.

7   Now, I'll go through the -- for the possession

8 with intent to distribute a quantity of crack cocaine,

9 marijuana and heroin, the total Offense Level is 31, and Mr.

10 Jennings' Criminal History Category is Roman Numeral VI, that

11 of a Career Offender. The custody range is 188 to 235 under

12 the guidelines. The supervised release term is 6 years.

13 Probation, he's not eligible. The fine range is $15,000 and

14 $2,000,000. Restitution is not an issue, and the special

15 assessment is $100.

16   Any objection to those advisory guideline

17 ranges, Mr. Webb?

18   MR. WEBB: Subject to what I just stated for the

19 record, no, Your Honor.

20   THE COURT: Any objection by the United States,

21 Mr. Lathan?

22   THE GOVERNMENT: No, Your Honor.

23   THE COURT: Okay. Then that's where we are.

24 I'm going to hear you in a moment, Mr. Webb.' I am familiar

25 with your client to the extent his background is in the

1 presentence report. He has -- he's 36 years old, he has his

2 GED. He is allegedly a validated member of the United Blood

3 Nations Street Gang. He has a long criminal record, but

4 that's encompassed in this Roman Numeral VI. I think he's

5 had 7 different gun convictions and at least several, 4 or

6 more, prior felony drug convictions.

7 I'll hear you, Mr. Webb, on what I should do. I

8 did receive letters. First I got a letter directly from Mr.

9 Jennings -- well, it's from Amy Davis, letters of character.

10 She's a cashier at the local mall, and the defendant is her

11 younger brother. And then I got a character letter by

12 himself, which I read. And also a letter from Shalonda

13 Vaughan in Wilmington, Carolyn Jacobs from Wilmington. I'll

14 hear you, Mr. Webb.

15 MR. WEBB: If Your Honor please, I also have a

16 letter that was handed to me today by Mr. Jennings, by Mr.

17 Jennings' mother, Ms. Fay Jones, who is in the courtroom

18 today. Please raise your hand or stand up.

19 THE COURT: You can hand it up to Madam Clerk.

20 MR. WEBB: Thank you. Your Honor made reference

21 to the fact that my client is a validated member of the

22 United Blood Nations Gang, but he's also a founder and member

23 of what's called the Henchman. And as I understand it, and

24 what I have been told over the 3 years or so that I've

25 represented Mr. Jennings, is the Henchman is a subset of this

6

1 | Blood Street Gang. In fact, what it is, is a community
2 | outreach program designed to reach young black men and young
3 | black women to try to keep them away from gang activity.
4 | Mr. Jennings, prior to his arrest in this
5 | matter, he did in fact serve as a mentor under this Henchman
6 | Program and he did that for 5 years. And he spoke to youth
7 | groups and to anyone who would listen. In fact, at the time
8 | of his arrest in the trunk of his car there were boxes of t-
9 | shirts that were designed to be given out to the Henchman
10 | youth groups.
11 | Your Honor has already made mention of the fact
12 | that he has obtained his GED while he has been out, or before
13 | his arrest. He was also at Cape Fear Community College in
14 | the Collision Repair Program. He's 36 years old. As Your
15 | Honor knows, he's had a checkered criminal history, but a lot
16 | of that was when he was in his teenage years.
17 | Today I'm just going to ask that we defer to
18 | Your Honor's discretion in terms of sentence. I'm not a big
19 | fan of the Sentencing Guidelines. Back there in the era when
20 | you and I were in the U.S. Attorney's Office we didn't have
21 | to deal with these arcane guidelines, and so I rely a great
22 | deal on the factors in 3553A. And I would ask that the
23 | cornerstone of Your Honor's sentence be a sentence that's
24 | sufficient, but not greater than necessary for Mr. Jennings
25 | in this case. So we'll just defer to Your Honor on that.

7

1   THE COURT: Thank you, Mr. Webb. Mr. Jennings,
2   do you have anything you want to tell me today?
3   THE DEFENDANT: Yes, sir.
4   THE COURT: I'll hear you.
5   THE DEFENDANT: To begin with, I'd like to
6   apologize to my family for being in this situation. Your
7   Honor, may I speak to just my family?
8   THE COURT: No, that wouldn't be appropriate.
9   THE DEFENDANT: I'd just like to say Ma, I
10   apologize for being in this situation, and I apologize for
11   not being a better son and, you know, just putting myself in
12   this situation, and you having to see me in this situation.
13   But also, he kind of misspoke earlier about the
14   Henchman. It is not a subset of the Blood Street Gang. It's
15   an independent non-profit community outreach program. And
16   what it stands for is highly educated negro sees his or her
17   mind elevating. And the goal with Henchmen, or my goal
18   was/is to uplift, elevate the minds of the young at-risk
19   youth. And basically it was a big responsibility, and it
20   just put me in a ill spot financially. And it's a crisis
21   going on in my community right now, financial crisis, family
22   crisis; it's just a lot going on out there that everybody --
23   it's like everybody has got to come together to fix the
24   problem. And it's like me, as one man, I tried to make a
25   difference, and I did. It's just that once I came to the

8

1 attention of Federal Agents they labeled Henchmen as a gang,
2 they labeled me as a gang leader, and they accused me of
3 distorting drug dealers and gambling houses and other
4 amenities, accusations are included inside my indictment.
5 The Government is relying heavily on them as reasonable
6 suspicion.
7   And I'd just like to say, Your Honor, I'm
8 standing here in front of you right now with a one-count
9 indictment for a small amount of drugs. And the majority of
10 my prior convictions came from my teenage years, like at a
11 time where honestly I really didn't know any better. And
12 right now I'm grown, I've got kids, teenage kids of my own,
13 and I don't want to see them make the same mistakes that I
14 have, you know. I apologize sincerely for my actions, and
15 you know, I just ask The Court for mercy and forgiveness.
16   THE COURT: Thank you, Mr. Jennings, you may be
17 seated. Mr. U.S. Attorney?
18   THE GOVERNMENT: Your Honor, I'm at a loss. The
19 Henchmen were a violent subset of the United Blood Nations,
20 specifically the Double Eye Bloods. And to stand here and
21 hear Mr. Webb -- for the first time -- I've never heard this
22 -- stand up in this court and make the claim that this was a
23 community outreach group, is -- it is not supported by fact,
24 it's not supported by any evidence; there has been no
25 evidence presented to The Court on that. And if The Court is

CAROLINA COURT REPORTERS, INC.
(252) 355-4700

9

1   inclined to believe that, then I hate to say it, but I would
2   suggest that another continuance of this sentencing hearing
3   is warranted, because that cannot stand. That assertion
4   simply cannot stand, because it is not true.
5   THE COURT: The Court bases no issue on that
6   type of matter, The Court is concerned principally about the
7   offensive conduct and the criminal history category, and
8   those -- neither impact that.
9   THE GOVERNMENT: Your Honor, the defendant is 36
10 years of age. He's a validated member of the United Blood
11 Nation Criminal Street Gang. Not only that, but a high
12 ranking member, Your Honor. His criminal history includes
13 convictions of 20 offenses, 8 felonies. It's a history that
14 is rife with violence, with convictions including resisting
15 an officer. 1997 charged with assault with a deadly weapon
16 inflicting serious injury, convicted of assault with a deadly
17 weapon. 1999 convicted of assault on a government official.
18 1999 the defendant was charged with robbery with a dangerous
19 weapon, assault with a deadly weapon, attempt to kill.
20 Defendant pleads guilty to assault on a government official,
21 common law robbery. 1998 the defendant is charged with
22 assault inflicting serious injury; he would ultimately plead
23 guilty to simply assault. And then in 2009, felony robbery
24 with a dangerous weapon, resisting an officer, hit and run.
25 Not only violence, but a history of firearms possession; two

CAROLINA COURT REPORTERS, INC.
(252) 355-4700

10

1 prior convictions for felon in possession of a firearm.

2   And then there's the drug trafficking, with

3 prior convictions for drug possession and drug trafficking.

4 1997, two convictions, 2000, 2012 -- in fact, the defendant

5 was on parole for a drug trafficking offense at the time he

6 committed this offense. So you have a history of drugs,

7 guns, violence. There's an interest that is unique to this

8 case for a sentence of incarceration that will adequately

9 protect the public from these crimes. There's also a unique

10 need for a sentence that will promote respect for the law and

11 afford adequate deterrence. The defendant committed many of

12 these crimes that I've gone through today with criminal

13 charges pending, or while the defendant was on post release

14 supervision, including the crime for which he was convicted

15 in this case, which was a drug trafficking offense committed

16 while the defendant was on parole for another drug

17 trafficking offense.

18   And let me give The Court one example. If I

19 could direct The Court to the top of page 7. When we speak

20 to the need to afford adequate deterrence and promote respect

21 for the law, in 2009 the defendant was convicted of robbery

22 with a dangerous weapon and various other offenses, and while

23 incarcerated incurs 82 infractions. And that's over what is

24 relatively a short period of time. That's a staggering

25 number of infractions for one to have committed in less than

1   5 years in the Department of Corrections. It's difficult to

2   fathom how one could even achieve that number of infractions.

3   And so it came as no surprise when the defendant is released

4   and he is almost immediately charged and convicted of felon

5   in possession.

6   Recidivism in this case is assured; it's a near

7   certainty. And it's a concern that The Court ought -- we

8   believe, to be taken into account in imposing the appropriate

9   sentence.

10

11·   There has not -- there is no cooperation to

12 report to The Court. The guideline range is 188 to 235

13 months, and that is a range that is supported not just by the

14 career offender designation, but every other factor that is

15 worthy of The Court's consideration supports a sentence

16 within that range. We'd ask The Court to impose a sentence

17 in the middle of that range. Thank you, Your Honor.

18   THE COURT: All right, you may stand, Mr.

19 Jennings. The Court adopts the findings in the revised   .

20 presentence report as credible and reliable, and based upon

21 those findings I've calculated the imprisonment range

22 prescribed by the advisory guidelines. I've considered that

23 range, as well as the other factors set forth in 18-USC-

24 3553A. Now, pursuant to the Sentencing Reform Act of 1984

25 and in accord with the Supreme Court decision in United

12

1   States V Booker, it is the judgment of The Court that the

2   defendant, Shawnee Otto Jennings, is hereby committed to the

3   custody of the U.S. Bureau of Prisons to be imprisoned for a

4   term of 188 months. Upon your release you'll be placed on

5   supervised release for a term of 6 years. Within 72 hours of

6   release you're to report in person to the Probation Office in

7   the district to which you are released. And while on release

8   you shall not commit another Federal, State or local crime,

9   possess a firearm or destructive device, and you shall comply

10 with the standard and the following additional conditions.

11 One, you'll participate in a program directed by your

12 probation officer for the treatment of narcotic, drug or

13 alcohol dependency, which will include testing, and may

14 require residential treatment. Second, you will participate

15 in a program of mental health as directed by your probation

16 officer. Third, you'll consent to a warrantless search by a

17 U.S. Probation Officer at his request, any law enforcement

18 officer, of your person and premises, including any vehicle.

19 You will participate in vocational training as directed by

20 your probation officer, and you will cooperate in the

21 collection of DNA. And it is required that you support your

22 dependents while under supervision.

23   It is further ordered that you shall pay to the

24 United States a special assessment of $100, which is due and

25 payable immediately.'

13

1   The Court finds that you do not have the ability

2 to pay a fine in addition to providing financial support to

3 your dependents, therefore no fine is being imposed. In view

4 of your cooperation denial of Federal Benefits is not

5 applicable.

6   Inasmuch as the range exceeded 24 months, the

7 difference between 188 and 235, I have sentenced you at the

8 lowest end of the guidelines due to the tardiness of the

9 United States Probation Officer in getting out the revised

10 presentence report, though both you and The Government agreed

11 to proceed today, and that's my basis. Otherwise it would

12 have been more in the middle. That concludes the statement

13 of your sentence.

14   Madam Probation Officer, do you have any

15 required change to further comply with the sentencing laws?

·16   PROBATION OFFICER: No, Your Honor.

17   THE COURT: Mr. Webb, do you have any remaining

18 legal objections to the sentence as just stated by The Court?

19   MR. WEBB: No, I do not, Your Honor. But I

.20 would like to ask if The Court would entertain a request that

21 Mr. Jennings be allowed while incarcerated to enroll in an

22 intensive drug treatment program. .

23   THE COURT: That was included in that statement.

24 Well, no, it wasn't. Excuse me, you are correct.

25   The Court, Madam Clerk, recommends the defendant

14

1   be exposed to the most intense drug treatment possible during

2   his incarceration.

3   　　　MR. WEBB: And one more item. I didn't hear in

4   the prior case, does The Court entertain a request for where

5   he might serve his sentence?

6   　　　THE COURT: I don't do that in drug and gun

7   cases.

8   　　　MR. WEBB: Okay, thank you, Your Honor.

9   　　　THE COURT: Does the United States have any

10   remaining objections, Mr. Lathan?

11   　　　THE GOVERNMENT: No, Your Honor.

12   　　　THE COURT: Then, Shawnee Otto Jennings, by

13   virtue of the authority duly invested in me I hereby impose

14   upon you the sentence I've just stated. I wish you good

15   luck. I have to tell you now, that if you believe your

16   underlying guilty plea was somehow involuntary, or if there

17   was some other fundamental defect in the proceeding, you may

18   have a right to appeal. If you believe the sentence I have

19   imposed is contrary to law you may have a right to appeal.

20   In any extent, if there's a basis for appeal you must file

21   your Notice with the Clerk of this court within 14 days of

22   today. And I ask Mr. Webb to confer with you, and if there

23   is a basis for appeal, to assist you in filing the Notice.

24   And after that it would be up to the Circuit Court to

25   ascertain who your counsel would be. That concludes your

15

1   sentencing hearing, Mr. Jennings. Marshal, you may take him

2   in your custody.

3   (HEARING CONCLUDED AT 2:12 P.M.)

4

5

6

7

8

9

10

11

12

13

14

15

16

17

18

19

20

21

22

23

24

25

Prologue... Code of Honor

After being sentenced to 188 months for drug distribution, I immediately began reevaluating my priorities and purpose in life.

What puzzled me the most was how the world continuously misunderstands and disrespects the code of honor. The words *love* and *loyalty* are no longer defined by sacrifices of sincere emotional commitment but instead by superficial surface-level type relationships. Of course, nobody's perfect, including myself, which is why I found it very necessary to reevaluate myself first and foremost before pinning this work of literal art.

Inside this book, you will find priceless jewels of knowledge and wisdom gained from personal experiences as well as a more in-depth understanding as to what the code of honor really stands for.

Unlike the *48 Laws of Power*, this isn't a book of deceptive manipulation tactics. This is a book of raw truth, honor, integrity, and righteousness deeply embedded within the spiritual aspects of the Yoruba African culture and designed to make the morals, principles, and values of the enlightened mind unbreakable.

Classified "Leader" by both local and federal authorities, I stood firmly as the United States Attorney desperately tried to convince the judge that I was indeed a menace to society. My independent community outreach program, HENCHMEN, had been labeled a gang and I, in turn, had been labeled a gang leader.

The judge's ruling was in favor of the government, which in turn enhanced my sentence from seven to fifteen and a half years. Now with more than fifteen years to serve, I've adopted writing as a hobby, a way to positively continue to promote "Highly Educated Negro Cee's His/Her Mind Elevate Nobly." And by doing so, I've defied both the laws of man and United States government. Although physically confined, I've broken the psychological chains of enslavement and escaped to share with you the Code of Honor—a code so powerful that when properly applied, you'll become incapable of being conquered by any oppressive forces.

The reevaluation of self during a time of suffering leads to a great awakening—the awakening of the mind's eye.

When I first started writing this book, I had initially intended for it to be strictly for the streets. I'm no saint or scholar nor do I pretend to be. However, after the completion of my first novel (*Family Always First: The HENCHMEN History*), it was as if I began to see the world with eyes of true understanding. My mind had become reawakened to an enhanced level of spiritual awareness, and writing strictly for the streets was no longer a top priority.

I felt it would be both contrary as well as counterproductive to realistically define the code of honor using only a street perspective. So in my attempt to fully define the code of honor, I have combined an array of revelations both street and spiritual to vividly express the oracles of honor, for true honor is a commandment of Almighty God reserved for things and people we hold in high esteem.

What Is the Code of Honor?

1) A set of principles that allows a person to remain both mentally and physically courageous while in the face of opposition and/or oppressive forces.

2) A sense of self-determination that serves as a motivational source of energy to destroy self-doubt when faced with an obstacle.

3) A level of enlightenment that can only be obtained through self-discipline to block all negative worldly distractions.

4) The rules and regulations within a society of people who constantly strive for perfection while never compromising their morals, principles, and values.

5) The characteristics of a righteous man in his righteous mind at one with his highest self, the universe, and destiny.

6) Vicariously representing righteousness without doubt nor fear; being ready and willing to sacrifice for whatever it is you believe in and stand for.

7) A commandment of Almighty God (the Alpha and Omega) reserved specifically for things and people we hold in high esteem. "*Honor* thy mother, thy father, thy neighbor, thy elders, and thy ancestors," said the Lord.

The Code of the Streets

Everyone knows the streets are full of codes and that these codes exist as a fundamental safeguard for individuals who've chosen to partake in illegal activity within the street life. These codes are protocol, the rules and regulations of the streets.

However, these codes have become a universal language spoken by many people of all races and nationalities. The code of the streets is no longer confined strictly to the streets, for many greats have emerged from the illegal street life and excelled to become very successful, and by doing so, they've expanded the exposure of the code. Some would argue that due to this overexposure, the code of the streets is indeed dead. I agree and disagree—and here's why.

You see, to me, the code is something that's embedded in your character. When you come from the streets and have that firsthand knowledge of experiencing living the street life. You learn very early in life how to hustle in order to survive. And everything you learn stays with you. It becomes a part of you. It never dies, no matter how big or small of a success you may become, you'll always live by and have respect for the code.

So no, the code itself isn't dead, and it'll never die, but street life in its current state of absolute chaos and confusion is indeed dead. You see, life is love, and love is what makes life worth living. But yet, upon closer examination, we all know there is no real love in the streets and that the streets don't love anybody. It's impossible to build a solid foundation atop quicksand; and that's exactly what the streets are—quicksand made to pull you under. Contrary to popular belief, the streets do not give a damn about who you are, what gang you claim, or how much money you have. If you do not have the right set of morals, principles, and values as well as the head (mindset) and heart (inner strength) to survive, they'll suck you under.

The streets scream, "Keep it real," but what defines that realness? And who's definition of real are we honoring? And how do you keep it real with something that's designed to destroy your life?

The streets don't love anbody, and the only way to keep it real with something that's designed to destroy your life is by fucking your life up. There's nothing real about dying before your time, being in and out of jail or killing somebody over some nonsense.

The game does not reward those who live by the code of the streets. It only rewards the individual who live by the code of honor.

Code of Honor (Rules)

1) Never betray the code of honor.
2) Never betray the trust of family.
3) Never lie nor steal from family.
4) Never accept defeat nor failure as a permanent reality.
5) Never speak, just to be heard; speak to be understood.
6) Never trust a rat, snake, or a coward.
7) Never compromise your morals, principles, or values under any circumstances.
8) Never follow a weak leader.
9) Never sell your soul.
10) Never put an outsider before family.
11) Never allow uncontrollable emotions dictate your actions.
12) Never disrespect what you stand for.
13) Never doubt your intuition or instinct.

Code of Honor (Expectations)

1) Always move with confidence and never hesitate when it's time to move.
2) Always be about your BI, and always keep your BI before pleasure.
3) Always respect those worthy of your respect (especially elders).
4) Always show strength in the presence of oppressors.
5) Always outthink, outfight, and outmaneuver the opposition.
6) Always uphold honor and honesty.
7) Always remain loyal to truth.
8) Always be your brother's keeper in a time of need.
9) Always take the initiative to get money, power, and respect.
10) Always shed blood when needs be to assure the safety and well-being of the family.
11) Always pay homage to fallen comrades.
12) Always respect what you stand for.
13) Always follow your intuition and instincts.

"Never Compromise Your Morals, Principles, and Values"

Morals, principles, and values define character, and character in turn is what determines one's legacy. A solid and strong character will leave a solid and strong legacy. Who you are, what you stand for, and how well you represent it are all merely a reflection of your individuality and belief system.

The gift of strong character is eternal life through one's legacy. The ability to live on even after death will only be granted to those who were willing to make great sacrifices while still alive.

When we speak of morals, principles, and values, we're speaking of an individual's belief system. The theory of eternal life through God and most religious concepts requires faith. And our faith requires that we believe. However, your faith must supersede all grounds of your physical existence. Additionally, your morals, principles, and values must be built firmly on solid grounds. You must remain 100 percent loyal to that in which you believe in at all times, never compromising your integrity. Being ready and willing to face all forms of opposition and/or oppression without fear of defeat and failure, for death is never feared by those who know their destiny. And when we accept destiny by the way of a righteous belief system, we're no longer subjected to doubt nor fear.

"Yea though I walk through the valley of the shadow of death, I will fear no evil; for thou art with me; thy rod and thy staff they comfort me" (Psalm 23).

The hidden message inside the Holy Scriptures gives mankind much insight and enlightment on matters of honor, though it is only

252

with the eyes of the understanding that one will comprehend the context correctly.

I say this not as a religious scholar but simply so that my audience can relate and fully understand that the legacy you leave will only be an equal equivalent to the life which you have lived.

Always uphold "honor." Never compromise your morals, principles, and values. And your legacy will live forever, eternally written in stone.

Top 5 Code of Honor Attributes

- Love—The highest most powerful form of emotional commitment.
- Loyalty—A form of dedication in which one never compromises their morals, principles, and values under any circumstances.
- Unity—To move and function as one—one mind and one body to accomplish one goal.
- Fearlessness—An act of extreme courage displayed while in presence of opposition.
- Honor—The essence of integrity and self-righteousness.

Who Is "Omega Blackpride"?

Every generation has its own view of history and a messenger who communicates the essence of historical events.

Omega Blackpride is a messenger committed to the elevation and enlightenment of young Black youth. Here, Blackpride uses his past experiences of misfortune as a platform to implant seeds of Black pride and African culture into the minds of his people. He also uses enhanced editorial skills to emphasize and shine light on controversial issues such as systematic oppression of the past, present, and even future generations of African Americans.

Omega Blackpride was born Shawnee Jennings Jr. in 1980 in Wilmington, North Carolina. After spending the majority of his adolescence and adult life in and out of confinement, he would later become known as OG. Frank White. In 2013, at age thirty-three, he was federally indicted for a single count of distribution of cocaine, heroin, and weed—and sentenced to 188 months.

During his latest stint of incarceration, Blackpride began studying the Yoruba African culture. He wears the crown of Orunmila, the Orisha chosen by the heavenly council to restore people of misfortune and said to have defeated death, made money his slave, and knows all the mysteries within the kingdom of heaven. He also has a very close relationship with Eshu, the most well-known spirit of the Yoruba religion. Eshu is a powerful spiritual spirit warrior who functions as a divine messenger and a gatekeeper. He can remove obstacles and open doorways into new opportunities—possessing the combined energies of both Eshu and Orunmila.

Omega Blackpride is both man and messenger. Omega Blackpride represents the resurrection and reawakening of the lost (fourth) generation. His past makes him the perfect messenger for his people.

In every generation, there comes a man with a voice, and not just an ordinary voice but a very powerful voice. A voice that's determined to be heard. This book is that voice—the powerful voice of Omega Blackpride.

Omega Blackpride isn't just my name; it's my vision—and may this vision be heard, accepted, and respected by all. Ashe, ashe, ashe!

CPSIA information can be obtained
at www.ICGtesting.com
Printed in the USA
BVHW071337221121
622225BV00001B/57